RICHARD RORTY

Bloomsbury Contemporary American Thinkers
The *Bloomsbury Contemporary American Thinkers* series offers concise and accessible introductions to the most important and influential thinkers at work in philosophy today. Designed specifically to meet the needs of students and readers encountering these thinkers for the first time, these informative books provide a coherent overview and analysis of each thinker's vital contribution to the field of philosophy. The series is the ideal companion to the study of these most inspiring and challenging of thinkers.

Daniel Dennett, David L. Thompson
Hilary Putnam, Lance P. Hickey
John Searle, Joshua Rust
Saul Kripke, Arif Ahmed

RICHARD RORTY

RONALD A. KUIPERS

BLOOMSBURY
LONDON · NEW DELHI · NEW YORK · SYDNEY

Bloomsbury Academic
An imprint of Bloomsbury Publishing Plc

50 Bedford Square 175 Fifth Avenue
London New York
WC1B 3DP NY 10010
UK USA

www.bloomsbury.com

First published 2013

© Ronald A. Kuipers, 2013

All rights reserved. No part of this publication may be reproduced or transmitted in any form or by any means, electronic or mechanical, including photocopying, recording, or any information storage or retrieval system, without prior permission in writing from the publishers.

Ronald A. Kuipers has asserted his right under the Copyright, Designs and Patents Act, 1988, to be identified as Author of this work.

No responsibility for loss caused to any individual or organization acting on or refraining from action as a result of the material in this publication can be accepted by Bloomsbury Academic or the author.

British Library Cataloguing-in-Publication Data
A catalogue record for this book is available from the British Library.

ISBN: HB: 978-1-4411-9238-7
PB: 978-1-4411-8238-8

Library of Congress Cataloging-in-Publication Data
Kuipers, Ronald Alexander.
Richard Rorty / Ronald A. Kuipers.
p. cm. – (Bloomsbury contemporary American thinkers)
Includes bibliographical references (p.   ) and index.
ISBN 978-1-4411-9238-7 (hardcover : alk. paper) –
ISBN 978-1-4411-8238-8 (pbk. : alk. paper) – ISBN 978-1-4411-7814-5 (epub : alk. paper) – ISBN 978-1-4411-4024-1 (ebook (pdf) : alk. paper)
1. Rorty, Richard. I. Title.

B945.R524K85 2012
191–dc23

2012020364

Typeset by Newgen Imaging Systems Pvt Ltd, Chennai, India

To Hendrik Hart, teacher, mentor, and friend

The best effort of a fine person is felt after
we have left their presence.
—*Ralph Waldo Emerson*

CONTENTS

Acknowledgments	ix
Introduction	1
1. Philosophy as Existential Quest: Rorty's Life in Thought	12
The Importance of Rorty's Emergent Intellectual Self-Concept	12
Formative Childhood Experiences and Parental Influence	17
Training in Philosophy: Hutchins College, The University of Chicago, and Yale	31
Professional Life: Before and After *Philosophy and the Mirror of Nature*	38
2. The Philosophical Therapist: Rorty's Critique of "Philosophy-as-Epistemology"	45
Changing the Subject: Rorty's Therapeutic Intention	45
What's the Malady? Rorty's Diagnosis of Philosophy-as-Epistemology in *Philosophy and the Mirror of Nature*	49
Philosophy from Descartes to Kant: Problematizing Dualism and Representationalism	55
What's the Therapy? Sellars, Quine, and Epistemological Behaviorism	67
Philosophy as Cultural Conversation: Allocating an Appropriate Place to Each	77

CONTENTS

3. The Liberal Ironist: Rorty's Cultural Politics	79
Putting away Childish Things	79
Substituting Freedom for Truth: From Theory to Narrative	84
Contingency: Language, Persons, and Communities without Skyhooks	90
Irony	98
Solidarity	103
Occupy Wall Street: What Would Rorty Do?	110
4. The Anticlerical Prophet: Rorty and Religion	114
Revisiting Rorty's Atheism: Complicating the Picture	114
Therapy or Prophecy? Rorty's Critique of the Western Ambition of Transcendence	118
Responsibility and the New	123
Transcendence as Ethical Alterity: Another Problematic God Substitute?	127
On Keeping the Word "God" in One's Final Vocabulary	133
Keeping Religion Private, or Keeping the Conversation Going?	140
5. What is Truth *For*? The Conversation Continues	149
Pinning Down Rorty's Philosophical Evasions	149
Normative Triangulation: Coherence, Solidarity, and Objectivity	153
Retrieving the Triangle: Ramberg on Rorty	159
What is Truth For? Returning Truth to the Service of Edifying Conversation	165
Conclusion: Pragmatism as the Apotheosis of the Future—Rorty, Hope, and the American Sublime	173
Notes	180
Bibliography	205
Index	211

ACKNOWLEDGMENTS

It is hard to believe that 20 years have passed since I first read *Philosophy and the Mirror of Nature* as a first-year Master's student in philosophy at the Institute for Christian Studies in Toronto. Since that time, Rorty's philosophical work has been a constant dialogue partner and reference point for my various forays into other areas of philosophy. I was privileged to meet him personally during the mid-nineties, when he was gracious enough to take me out to lunch on the campus of Stanford University. Unfortunately, our paths never crossed again. I owe a debt of gratitude to Rorty himself for his important contribution to philosophical discourse, one that continuously challenges settled assumptions and encourages readers to explore fresh intellectual paths.

The teacher who first impressed upon me the significance of Rorty's intellectual contribution was my graduate supervisor at both the Master and Doctoral levels, Hendrik Hart. As I explain in the introduction, Henk helped me past my first, rather allergic, reaction to Rorty. For this patient mentoring I will be forever grateful, for I could not now imagine my intellectual life without the edifying influence that Rorty's work (not to mention Henk's) has had upon it; for this reason I have dedicated this book to Henk.

For the last 20 years, my intellectual home as both a graduate student and a professional scholar has been the Institute for Christian Studies in Toronto, an oddly named, quirky school of interdisciplinary philosophy and theology started by a progressive community of Dutch Christian Reformed immigrants in the late 1960s. This community, in which I was also raised, deserves much credit for continuing to support this somewhat subversive and at times controversial outpost of Christian higher education. This book, and those of my faculty colleagues past and present, would not be possible without that support. I would also here like to thank the Institute itself for granting me a sabbatical leave for the 2011–12 academic year, during which time the bulk of this book was written. On this note, I must also thank our Associate Academic Dean and Registrar, Shawn Stovell, for his help in protecting this leave from many of the normal incursions and pressures that might have otherwise impinged on this valuable and necessary mental space.

Several people provided useful comments on some or all of this book while in the draft stage. I would especially like to thank my brother-in-law, Ralph Witten, Associate Chair of the Liberal Arts Department of the Northern Alberta Institute of Technology, for reading the manuscript in its entirety and offering timely comments and stimulating conversation. This interaction helped make the book a joy to write. My research assistant, Andrew Tebbutt, also read the entire manuscript and thankfully followed my encouragement to take his gloves off when it came to offering his criticisms. My colleague at the Institute, Robert Sweetman, made valuable comments on a section of Chapter 2 dealing with Rorty's reading of Aristotle, and Barry Allen of McMaster University helped me parse my reading of Donald Davidson in Chapter 3.

Over the years, there have been several other significant scholars whose work on and opinion of Rorty has influenced my own. Among these I thank especially my undergraduate philosophy professor D. Vaden House (the author of *Without God or his Doubles: Reason, Relativism, and Rorty*), Carlos Prado, Professor *Emeritus* at Queen's University, Tom Reynolds of Emmanuel College at the University of Toronto, Jeffrey Stout of Princeton University, and G. Elijah Dann, author of *After Rorty: The Possibilities for Ethics and Religious Belief* (and other works on Rorty). In this group I would also place the various students who have participated in my "Pragmatism and Religion" seminar at ICS in the past. In particular, Murray Johnston composed a significant paper on the role of novelty and futurity in Rorty's thought that confirmed some of my hunches and also influenced my ongoing interpretation of Rorty. Daniel Mullin, whose excellent PhD thesis on democracy and secularism I am now supervising, has also stimulated my thoughts on Rorty. I am not exactly sure where in the following text to pin their influence, so I simply acknowledge it here.

ACKNOWLEDGMENTS

For intellectual friendship of a more general, but no less important, nature, I would like to thank my other faculty colleagues at the Institute: Doug Blomberg, Rebekah Smick, Shannon Hoff, Lambert Zuidervaart, Nik Ansell, Isabella Guthrie-McNaughton, and *Emeritus* Professor James Olthuis (who directed my attention to significant essays by Simon Critchley on Rorty). I single out Lambert and Nik especially for serving as provocative and critical conversation partners concerning all things "Rorty." Beyond the Institute, I wish to express gratitude to Simone Chambers of the Department of Political Science at the University of Toronto for sustained conversations regarding topics of mutual interest, and for her encouragement of my work in critical theory as well as pragmatism, and John Caruana of the Philosphy Department at Ryerson University for ongoing discussions in political theology.

Some fragments of Chapter 4 appear in an essay called "Rorty on Transcendence" in the edited collection *Looking Beyond? Shifting Views of Transcendence in Philosophy, Theology, Art, and Politics* (Amsterdam: Editions Rodopi, 2012). I am grateful to the editors and publishers at Rodopi for their permission to reprint this material. I would also like to thank Willie VanderMerwe and Wessel Stoker, organizers of the conference at the VU University, Amsterdam, whose proceeds form this collection, for inviting me to give this paper, as well as Govert Buijs for his helpful comments on it at the conference.

I would also like to thank the editorial staff at Bloomsbury for all of their help and support in seeing this manuscript through to completion, especially Sarah Campbell and Rachel Eisenhauer. I also thank the editors for granting a generous 4-month extension to my original deadline.

Finally, I would like to thank my most intimate support network. My daughter, Olivia, and my son, Ben, provide more joy to my life than they can know, and are a constant reminder to myself of the miracle of natality and the openness of the future. It may be a cliché, but there is nothing quite like seeing the world through the eyes of a child; getting down on the floor with the legos and the tea sets has provided me with a welcome sense of perspective. Plus, they are both hilarious, and crack me up all the time. Thanks cannot begin to express what I owe my wife of nearly 20 years, Cheryl Hanson, whose grace frees me from the burden of assuming this unmanageable debt, and whose beauty, wit, and intelligence leave me wondering in amazement at how quickly the time has gone. Yet I still must thank her for her unwavering belief in my calling to the (in some ways) difficult and lonely life of scholarship, as well as for the numerous other ways she holds me up.

This introduction to Rorty's thought does not pretend to be an exhaustive account of his philosophy, as more can always be said. This is the part where I as author usually claim sole responsibility for any sins of omission or commission to be found in the text. Yet I have always found these claims curious, for no author is an island, and a book is really just a moment in a larger, unfinished conversation. So if you think about it, all the people I here acknowledge and more besides have a share in the blame for any such sins, but because my name is the only one of this group on the front cover I will gladly take the heat. Be that as it may, what I have sought to do in the following pages is to create a thick intellectual portrait that will help the reader attune her or himself to Rorty's distinctive voice. Criticism begins with sympathy, and while I do not deny that there are many aspects of Rorty's work that one might wish to criticize, I have here made the hermeneutic decision to restrict myself mainly to helping the reader develop a sympathetic ear for what Rorty was trying to do (with the exception of a few, irresistible moments). My hope is that this strategy provides the best platform for subsequent critical interaction with his work.

INTRODUCTION

In the world of philosophy, not to mention other academic enclaves, the name "Richard Rorty" has come to acquire a certain mystique. Part of the reason for this surely has to do with the fact that he is hard to place on the spectrum of twentieth-century intellectual opinion. His work, often poorly understood, has garnered him the reputation of philosophical "bad boy." He is often portrayed as an ungrateful *enfant terrible* who is simply out to denounce the cherished shibboleths of modern professional Anglo-American philosophy. Those who view Rorty in this light understand him to be in league with other philosophical radicals like Jacques Derrida or Michel Foucault. On the other hand, another group of critics view him as a culturally conservative, if not reactionary, thinker, especially when he defends the American political record against what he takes to be the *faux* radicalism of the late twentieth-century cultural Left. To complicate matters, at the same time that he was being criticized and denounced by such a diverse array of critics, the *New York Times Magazine* hailed him as "the most influential contemporary American philosopher."[1] Whatever else he might have accomplished over the course of his illustrious career, Richard Rorty certainly had no trouble making waves.

Now someone who simply likes making waves for their own sake, out of the sheer desire to create havoc, is often best left ignored. "Let him thrash around," we say, "he'll tire himself out eventually." But sometimes there is an important point in making waves, and I suggest that this is definitely the case with Rorty. Rorty did not enjoy, and even lamented, the fact that many people found much of his work to be so upsetting. Yet he carried on all the same, which speaks to the fact that his work was inspired by a deep sense of vision and conviction, to which he strove to remain faithful. This introduction to Rorty's thought hinges largely around the attempt to uncover and unpack this sense of vision and conviction.

To this day, the majority of Rorty's philosophical critics balk primarily at his dismissal of the topic of truth, his attempt to replace the notion of objectivity with that of intersubjectivity or solidarity. How could any philosopher seriously recommend, as Rorty does, that we stop talking about truth, that we stop paying so much attention to the question of what truth is, or to the related question of how we are to know when we have grasped it? Only rarely do such critics stop to ask themselves what might have motivated an otherwise highly intelligent philosopher to flirt so dangerously with what they take to be an explicit piece of self-defeating incoherence; for, presumably, Rorty must think that his stated rejection of truth as a culturally important topic is itself *true*, that is, objectively true. Yet what could that possibly mean once he has rejected the very notion of objectivity itself?

As we shall see in this book, Rorty does in fact have a response to this line of criticism, even if in the end he fails to satisfy the sort of philosophical critic who launches this charge. In fact, this very failure is instructive, for it illustrates the existence of a paradigmatic difference between Rorty and many of his critics in Anglo-American philosophy. Briefly stated, in this dispute Rorty is recommending a change of subject to his philosophical peers. He is thereby attempting to engage in a form of philosophical therapy that is intended not to solve, but rather to dissolve, the epistemological problems his critics think need solving, to get them to recognize the fruitlessness or pointlessness of asking certain kinds of questions about the nature of truth and human knowledge. His epistemological arguments—or better, his arguments against the usefulness of certain epistemological concerns in professional philosophy—are best read, then, not as attempts to advance an alternative conception of truth and objectivity, but as attempts to coax philosophers to circumvent rather than address traditional epistemological questions concerning the nature of truth.

Yet any introduction to Rorty's thought would be woefully incomplete if it simply limited itself to an examination of these epistemological issues. Instead, these epistemological disputes must be understood as invitations or gateways to Rorty's richer and deeper orientation toward a variety of concerns, including moral, political, and religious concerns. If one simply takes sides at the point of this seeming impasse over the question of truth, one would miss out on the larger and very interesting cultural conversation that Rorty carried out with his time in thought. So, while Rorty does indeed have *reasons* and *arguments* by which he criticizes traditional philosophical understandings of truth, he also has moral, political, and dare I say spiritual, *motivations* for doing so. Any reader who would understand Rorty must appreciate these motivations, over and above understanding the arguments themselves.

In taking such a stand against key professional concerns in his chosen academic discipline, Rorty hoped to clear the way for more relevant yet still thoughtful conversations concerning the problems of our time. It is somewhat ironic, then, that his reputation in academic circles, a reputation for which he himself bears some responsibility, often served to block these very conversations, and so block many people's attempts to understand his work. How might one get past this block? It is my conviction that the hermeneutic key to understanding Rorty's philosophy lies in acquiring the ability to hear his unique and highly distinctive voice. This achievement is harder than it might first appear, for although Rorty's philosophical style is disarmingly direct, and his prose plain-spoken, his work remains metaphorically rich, complexly layered, and elusive. Furthermore, his candor can often be mistaken for glibness or insensitivity, when the opposite is in fact the case. It is my guess that many intelligent readers have failed to acquire an ear for Rorty's distinctive voice precisely because his smooth and easy-to-read style gives them too much confidence that they have fully understood his position, when in fact they may have missed the forest for the trees, or the implicit suggestion and nuance for the explicit, forthright articulation.

Let me illustrate this conjecture with an example. Popular philosophical lore credits Rorty with an infamous philosophical quip that runs something along these lines: "truth is what your peers will let you get away with saying."[2] Such a comment can easily be taken, and has been by many critics, as a pernicious little piece of relativism, one that reduces truth to arbitrary social convention, however achieved. Such a reading, however, assumes that Rorty has no normative understanding concerning those trials of strength and resilience through which our claims to knowledge are tested. Of course he does. Yet the very offhand way in which he puts the point does little to encourage an unsympathetic reader to investigate whatever else might lie behind it. And there's the rub; if one can find a way to become less inclined to dismiss him, one discovers the possibility of interpreting such comments in an alternative, more sympathetic light. For instance, one begins to see how the sentiment in question is an extremely condensed and colloquial version of a much more sophisticated philosophical position. Rather than reading it, in the traditional philosophical manner, as providing an essentialistic (not to mention relativistic) *definition* for a substantive named "truth," it is possible to read it instead as a highly condensed summary *description* of the social justificatory process through which our knowledge claims earn the honorific status "true." Rorty's claim here is, then, not so much about what truth *is* (a point which the inaccurate paraphrase occludes), as it is about the way in which he thinks the word "truth" gets used in those justificatory contexts in which it is invoked. He is also making the further point that he does not think it is possible for us to transcend these justificatory contexts in order to determine if our statements correspond to a reality that is completely independent of them. As he elaborates a couple of pages after the infamous quote: ". . . to say that truth and knowledge can only be judged by the standards of the inquirers of our own day is not to say that human knowledge is less noble or important, or more 'cut off from the world', than we had thought. It is merely to say that nothing counts as justification unless by reference to what we already accept, and that there is no way to get outside our beliefs and our language so as to find some test other than coherence."[3] Whether or not one ultimately agrees with Rorty's take on this matter, the lesson to be learned is that his deeper position is significantly more sophisticated and nuanced than what gets captured in his catch phrase—however pithy—when taken on its own.

I do not intend to be presumptuous in voicing the suspicion that Rorty's rhetoric has misled more than one critic, for I once fell into a similar trap myself. It might help, then, to recall the memory of my first encounter with Rorty's writings. I was first introduced to Rorty's work in a serious way in the early 1990s, as a Master's student in philosophy at the Institute for Christian Studies (ICS) in Toronto. My supervising professor, Hendrik Hart, had around that time become quite taken with Rorty, especially the books *Philosophy and the Mirror of Nature* and *Contingency, Irony, and Solidarity*. Hart, a Calvinian Christian, found in Rorty, an outspoken atheist critic of religious culture, an unlikely ally for his own Wittgensteinian critique of philosophical foundationalism in analytic philosophy of religion. The curriculum of ICS at the time required all Master's students to pursue a guided reading seminar with their supervisor, and Hart was then in the habit of using this curricular requirement to "Rorty up" his students so that they could quickly get themselves into the same philosophical conversation that he had come to find so fruitful and exciting.

I must confess that my first reaction to Rorty's work was almost completely allergic. It was not so much Rorty's critique of rationalism or foundationalism that I found to be particularly upsetting, for I was then sufficiently "with" so-called postmodernism to consider that aspect of his thought to be simply *de rigeur*. (I now fully agree with Rorty that the word "postmodern" is too broad and vague to be of much use.) Rather it was what I then took to be Rorty's glib affirmation of a rather bland version of political liberalism that really irked me. For at that time I was, and still to a certain extent am, that sort of Christian called a Christian Socialist (basically the kind that worries about suffering in the world, at a systemic level, and thinks something ought to be done about it, at a systemic level). As such, I simply could not abide what I took to be Rorty's wilful blindness toward the contribution of American foreign policy to disastrous levels of oppression and misery the world over. If Rorty had known me at the time, he would have simply considered me to be a competitor in what he called the "America sucks sweepstakes."[4] (By the way, if this is not your particular issue, don't worry; there is more than enough material in Rorty's *oeuvre* to irritate you somewhere along the way.) Anyway, I went back to Professor Hart, and I had complaints.

Hart simply advised me to reexamine the texts I didn't like, and wrestle with them in order to see if there might not be a way to read them differently (he suggested several directions). Once I discovered one such promising angle, he advised me to reread everything I had been assigned in the light of it, and then assess to what extent my original interpretation had changed. Hart's advice was a very gentle way of telling me that, in spite of my confidence in my own initial reading, my first pass at Rorty had failed to capture the depth and nuance that was in fact there to be found. I will always remember the result of this second reading, for it was extremely humbling; it was as if scales had fallen from my eyes, and I was reading an entirely different philosopher.

The only reason this story might be interesting or helpful to the new reader of Rorty has to do with the lesson I think it carries for someone thus uninitiated: one can almost always count on Rorty's thought to be richer and more complex than it at first appears. This is why I think it is important to acquire the ability to hear his unique voice. For it is only when one has been able to do so that one will be able to sound out this deeper register in Rorty's work, and it is only when one has become attuned to this deeper register that one can begin to acquire some sympathetic appreciation for his unique sense of vision and conviction to which I alluded above.

I have therefore chosen to organize this book-length introduction to Rorty's thought around the question of voice. In the first chapter, "Philosophy as Existential Quest," I present something of a biographical character sketch, or intellectual portrait, in order to provide a holistic, if somewhat curtailed, portrayal of Rorty as a person. I understand that there is no small amount of controversy with regard to the question of the direct relevance of a philosopher's biography to his or her thought (Rorty himself had suspicions concerning this matter, especially with respect to the work of the German philosopher Martin Heidegger), and that there are different schools of thought with respect to the nature of that relevance, if in fact there is any. Of course, I think there is something to be gained from understanding the details of a philosopher's life for the project of understanding a philosopher's thought, otherwise I would not waste a chapter on this topic. All the same, it is wise to avoid making direct speculative connections between such biographical details as, say, the fact that Rorty was bullied in grade school, to, say, his understanding of the religious Right in America as a cabal of fascist bullies. Instead, I will restrict my focus to those biographical details Rorty himself sought fit to publish or speak publicly about (which, ironically enough, includes the fact that he was bullied in grade school). In addition to those sources, I will here lean heavily upon Neil Gross' remarkable sociological study of the historical development of Rorty's thought and emergent intellectual self-concept, simply entitled *Richard Rorty: The Making of an American Philosopher*. As Gross explains, Rorty eventually came to see himself as a Left-wing American patriot, an anticommunist social democrat who was deeply concerned with issues of social justice and the positive role that the United States could, and sometimes did, play on the world stage.[5]

As will become clear in this chapter, this intellectual self-concept emerges from roots that extend deep into the formative experiences of Rorty's childhood. As the only child of highly intellectual, politically engaged parents, the young Rorty had a wealth of cultural resources upon which to draw while growing up. From out of this context, one comes to understand Rorty's desire to study philosophy, at least at the beginning, as part of a quest to work through certain vexing existential and spiritual concerns that already pressed themselves upon him in his early adolescence.

The following three chapters (2–4) take up key aspects of Rorty's thought, presenting them in the form of different philosophical *personae*: the philosophical therapist (Chapter 2), the liberal ironist (Chapter 3), and the anticlerical prophet (Chapter 4).[6] This approach also supports my attempt to organize the chapters of this book around the question of voice, because, as the Latin word *persona* suggests, Rorty's voice can be heard "sounding through" these different "masks," masks he uses to communicate and dramatize various aspects of his thought. By invoking the metaphor of "mask," however, I do not mean to imply that there is a "real" Rorty hiding and waiting to be discovered behind these various masks. Rather, it is this peculiar combination of masks that constitutes the very Rorty the reader hopes to meet, and it is also this peculiar combination that accounts for the oft-remarked originality of his work. It was this combination, I dare say, that led the literary critic Harold Bloom to describe Rorty, on the back-cover endorsement of *Contingency, Irony, and Solidary*, as "the most interesting philosopher in the world today." Chapter 5, the final chapter, returns to an examination of Rorty the philosopher, someone who would not simply try to evade criticism through therapy, irony, or prophecy, but a thinker who shows he is also willing to change his mind when his critics do in fact strike their mark. In particular, this chapter explores the significance of a late philosophical exchange between Rorty and Bjørn Ramberg which, interestingly, leads Rorty to significantly alter his habitually dismissive attitude toward the question of truth.

In Chapter 2, "The Philosophical Therapist," I focus explicitly on Rorty's emerging quarrel with the main epistemological currents of analytic philosophy. This chapter therefore focuses on explicating the extended argument Rorty presents in *Philosophy and the Mirror of Nature* and elsewhere, in which he engages the work of such analytic philosophers as Wilfrid Sellars and W. V. O. Quine in an attempt to show that the epistemological problems that

American analytic philosophy inherited from such logical positivist philosophers as Rudolph Carnap have exhausted themselves. As this book is an introduction, I make no attempt to exhaustively cover the technicality of these complex philosophical debates; at the same time, I strive to do justice to Rorty's emergent position with respect to them. What is important to understand for the beginning reader, I think, are the general reasons behind Rorty's growing disaffection with the state of the art in Anglo-American philosophy, and the concomitant desire to change the topic of intellectual inquiry in that milieu. Rorty's attempt to articulate such an alternative reawakens his abiding interest in the work of such first-wave American Pragmatist philosophers as William James and John Dewey. (Indeed, his discussion of these thinkers has been credited as a key reason for the renewal of interest in this uniquely American contribution to philosophical discourse.) By the end of *Philosophy and the Mirror of Nature*, Rorty has laid the groundwork for a more pragmatic understanding of knowledge and justification, one that stresses the importance of peer conversation and reason exchange (what Dewey called "warranted assertability") over against objective confrontation with a supposedly mind-independent world.

Rorty's preference for conversation over confrontation in his understanding of knowledge leads naturally into an exploration of his social and political thought. Chapter 3 thus focuses on the Rortyan persona of "The Liberal Ironist," the public intellectual who actively participates in cultural politics, or "talk about what we should be talking about." Notwithstanding such participation, one might perhaps be forgiven for thinking that Rorty did not have much, if anything, important to say regarding social and political matters.[7] Because so much of his philosophy is considered to be therapeutic in intent, his work is often read as rather quietist in nature. He does, in fact, reject the idea that anything of world-historical import hangs on the resolution of internecine disputes in a philosophical profession that he came to regard as excessively professionalized and too-narrowly specialized. At best, such philosophical reflection can be used to relieve the confusion philosophers experience concerning the problems they inherit by demonstrating how these problems are actually pseudo-problems that can be circumvented as opposed to resolved.[8] Yet the importance of this kind of activity, for Rorty, is not simply that it provides the sort of relief from intellectual pain that Wittgenstein sought, but that it can free us up to devoting our intellectual energy to more pressing (dare I say real) social and political concerns. So, while Rorty's understanding of what professional philosophy, not to mention theory in general, is able to accomplish politically is indeed quietist, that fact alone does not make him out to be a quietist himself, nor does it make him a quietist with respect to his understanding of the potential benefit that flows from intelligent discussion of the many problems humanity now faces. Rorty himself devoted a significant portion of his own intellectual energy to addressing some of these concerns. This chapter will focus especially on the peculiar way he champions the themes of solidarity, freedom, and democracy, in the context of his defense of a political liberalism that distinguishes and seeks to protect both private and public dimensions of collective human life.

In Chapter 4, I introduce the somewhat oxymoronic persona of "the anticlerical prophet," in an attempt to clarify what I take to be Rorty's ambivalent attitude toward the important cultural "dialogue" (some might instead say "war") currently taking place concerning matters of religion and faith. While most of the time Rorty comes across as a rather outspoken critic of religious culture, he also claims to follow John Dewey in being suspicious of more strident forms of militant atheism; and at times, if one listens carefully, one can detect the articulation of a kind of "hope against hope" that has a rather expectant or proleptic, if not quite messianic, character (this might be the most controversial claim I make about Rorty in this book, so *caveat emptor*). In essays like "Religion as Conversation-Stopper," however, Rorty pulls no punches in his assessment of the threat he thinks that religion poses to the realization of a vibrant and flourishing democracy. Indeed, Rorty understands monotheistic religions, especially Christianity, to represent little more than popular variants of a pernicious metaphysical ambition of transcendence, and so they must be thrown out along with the bathwater of objectivity and the correspondence theory of truth. It is Rorty the anticlerical prophet who rejects transcendence in the name of human self-reliance, an ideal that is intimately linked to his pragmatic affirmation of human responsibility. Rorty understands the metaphysical ambition of transcendence that he sees motivating both philosophical and religious insistences on the importance of Truth as simply exemplifying the human propensity to submit—and in so doing to give away our freedom as well as our responsibility for that freedom—to unanswerable, nonhuman authority. In fact, Rorty's very embrace of pragmatism is motivated by his desire for liberation from these authoritarian bonds.

In these moments, Rorty feels compelled to assume the mantle of the prophet, one who points us away from our vain metaphysical pursuit of truth as correspondence and instead turns our attention in the direction of a utopian, post-Philosophical future in which human beings have, at long last, "gotten out from under the thought of, and the need for, authority."[9] At the same time as he put on this mantle, however, he continued to engage in sympathetic conversations with religious philosophers like Gianni Vattimo and Nicholas Wolterstorff, and in these engagements one can discern in Rorty a sensitive, if not explicit, understanding of another possibility for religious culture than the Platonic ambition of transcendence that he constantly derides. This chapter seeks to shine a light on this sensitivity, not so much in order to paint Rorty in a quasi-religious light, as to mark out a certain terrain upon which religiously oriented thinkers might engage Rorty's thought in a fruitful, nonallergic fashion.

As already mentioned, Chapter 5 introduces and explores an important exchange between Rorty and Ramberg, a sympathetic critic who thinks Rorty still has one more lesson to learn from Donald Davidson's coherence theory of truth. In exploring this exchange, the chapter also introduces the work of a younger generation of thinkers who have been strongly influenced by Rorty, a group that, in addition to Ramberg, includes Rorty's former Princeton colleague Stout, and his former graduate student Robert Brandom. While demonstrably appreciative of Rorty's overall philosophical contribution, these thinkers continue to raise concerns about his wholesale rejection of the usefulness of any conception of objectivity, or what Stout calls "our interest in getting things right."[10] The main issue here involves Rorty's reading of Davidson, and whether or not Rorty successfully enlists Davidson's philosophy in support of his own version of pragmatism. As Davidson himself characterizes the potential disagreement between them, "where we differ, if we do, is on whether there remains a question how, given that we cannot 'get outside our beliefs and our language so as to find some test other than coherence', we nevertheless have knowledge of, and talk about, an objective public world that is not of our own making."[11] This chapter explores the way in which the aforementioned thinkers, most especially Ramberg, push Davidson's suggested difference between himself and Rorty, thereby returning us to a discussion of truth as objectivity, albeit one that might still fit within a pragmatist framework.

It is perhaps curious, yet somehow fitting, to both begin and end an introduction to the philosophy of Richard Rorty with the question of truth, for in spite of his recommendation that we drop this question, and despite his hope that human culture might one day be "de-metaphysicized," much of Rorty's more positive work, including his engagement with his critics, flows from and to his peculiar way of handling the question concerning truth. Rorty often advised that if we take care of freedom, truth would take care of itself.[12] This typically off-hand comment harbours and summarizes a wealth of learning and insight, the significance of which is often missed. As I discuss in Chapter 5, the many things Rorty does have to say about truth constantly push the pragmatist question, "What is truth *for*?" My hope for this book is that it will help new readers catch a glimpse of the significance of that question, and give them a firm grasp of the insights that motivated Rorty, in his inimitable fashion, to pose it.

CHAPTER 1

PHILOSOPHY AS EXISTENTIAL QUEST: RORTY'S LIFE IN THOUGHT

THE IMPORTANCE OF RORTY'S EMERGENT INTELLECTUAL SELF-CONCEPT

Before delving directly into the biographical sketch promised in the Introduction, I would first like to say something about my purpose in providing one. For what might be the point of offering such a sketch, beyond simply satisfying an idle curiosity about the personality and character of the figure behind the philosophy? Is there an important, illuminating connection to be made between the life of the thinker and the thought itself, or can we safely ignore this question and instead head straight for Rorty's arguments, assessing them on their own merits? While I do not deny the possibility of restricting oneself to the latter effort, I have become convinced that knowing a little bit about what made Rorty "tick" as a person (and, perforce, as a scholar) does much to help one become better attuned to his unique philosophical voice. Put more precisely, an understanding of Rorty's sense of intellectual identity (or what Neil Gross refers to as "intellectual self-concept") provides an important key to understanding his thought.[1]

But what exactly is it about Rorty's life and/or his philosophy that makes a discussion of biographical details important for understanding his thought? I contend that the provision of such a biographical sketch will help illuminate the consistent sources and motivations that run throughout the various threads of Rorty's philosophy, connecting what may otherwise seem to be highly diverse twists and turns that his thought has taken through the years. In saying this, it is interesting to note that Rorty himself hesitated when it came to the issue of making direct connections between the life of a thinker and the nature and value of his or her thought. This hesitation stems largely from his deep admiration for the scholarship of the German philosopher Martin Heidegger, who in addition to being a thinker of some profundity, was also an active Nazi functionary in the early 1930s, one who never officially renounced or otherwise apologized for that association. Many argue that Heidegger's involvement with Nazism irreparably taints his thought. (The critical theorist Theodor Adorno famously quipped that Heidegger's philosophy "is fascist to its innermost cells.") In a *New York Times* review of Rüdiger Safranski's intellectual biography of Heidegger, Rorty expresses this hesitation, stating that "[m]any people who learn that Martin Heidegger . . . lied over and over again about his Nazism, and that he did his best to ignore the murder of the European Jews, conclude that his writings can be neglected. For those who care about philosophy, however, things are not that simple." In the difficult case of Heidegger, Rorty concludes that one can still appreciate his genuine philosophical insight without necessarily turning a blind eye to his damning political actions. Rorty goes even further than this, however, suggesting that knowledge of such biographical details can actually be useful in our attempt to understand a philosopher's work. For example, he applauds Safranski's success in creating a narrative that entwines scholarly interpretation of Heidegger's philosophy with a critical analysis of key events in his life: "If you should decide that you ought, despite everything, to read Heidegger's books," says Rorty, "this biography will give you a good running start."[2]

But who cares what Rorty thinks? After all, one need not agree with his opinion on the relative importance of biographical information in order to come to one's own conclusion concerning its relevance. Be that as it may, Rorty must have considered the provision of such information to be even more important than he rather reluctantly admits in his discussion of Heidegger, for in order to help his readers understand his own thought, he made sure that they would have ready access to such information. Not only did he compose a highly personal autobiographical essay called "Trotsky and the Wild Orchids," he also opened all of his files to the sociologist Neil Gross, giving the latter "carte blanche" to write whatever he saw fit for his portrait of Rorty. Evidently, then, Rorty thought that the provision of such material would also give readers of his own work "a running start."

Rorty claims to have composed "Trotsky and the Wild Orchids" out of a felt need to address the varied suspicions of his many critics, and thereby place his philosophy in a more sympathetic light.[3] A similar point could be made regarding his cooperation in Gross' project. Taken together, both of these pieces provide unique insight into Rorty's motivations for practicing philosophy, and as such they help us make better sense of his highly original contribution, a contribution that sought to juxtapose, if not integrate, a complex array of philosophical voices and traditions. Both pieces help us see that Rorty's wide-ranging forays into diverse branches of philosophy stem organically from certain existential and spiritual questions that arose during his childhood and adolescence, with all the cultural resources available to an only child of two intellectually gifted, socially concerned, and politically active parents.

In *Richard Rorty*, Gross asks a deceptively simple compound question: "But who is Richard Rorty, and what is so significant about his philosophy?"[4] The very way in which the question is phrased also hints at the idea that knowing something about who Rorty *is* will help one understand the significance of his philosophy. According to Gross, an understanding of key aspects of Rorty's life will uncover the slow development of what he calls Rorty's "intellectual self-concept." Centered around the development of this latter theme, Gross' book is not so much a piece of traditional intellectual biography as it is a sociological case study (in a genre of sociology known as "the sociology of ideas") that attempts to show the crucial role that a thinker's emerging intellectual self-concept plays in shaping her career path and sense of professional vocation. The effort to discover and define Rorty's particular intellectual self-concept determines the selection and discussion of biographical details that Gross uses.

According to Gross, the emergence and crystallization of Rorty's intellectual self-concept played a decisive role at a key moment in his career as a professional academic philosopher. This moment is none other than the infamous and oft-discussed "shift" in Rorty's thought, signaled by the publication of *Philosophy and the Mirror of Nature*, "from technically oriented philosopher to free-ranging pragmatist. . . ." According to Gross, this transition reflected "a shift from a career stage in which status considerations were central to one in which self-concept considerations became central."[5] What is more, in tracing the seeds of this emerging self-concept back to Rorty's childhood, Gross is able to highlight the larger biographical context against which this intellectual shift occurs; in this light, the shift can be seen as less radical than some have supposed, one that in fact is even continuous with a larger existential quest that got Rorty interested in philosophy in the first place.

So, because understanding the nature of this shift is also a crucial part of understanding Rorty's philosophy, some knowledge of the key biographical details that contextualize it becomes important. As I noted above, an awareness of this context places this shift in a different light than the one under which it has frequently been viewed. Many Rorty commentators have tended to view him, for good or ill, as a once-favoured son of the analytic philosophical establishment in the United States who then went on, in a radical gesture, to betray that philosophical school in favour of pragmatism. In Gross' narrative, however, the shift in question appears to be rather less dramatic than the aforementioned popular account suggests, for it connects Rorty's emerging intellectual self-concept with certain values that he acquired already in adolescence as a result of his parents' profound influence. When viewed through this sociological lens, Rorty's immersion into the technical debates of analytic philosophy of mind in the 1960s and 1970s, while not in radical discontinuity with the philosophical questions he had been cultivating since his youth, begins to appear as something of an exception in his career as a philosopher, and not the rule that he would then later radically abandon.

So what is this all-important intellectual self concept? As I mentioned earlier, Gross gives it the moniker "leftist American Patriot." As a description of a persona that unites all of Rorty's other personas, this moniker is a pretty good one (even if, as we shall see, it emphasizes Rorty the public intellectual over Rorty the idiosyncratic romantic). For starters, it contains that whiff of paradox that accompanies other monikers Rorty applied to himself, such as "postmodern bourgeois liberal" (even if the latter ascription was more of a jest than anything else). These days, progressive liberal types, especially outside of the United States, tend to regard American patriotism as the exclusive purview of those on the Right. This hint of paradox, then, is a good way to allude to the complexity of Rorty's views in a brief formulation. Second, and more importantly, Gross' moniker displays the proximity that exists between Rorty's political and philosophical views (even though, as we shall also see, Rorty questioned the idea that any necessary connection must exist between them), a proximity through which the emergence of one (the politically tinctured intellectual self-concept) leads to a decisive shift in the other (the philosophical orientation). Rather than suggesting the idea that a certain brand of politics dictates the assumption of a particular philosophical stance, or vice versa (a conclusion Rorty himself repeatedly criticized), the connection I am suggesting here merely argues for the integrity of Rorty's intellectual persona, an integrity according to which a change in one area brings about a concomitant shift in other areas.

Rorty himself focuses on the idiosyncrasy of his political views as a key to understanding the trajectory of his developing contribution to philosophy. As I mentioned in the introduction, Rorty regretted the fact that many people found his work to be so upsetting. In response to this state of affairs, he took the rather dramatic step of composing the aforementioned autobiographical essay "Trotsky and the Wild Orchids." The importance of the following passage, in which he elaborates upon his motivation for composing this essay, can hardly be underestimated when it comes to the project of understanding the impetus that lies behind Rorty's work in philosophy:

> I am sometimes told, by critics from both ends of the political spectrum, that my views are so weird as to be merely frivolous. They suspect that I will say anything to get a gasp, that I am just amusing myself by contradicting everybody else. This hurts. So I have tried, in what follows, to say something about how I got into my present position—how I got into philosophy, and then found myself unable to use philosophy for the purpose I originally had in mind. Perhaps this bit of autobiography will make clear that, even if my views about the relation of philosophy and politics are odd, they were not adopted for frivolous reasons.[6]

The simple sentence "This hurts" at the fulcrum of this paragraph stands out as a testament to the fact that Rorty cared deeply about the way in which his peers received his contribution to philosophical discourse and general intellectual debate, and he did so not simply out of a concern to cement his professional reputation or to secure his place in intellectual history, either. Rather, Rorty was, among other things, a social philosopher who wished to contribute to the betterment of the society for which he wrote. For this reason, the fact that he witnessed so many prominent colleagues writing his work off as frivolous caused him no small amount of concern. If, in the process of writing his books and essays, he was also making waves, he was convinced that he was not making them for frivolous reasons. So it upset him when his peers in the academy viewed him as a mere attention seeker who was just thrashing around.

In the end, then, the provision of a biographical sketch such as the one I provide below will serve to demonstrate Rorty's integrity as a thinker, and in doing so help the new reader get past some of the common stumbling blocks that have often stymied many of Rorty's commentators. To that sketch I now turn.

FORMATIVE CHILDHOOD EXPERIENCES AND PARENTAL INFLUENCE

In "Trotsky and the Wild Orchids," Rorty portrays two sides of himself that, already in his youth, he desperately sought to integrate. One side, which we might describe as the "social" side, involved his internalization of his parents' Left-leaning political values and concern for social justice (symbolized by the figure of Leon Trotsky). The other side, which we might describe as the "idiosyncratic" side, involved what Rorty describes as his "private, weird, snobbish, incommunicable interests," interests that were nevertheless deeply important to his sense of personal identity (symbolized by his fascination with the wild orchids that grew in the mountains behind his northwestern New Jersey home).[7] One might even understand these two sides of Rorty's personality as symbolized by the two geographical regions between which his family split their time during Rorty's formative childhood years— the city of New York (Brooklyn) and the rural community of Flatbrookville, New Jersey.[8]

Rorty describes the "social" side of his emerging sense of self by relating impressions of the time he spent with his parents in New York, where both were associated with that vociferous circle of scholars and literary critics dubbed "the New York intellectuals."[9] Rorty describes the effect that his parents' Leftist political passions and commitments had on his nascent understanding of what made life meaningful. At the age of 12, he tells us, the "most salient" books on his parents' bookshelf were two red-bound volumes that comprised the report of the Dewey Commission of Inquiry into the Moscow Trials entitled, respectively, *The Case of Leon Trotsky* and *Not Guilty*. "I thought of them," says Rorty, "in the way in which other children thought of their family's Bible: they were books that radiated redemptive truth and moral splendour." During the early 1940s, Rorty would deliver drafts of press releases from the Workers' Defense League in New York, where his parents worked, to the offices of Norman Thomas (the socialist candidate for president) as well as to the Brotherhood of Sleeping Car Porters. During these subway trips, he would read the documents he carried, documents that chronicled the often violent and oppressive struggle for workers' rights in America: "they told me a lot about what factory owners did to union organizers, plantation owners to sharecroppers, and the white locomotive engineers' union to the coloured firemen. . . ." Due to formative experiences like these, Rorty explains that "at 12, I knew that the point of being human was to spend one's life fighting social injustice."[10]

Yet the youthful Rorty's sense of the meaning of life was also troubled by more idiosyncratic pursuits that he had difficulty squaring with his parents' emphasis on the pursuit of social justice. Nevertheless, he still felt that these idiosyncracies were as important as his budding sense of social concern. A few years after running messenger errands for the Workers' Defense League, these personal pursuits were exemplified by a preoccupation for the wild orchids that grew in the mountains around his rural New Jersey home. "I was not quite sure why those orchids were so important, but I was convinced that they were," says Rorty. However important these flowers seemed to him, he still could not escape the uncomfortable conclusion that his interest in them was simply eccentric. "I was uneasily aware . . . that there was something a bit dubious about this esotericism—this interest in socially useless flowers."[11] This anxiety began to take on the form of an intellectual problem for the young Rorty, which he describes as follows:

> I wanted to find some intellectual or aesthetic framework which would let me—in a thrilling phrase which I came across in Yeats—'hold reality and justice in a single vision'. By *reality* I meant, more or less, the Wordsworthian moments in which, in the woods around Flatbrookville . . ., I had felt touched by

something numinous, something of ineffable importance. By *justice* I meant what Norman Thomas and Trotsky both stood for, the liberation of the weak from the strong. I wanted a way to be both an intellectual and spiritual snob and a friend of humanity—a nerdy recluse and a fighter for justice.[12]

Here in a nutshell Rorty relates the emergence of an intellectual problem that would, in some form, remain with him throughout his philosophical career. (For example, his ultimate inability to synthesize these two dimensions of his life goes some way in explaining his endorsement of liberalism's private–public distinction, as well as his portrayal of the figure he calls the "liberal ironist" in his book *Contingency, Irony, and Solidarity*.)

As the foregoing childhood reminiscences demonstrate, one can hardly underestimate the profound influence that Rorty's parents, James Rorty and Winifred Raushenbush, had upon the formation of the existential and intellectual concerns that would eventually lead him to pursue the study of philosophy. Gross' study bolsters this impression by devoting discrete chapters to each parent. Both James and Winifred were clearly interesting intellectual figures in their own right, and not just because they acted as the primary influencers of their arguably more famous son. As mentioned, Rorty's parents were on the margins of the group known as the "New York intellectuals," which included such luminary figures as Mary McCarthy, Lionel Trilling, Sidney Hook, and Daniel Bell, and which was associated with such publications as *The Nation* and *Partisan Review*. A diverse group of thinkers with a variety of intellectual interests, the New York intellectuals formed out of the scholarly ferment bubbling under at places like City College in New York, one of few schools that was happy to accept Jewish students in the 1930s. As Gross explains, the Jewish experience of many of the group's early members was determinative for the Left-leaning outlook of the group: "If their politics ran to the far left of the political spectrum—and it did—it was because many newly arrived eastern European immigrant families regarded socialism not as a foreign idea but as part of their ethnic heritage. Radicalism and Judaism went hand in hand, both in the cultural imaginary and in social reality."[13] For non-Jewish intellectuals like Rorty's parents, who did not share this cultural background, the group was attractive insofar as it gave voice to their sense of cultural marginalization.

Moreover, the Jewish intellectuals in the group, again because of their European cultural background, could provide more easy access to the work of such influential European figures as Marx, Nietzsche, and Freud, thinkers who in different ways also spoke to the New York intellectuals' sense of cultural estrangement.[14]

While many of the New York intellectuals were attracted to socialism, which surely must have seemed prescient to them given the economic collapse that brought on the Great Depression, they also gave their Leftist politics a uniquely American twist, one that eschewed ideological group-think, valued pragmatic experimentalism, and was highly suspicious of the attempts of the American Communist Party to suppress dissent. (Gross reports that James Rorty suffered from one of the party's several purges, specifically for championing the poetry of Robinson Jeffers, whom the party saw as having fascist tendencies.[15]) The socialism of the New York intellectuals thus fit better with Trotskyist sensibilities, and this tendency was confirmed once the events of the Great Purge and other Stalinist atrocities came to light. According to Gross, "James Rorty and Winifred Raushenbush never lost their leftist leanings, but like many other New York intellectuals they eventually became fiercely anti-Communist."[16]

In addition to this taste for socialist politics, Gross also emphasizes the value the group placed on passionate, rational discussion of political, aesthetic, and other intellectual ideas. James and Winifred shared this commitment to passionate argumentation, even if, as Gross points out, they owed their radical outlook to more sources than the "expansive philo-semitism" of the group's non-Jewish members:

> Rorty and Raushenbush came to their radicalism by other paths. For [James] Rorty, it was his parents' political iconoclasm, along with his father's thwarted literary ambitions, that drove him into radical politics and writing. For Raushenbush, it was her parents' zeal for social reform. Like others in the New York intellectual circle, though, they partook of the cultural practice of "arguing the world" and made a home where radical social criticism, politics, and literature were bread-and-butter topics of discussion. Their ideas and beliefs—and the passion with which they argued for them—would not fail to impress their only child.[17]

Clearly, it is hard to underestimate the influence this level of cultural discourse would come to exercise on the thoughts and feelings of the precocious youngster whom both parents affectionately referred to as "Bucko." A closer look at the life and cultural contribution of each parent, then, will give us a stronger sense of the particular nature of that influence.

* * *

After graduating from Tufts College in 1913, James Rorty's first job was as an advertising copywriter with the H. K. McCann advertising agency in New York. He later served with distinction in the ambulance corps during the First World War, and after he returned from Europe he subsequently moved to California, once again taking up work as an advertising copywriter in San Francisco. Although employed in the advertising industry, Gross informs us that "Rorty's politics were already left of center."[18] Immediately after returning to New York from the war, he roomed in the same house as the renowned critic of capitalism Thorstein Veblen, and frequently attended Veblen's lectures at the New School for Social Research. In addition to his growing sympathy with Veblen's critique of capitalism, the net effect of Rorty's military experience also led him to distrust the conformism and group-think he felt the army encouraged, a distrust that ultimately culminated in a deep concern for the maintenance of a robust sense of individual authenticity, as well as a lifelong commitment to pacifism.

In discussing these various existential influences on James Rorty's postwar social and intellectual views, Gross notices the emergence of a tension, one strikingly similar to the one between the personal and the social with which his son would later struggle: "Already evident in his condemnation of militarism . . . was a tension that would beset [James] Rorty's work to the end: his sense that the sanctity of the individual must be preserved and at the same time his recognition that individualism is politically debilitating."[19] It would seem that perhaps, in a way similar to his son, the father also had trouble squaring his concern for the maintenance of individual authenticity with a larger concern for social justice, insofar as the latter concern transcends the realm of the merely individual. Yet as Gross points out, there seems to be more to this tension than simply a competition between a concern for individual expression, on the one hand,

and a concern for social justice, on the other. For example, Rorty came to be critical of the army because, on his view, "it turns out an extraordinary quantity of morally and spiritually diminished individuals" and is for that reason "hostile to individuality."[20] Yet at the same time Rorty's wartime experiences confirmed to him the contrary fact that there was much that was unique and distinctive about his fellow soldiers, more than the army ever took into account. Reflecting on these wartime experiences, he claimed that "my countrymen are in their way as vivid, as rich in individual personality as the French," but he would then go on to lament that, with the war now over "the individual once more becomes a factor in the political algebra of our country."[21] It seems then that the elder Rorty was struggling to affirm individual variation in democratic society in a way that strengthened rather than weakened the solidarity of the citizens that composed it; he was therefore concerned that his interest in promoting the sanctity of the individual would not slide into the social fragmentation wrought by an unhealthy individualism devoid of any common moral purpose, a tendency he saw exacerbated by capitalism's interest in reducing inescapably unique individuals to interchangeable figures in an impersonal political and economic calculus.

Perhaps in a way similar to John Dewey (not to mention Ralph Waldo Emerson or Walt Whitman), the elder Rorty too sensed the important connection between the health of any democratic society and the simultaneous flourishing of a robust sense of individual personality and uniqueness among its citizens. While Dewey lamented the sense of isolationist, atomized individualism that seemed to flow from the Western understanding of mind as something set over against one's community and one's natural surroundings, he nevertheless insisted that an alternative, more healthy concern for individual freedom would strengthen the fellow-feeling of the democratic citizen, enhancing the solidarity of the resulting community. For Dewey, a solidaristic community that was rife with individual variation was far more preferable to the uniformity imposed by a more authoritarian society: "A society based on custom will utilize individual variations only up to a limit of conformity with usage; uniformity is the chief ideal within each class. A progressive society counts individual variations as precious since it finds in them the means of its own growth."[22] The tension that both Dewey and the elder Rorty appear to be here confronting is that quintessentially American struggle to envision and achieve a society that is able to maximize the balance between acting with common democratic purpose, while at the same time creating sufficient scope for individual freedom and variation—a society able to resist the twin dangers of individualistic fragmentation, on the one hand, and conformist authoritarianism, on the other.

Unlike Dewey, however, James Rorty was more pessimistic about the kind of individualism he witnessed emerging in American society. For him, such individualism no longer resembled the healthy sort of variation that Dewey thought essential to the growth of a robust democratic culture. Instead, the individual variation he witnessed struck him as aimless and decadent, devoid of larger purpose or meaning. In 1934, shortly after Richard's birth (in 1931), and on the heels of the publication of his book *Our Master's Voice: Advertising* (an insider's indictment of the poisonous social effects of that industry), Rorty embarked on a 7-month automobile tour of America, probing the thoughts and aspirations of his depression-era compatriots. He embarked on this trip in pursuit of a larger political agenda, hoping to discover whether his fellow citizens had the inner resolve to resist capitalism and thereby overcome the social malaise that, in his view, this flawed economic system had visited upon his country.[23] His conclusions were not encouraging. In one memorable passage, he summarizes his impression of the various hitchhikers to whom he had given rides along the way:

> Often, driving alone across the lonely distances of the West, the faces and figures of these chance acquaintances swarmed before my eyes, like gnats in the sun. What profound failure of American life did this drift of human atoms signify and embody, and to what would it lead? The West was newer and I felt it more there, but even east of the Mississippi it was much the same. The people had not possessed the landscape, nor had the landscape possessed them. The balance was indeed broken. Would the landscape some day reject all these people, all the vulgar and unfeeling falsities they had created and permitted, just as it had rebuked and rejected me? Certainly some profound profanation of the human spirit had occurred, some fundamental dislocation of the natural ecology. . . ."[24]

This pessimism was emblematic of Rorty's larger social outlook. His cross-country tour did little to convince him that a genuine workers movement in America could resist the inevitable depredations of a capitalist economy: "Our domestic situation is that of a progressively deteriorating social and economic anarchy, with a definite drift toward fascism."[25]

As we have just seen, James Rorty's rather pessimistic social criticism also had an ecological bent. Part of the American malaise, he felt, had to do with the fact that "the people had not possessed the landscape, nor had the landscape possessed them." This ecological sensibility also shows up in Rorty's poetry. Alongside the many pieces of Veblen-inspired social criticism he wrote for the Left-wing magazine *The Nation* during the 1920s, he also published two collections of poems that reflect a romantic sensibility regarding the importance of humankind's relationship with nature, and the dangers of our current alienation from it. Perhaps this ecological sensibility constituted the "intellectual or aesthetic framework" in which the elder Rorty hoped to reconcile the poles of the tension he experienced between the individual and the social. Whatever might have been the case, in Gross' estimation "there could be no mistaking Rorty's strong personal attachment to nature or his belief that human kind is at its best when it is in communion with the natural."[26]

So in the elder Rorty's Left-wing politics, in his struggle with a tension between the individual and the social, and in his ecological sensitivity, we see themes that would surely not fail to impress themselves on his son. In addition to these, and as part of his larger social outlook, one also finds in the elder Rorty a suspicion of an obsession with scientific objectivity and purported value neutrality then coming into vogue in American academic circles, especially in such social sciences as economics and sociology. (This is a suspicion he also shared with his wife, Winifred.) Rorty viewed this obsession with objectivity and its concomitant claims to value neutrality as something of a moral dodge; in a time of crisis, he felt, it is important to choose sides, otherwise one's work will inadvertently serve the interests of those who prefer to maintain an unjust status quo. In *Our Master's Voice*, Rorty voices the suspicion that many social scientists of his day, such as the economist Leverett Lyon, used the guise of objectivity and value neutrality to sustain and promote the interests of anonymous capital. The elder Rorty shared Dewey's concern that academicians of this ilk refuse their responsibility to move outside the narrow circle of the empirically descriptive, in order to address in a normative fashion the damages inherent in the situations they are seeking to describe. As Gross explains, Rorty "criticized academics for embracing notions of objectivity rather than putting their knowledge to use in the service of countering ideological distortions."[27] In *Where Life is Better*, Rorty repeats this critique of the preference for value-neutral inquiry, regnant among the sociologists of his day, in words that echo Marx's Eleventh Thesis on Feuerbach ("the philosophers have only interpreted the world, the point is to change it"): "[T]hey are more interested in what is happening and in what is likely to happen than in *making* things happen—that they leave to politicians. It does no good to point out that no science and no art begins and ends with fact-finding; that some sort of social philosophy must guide the collection of facts and control their interpretation and use."[28] As we move deeper into this introduction to the younger Rorty's thought, we should keep in mind his parents' suspicion that (social) scientific claims to objectivity and value neutrality were little more than ideologically distorted attempts to evade one's moral duty to challenge the inequities of an unjust economic system: What of his parents' suspicions with respect to this matter would remain in their son's own critique of the philosophical preoccupation with truth and objectivity?

Finally, it is important to note that the elder Rorty's deep-seated pessimism does not simply boil down to a sophisticated, intellectual version of hopeless despair. Rather, his pessimism also bears witness to an unsentimental hope, or hope against hope, as one can glean from the concluding paragraphs to *Where Life is Better*:

> Wheel in a wheel. To travel over America is to see these wheels grinding faster and faster; to know that they cannot be reversed or stopped; to be shaken and terrified again and again by contemplating what their grist may be. Certainly in days to come, there can be no escape, no peace, no neutrality for anybody.
>
> Life can be made better in America. Indeed, America can be made quite magnificent. But not by those who dream dead dreams, who plead exemption from struggle on one ground or another, who cry for peace but will not pay its price. . . .

How childish are such pleas! Only when we have ceased to make them can we claim that as a people we have come of age and are worthy to challenge fate.[29]

In spite of his pessimism, the elder Rorty still points to a difficult path of possibility. This too, I think, is a sentiment that would not fail to influence the work of his son, for whom the maintenance of social hope in the face of difficult if not impossible circumstances remained a constant theme.

* * *

When it comes to assessing the intellectual influence of Rorty's mother, Winifred Raushenbush, Gross points out the limitation inherent in the fact that the volume of her published work, due to different ambitions and opportunities, is far less than that of her husband, with the result that "the content of her thought cannot be fully reconstructed."[30] Gross goes on to suggest, however, that it would be a mistake to conclude from this state of affairs that James' intellectual influence on their son was greater than Winifred's. In fact, Richard Rorty's first wife, the philosopher Amélie Rorty, offers the contrary impression, informing Gross that "Winifred's more thorough intellectual style relative to that of her 'iconoclastic, temperamental, and intuitive' husband impressed itself upon Richard."[31] And although her list of publications wasn't as long, Gross adds that "she was every bit as radical as her husband, and her intelligence and writing as sharp."[32]

Winifred Raushenbush was the daughter of Walter Rauschenbusch (1861–1918), the leading figure of the nineteenth-century social gospel movement in America (she dropped both instances of the letter "c" from her surname in an effort to anglicize it). While she shared her father's passion for advancing the cause of social justice, she also bridled at his rather Victorian understanding of gender roles. Although she rejected the label "feminist," Gross reports that she was "deeply affected by the emerging feminist movement . . . and saw its implications to go beyond the question of women's suffrage" (which her father had also supported).[33] In addition to her work as a suffragette, Raushenbush became interested in promoting and exploring an expanding range of existential possibilities for women. In her own case, the field for such exploration opened rather dramatically once she left home to attend Oberlin College, a time when her budding experiments in self-liberation put her in conflict on more than one occasion with her parents' Victorian emphasis on self-control. Even so, Raushenbush was interested in more than the aimless exploration of individual moral license. What distinguished her ethic of self-liberation from "more hedonistic strands of bohemianism," Gross says, was "the recognition that self-liberation, in politics and personal life, should be measured and serve some higher purpose." Accordingly, Gross describes Raushenbush's experimental interest in personal development as an interest in "controlled self-liberation."[34]

According to Casey Nelson Blake, the generational shift that played itself out rather tragically in Raushenbush's stormy relationship with her father involved not so much a rejection of the need to strike a proper balance between personal development and social concern, as it involved a disagreement about the means and institutions through which such a balance might be struck. Like others of her generation, Raushenbush "took up the progressive cult of the school as the site where a private life of self-fashioning met a public realm of social-scientific reform."[35] In contrast to her father, Raushenbush understood the school, and not the family, to be the incubator of both new forms of individual excellence as well as new models of civic virtue (both of which she still saw as somehow going together). Her personal interest in "controlled self-liberation," then, also found an outlet in her growing intellectual interest in the study of progressive social-scientific reform. In particular, she became attracted to the study of sociology, especially the work of the Chicago School led by Robert E. Park.

After leaving Oberlin, Raushenbush moved to Chicago, where, from 1919 to 1925 she worked intermittently for Park as a research assistant on various projects, including a study of the immigrant press and a survey of race relations along the Pacific coast. During this time, she cultivated what would become a lifelong interest in race relations and civil rights, even taking up a position with the Chicago Commission on Race Relations. Raushenbush claimed that her intellectual life really began when she moved to Chicago. Although she eventually decided against attending graduate school and pursuing a career in the academy, she clearly continued to imbibe much of the intellectual resources this culturally vibrant city had to offer. As Gross clarifies, the fact that she was not bent on entering the academy "was as much a function of her preferences for direct political action as a reflection of the conditions of possibility she would have faced on the academic labour market. . . ."[36] Notwithstanding her reservations regarding professional academic life, it is clear that she considered learning to be a lifelong affair, as evidenced by her continued professional association with Park. In an unpublished document, she goes so far as to claim that Park gave her "an apprenticeship in sociological research undoubtedly very similar in kind to that of many of his other students."[37]

In the mid-1920s Raushenbush participated in Park's Survey of Race Relations, work that took her to California (where she met James), and which resulted in the publication of several articles for *Survey Graphic*. When the Survey was completed, Raushenbush then moved with James to New York. Although she remained appreciative of Chicago School sociology, in New York Raushenbush, like her husband, grew increasingly impatient with sociologists and other social scientists who she felt hid behind a veneer of professionalism and specialization that kept them from contributing to the work of transforming an unjust society. In a 1931 piece for the *New York Herald Tribune*, Raushenbush concluded that "the academician—that is, the social scientist—dodges the very simple preliminary task of the thinker—that of counting up all the factors in the situation on the fingers of his hands. . . . He confines himself to the mole hill of his speciality or a field of mole hills, and ignores the mole hills in adjoining acres."[38]

While Raushenbush chided the social sciences of her day for refusing the responsibility of orienting social workers and other activists to the task of social transformation, she was also critical of the approach taken by many of the political radicals she came to know in the New York intellectual circle. Specifically, she grew rather skeptical of the shape of their Marxist utopianism. As Gross notes, it is not that she objected to utopian dreaming in principle, rather she felt that "utopians consistently overestimated their capacity to impose their preferred political and social systems on societies whose cultures would be resistant."[39] Raushenbush here strikes a chord, as Gross also notes, that would later become important to her son, and one that distinguished her approach to political activism from that of her husband. While both advocated for social reform, "Raushenbush insisted that such change be effected from the bottom up, not simply through the banding together of writers and intellectuals to bring attention to an issue, as had been James Rorty's preferred strategy, but through the coming together of ordinary citizens guided by the dictates of conscience and social-scientific knowledge."[40] Richard Rorty's legendary skepticism regarding the actual or possible existence of an intellectual vanguard in politics seems to be presaged by his mother's doubts about the efficacy of a top–down version of utopian dreaming. As we will discover, he often criticized the assumption that social change could be made to happen that way, and instead thought that much more is required to alter the temperament of a people than simply the intellectual effort to *argue* them, from the "top down" as it were, into adopting an alternative point of view.[41]

Another point of potential intellectual influence between mother and son can be found in Raushenbush's aesthetic interests. Her rough equivalent of her son's wild orchids was women's fashion, a topic she wrote about on more than one occasion. Although she shared her husband's Veblenesque critique of the keeping-up-with-the-Joneses' style of crass consumerism promoted by the fashion industry, her opinion of women's fashion as a culture critic softened over time.[42] Gross notes that, even in her earlier critical pieces, "Raushenbush was an admirer of the aesthetic aspects of fashion, however critical she might have been of the institution."[43] Because of this combined criticism and appreciation, it became important for her to assess the social, as well as the aesthetic, merit of fashion, and thus to move beyond what might simply have been an esoteric interest in it. In 1942, she published a book entitled *How to Dress in Wartime*, her first solo-authored work, in which she expressed the idea that women's fashion in America could be read as a cipher of that country's democratic progress toward minimizing class differences. According to her, fashion in America encouraged freedom of individual expression while at the same time granting all classes of women access to similar styles of clothing (if not quality of material). As Gross notes, "Raushenbush was not suggesting that every American should dress alike—quite the opposite. But that middle- and upper-class women had equal access to similar styles . . . could, in her view, go so far as to serve as one more indication that 'the moral axis of the world no longer lies in Europe . . . [but] seems to rest here'."[44] In describing Raushenbush's shifting thoughts on the fashion industry in this way, Gross suggests that she was, with her husband, moving toward a more patriotic version of Left-wing politics, one that was more willing to celebrate America's moral worth and political achievements, including its ability to create space for individual freedom and variation, without at the same time neglecting larger social concerns.

In moving with her husband toward this more patriotic, not to mention anticommunist, Leftist political position, Raushenbush displayed a continuous and concerted effort to fit the progressive social views she inherited from her father with her strong insistence on the importance of free individual expression. There is evidence to show that, perhaps unlike Rorty himself, she continued to strive to integrate both of these dimensions throughout her life. As with her husband, this attempt at integration seems to have turned on an emerging ecological sensitivity (which is perhaps also reflected in their preference for rural life). In a biography of Park that Raushenbush wrote late in life, she commends what she describes as Park's pioneering ecological vision. In drawing attention to this aspect of Park's perspective, Gross claims that Raushenbush established a connection between her work on this biography and her larger political agenda: "Beyond the view that sociology should guide social reform, she now took the position that what was to be most appreciated about Park was his ecological perspective, a framework for understanding the natural and social worlds that could serve as a powerful antidote to Communism."[45] In addition to the idea that this ecological perspective could serve as an antidote to communism, Blake notes that, for both her and her husband, this perspective also illuminated a promising path toward achieving the sought-after synthesis of the personal and the social. As Blake summarizes: "In their old age, Winifred and James Rorty speculated in private about a new synthesis of religion and politics, of ethics and public action, that would in effect revive the social gospel on the basis of an ecological politics and a syncretic mystical religion. They came to believe that an ethic of public obligation was the only way to organize and give meaning to the search for personal fulfillment."[46]

* * *

Hopefully, this excursus into the intellectual lives of Rorty's parents provides a sense of the sort of intellectual environment in which he was raised, helping to further contextualize the autobiographical reflections about his work that he offers in "Trotsky and the Wild Orchids." Gross notes several examples in which the young Rorty makes use of the rich cultural capital afforded him by his parents, mentioning several quite sophisticated editorials written for his school newspaper, the *Minisink Valley News*, from 1943 to 1944. Gross mentions one undated article in particular that "would have made Walter Rauschenbusch proud," in which the young Rorty observes that the American war effort might be compared "to that which Jesus fought": "Christ might be compared to an underground leader who fought to liberate the oppressed in the Roman-occupied country of Palestine.... His doctrine of liberty for the common man is what the Russians, the French, the Chinese, and we here in America fought for in our respective revolutions."[47] Gross argues that the relative sophistication and subject matter of writings such as this reflect the influence of Rorty's parents, who passed along to him "their facility with writing, critical analysis, and political discourse."[48]

Knowing more about Rorty's parents, it also seems natural that their intellectually precocious child would come to sense the importance of searching for an intellectual or spiritual framework that would integrate the pursuit of personal freedom, self-exploration, and experimentation with larger questions of meaning and purpose, that is, "the big picture." And, as Rorty claims, this is precisely what he went to the University of Chicago hoping to find.

TRAINING IN PHILOSOPHY: HUTCHINS COLLEGE, THE UNIVERSITY OF CHICAGO, AND YALE

"At fifteen I escaped from the bullies who regularly beat me up on the playground of my school (bullies who, I assumed, would somehow wither away once capitalism had been overcome) by going off to the so-called Hutchins College of the University of Chicago."[49] With these words, Rorty abruptly reports what can only be considered a major life transition. In September of 1946, he left his home and school in New Jersey to begin a unique undergraduate program at the University of Chicago. Started by Robert Maynard Hutchins, who assumed the presidency of the University in 1929, the school was designed around a classical, interdisciplinary curriculum that sought to provide historical context for modern contributions to knowledge in the social and natural sciences. The school was also unique in that it permitted entry to students after their sophomore year of high school, as it was Hutchins's view that "gifted students were ready for college-level work earlier than the American education system allowed for."[50] Because Rorty's parents viewed their son as suitably gifted, they decided, surely not without some apprehension or misgiving, that he would be more sufficiently challenged in the educational environment available at Hutchins. Rorty himself was eager to go.[51]

Although in retrospect he describes his move to Chicago as an "escape," all was not smooth sailing for this bookish 15-year-old living away from his parents for the first time. Gross reports that by the fall of his third year at Hutchins (1948) Rorty suffered through a serious bout of depression. The situation was dire enough for his parents to take their concerns about it to their family doctor, who strongly advised them to take Richard out of school while he was suffering through it. While in the end he remained in school, the 1948–9 academic year (the final year of his bachelor's program) was a difficult one for him. In the first semester, he received two C's in philosophy courses, which, in a letter to his mother, he worried would "stand on my record and be something of a constant drag in the future."[52] In spite of these two grades, he nevertheless seems to have been bitten by the philosophy bug, indicating as early as the spring of 1948 a desire to pursue studying it at the graduate level. As Gross describes: "Notable about this period in Rorty's undergraduate career is that through the haze of his depression, he was somehow able to formulate the aspiration to become a philosopher and develop a specific plan for doing so."[53]

Throughout his time at Chicago, Rorty's politics never strayed very far from the Leftist patriotism he had learned from his parents. Yet his philosophical studies did make him critical of what he considered to be the rather weak philosophical foundations underpinning his parents' social and political views. His new intellectual context at the University of Chicago helps explain this development. When Hutchins took over as President, one of the tasks he undertook was to reorient undergraduate humanities education in a more classical direction, away from the emphasis on disciplinary specialization that was coming into vogue at major American research universities. In doing so, he relied on the advice of his friend Mortimer Adler, a neo-Thomist who was also an outspoken critic of Dewey and Dewey's lasting influence at the University (Dewey had already left Chicago for Columbia in 1905).[54] In "Trotsky and the Wild Orchids," Rorty describes the academic environment he encountered at Chicago as follows: "When I got to Chicago (in 1946), Hutchins, together with his friends Mortimer Adler and Richard McKeon . . ., had enveloped much of the University of Chicago in a neo-Aristotelian mystique."[55] Although Adler may have been the most hostile opponent of Deweyan pragmatism (the unofficial philosophy of his parents' New York intellectual circle), Rorty notes that all three men were united in their criticism of Dewey:

> All of them seemed to agree that something deeper and weightier than Dewey was needed if one was to explain why it would be better to be dead than to be a Nazi. This sounded pretty good to my 15-year-old ears. For moral and philosophical absolutes sounded a lot like my beloved orchids—numinous, hard to find, known only to a chosen few. Further, since Dewey was a hero to all the people among whom I had grown up, scorning Dewey was a convenient form of adolescent revolt.[56]

All that remained, says Rorty, was whether this revolt would assume a religious or philosophical form. He appears to have taken the religious option seriously, noting, with respect to it, his admiration at the time for the poetry of T. S. Elliot and his fascination with the character of Alyosha in Dostoevsky's *The Brothers Karamazov*. In the end, however, he explains that "a prideful inability to believe what I was saying when I recited the General Confession gradually led me to give up on my awkward attempts to get religion. So I fell back on absolutist philosophy."[57] Gross summarizes that, due to the intellectual influence of his new academic environs, "Rorty was becoming convinced that there were timeless truths about human existence [that] it was the job of the philosopher . . . to discover."[58]

So it was an intellectual motivation still very much in line with the one he felt during high school that encouraged Rorty to pursue graduate study in philosophy. His parents were immediately supportive, although his mother characteristically expressed a worry about the negative consequences of academic isolationism and elitism. One of the challenges he would have to meet, she told him, would be to prevent the danger of a life spent in the university causing him to lose touch with the nonacademic world: "If you stick to universities by way of evading this problem—which is what many maybe most academicians have done . . . —that would not be good . . . . I am confident that you will take this hurdle in your own good time and that you will not cramp the so far beautiful development of your life by an evasion."[59] His mother's sense of intellectual responsibility to the wider world beyond the academy would not be lost on Rorty, who often composed reflections for a more general audience, and took the task of being a public intellectual seriously. It seems he was able, by and large, to avoid the evasion his mother worried about, as he would go on to become one of the most widely read philosophers outside of the academy in his day.[60]

Although Rorty always had the option to stay on at Chicago for his Master's education, given his recent mental health issues his parents thought it might be better to explore other options closer to home. They engaged their social network, including James Farrell and Sidney Hook, in an attempt to help Rorty gain admittance to Harvard or Columbia, two schools in which he had expressed interest. The advice of Hook and Farrell was not exactly encouraging, largely due to the fact that Rorty's peculiar academic profile strayed so far from current academic norms. He therefore followed the default route and stayed on at Chicago. As Gross explains, "[t]he Hutchins College program was too out of sync with the rest of the American University system for other schools to know what to do with someone who had graduated at age eighteen after only three years of coursework. Richard decided to stay on at Chicago, and the experiences he underwent during his next three years there would prove formative for his later thought."[61]

Unlike many other philosophy departments in America at this time, the University of Chicago's department resisted the trend toward a near exclusive focus on the technical domain of analytic philosophy. As Gross puts it: "In a field increasingly defined by logical positivism, Chicago maintained an eclectic orientation."[62] Although one of the founding figures of logical positivism, Rudolf Carnap, held a position there, thanks to the impress of Hutchins, Adler, and McKeon, the faculty remained strong in ancient philosophy and the history of philosophy generally. As well, the presence of a philosopher like Charles Hartshorne, under whom Rorty would write his Master's thesis, ensured that American pragmatism as well as the metaphysics of Alfred North Whitehead remained part of the discursive air as well. Yet the real division in the department was between the "moderns" (represented by Carnap) and the "ancients" (represented by McKeon), with the latter group receiving most of the departmental emphasis and thus a higher share of the more serious students. Eschewing the "presentism" of the logical positivists, Rorty joined ranks with those students and professors "who insisted that philosophical insight was a matter of erudition with respect to the history of philosophy."[63] Although Rorty took a wide variety of courses, he especially enjoyed the ones he took on the philosophy of other historical periods, including medieval philosophy. "It soon became clear to Rorty," Gross says, "that his *métier* was historically oriented philosophizing."[64]

Yet Rorty was not interested in becoming a specialist in the philosophy of any historical period. Rather, around this time he acquired a taste for synoptic works that offered a panoramic view of the history of philosophy, like Hegel's *Phenomenology of Spirit*.[65] Socially speaking, he spent more time outside the department with students in the Committee on Social Thought, many of whom, including Allan Bloom, were disciples of Leo Strauss.[66] While Rorty did not consider himself to be such a disciple, he mentions in more than one interview that he appreciated being around the intellectual prowess of the other members of this group: "Strauss's students were the brightest people in the university," he says, "so I was glad to be part of his circle, even though I never really grasped his point of view."[67] One can easily imagine, however, that during a time when Rorty was doing his best to be "some kind of Platonist,"[68] he would seek out just the sort of conversations that were taking place in Strauss's orbit.

Rorty's preference for the company of students in the Committee on Social Thought represents something of a tendency in his attitude toward academia. Throughout his career, he seems to have preferred the company of broader, more interdisciplinary thinkers to that of specialist, technical philosophers; his interest in synoptic views of philosophical history chimes with this preference for generous scope over technical detail. At the University of Chicago, Rorty came to describe this preference in terms of a rearguard defense of the very metaphysics that was one of the logical positivists' main targets. While Rorty had kind words for Carnap, whom he credits for giving him his "first lessons" in analytic philosophy, the fact that his sympathies lay more with the broad, metaphysical interests of someone like Hartshorne is evident in a 1950 letter he wrote to his mother. In it he describes a paper he wrote for Carnap, claiming (in characteristically self-deprecating fashion) that it will have little interest to anyone "except the little clique of reactionary metaphysicians (the rank to which I aspire) who are trying to stop the positivist invasion."[69] These "metaphysical aspirations" would culminate in a thesis on the metaphysics of Whitehead, specifically focusing on the latter's treatment of the theme of "potentiality." The thesis argues, in an attempt to augment rather than refute Whitehead, that "real potentiality" as opposed to "ideal potentiality" is the true ground of human freedom.[70]

After receiving his MA from the University of Chicago, Rorty went on to pursue doctoral studies at Yale. His decision to attend Yale University would prove just as fateful for his future career path as would his choice of the University of Chicago, allowing him to continue to steep himself in philosophical subjects outside the parameters of analytic philosophy. Like Chicago, the philosophy department at Yale understood itself as somewhat of a foil to the analytic emphasis that had been sweeping through other philosophy departments, most notably at Yale's perpetual rival, Harvard. Once the home of such pragmatists as William James and Josiah Royce, not to mention the speculative metaphysics of Whitehead, Harvard's department in the 1950s had become dominated by, if not precisely the program of logical positivism, "a technical vision of philosophy" that emphasized symbolic logic and considered natural scientific understanding as the paradigm of knowledge. "In this context," says Gross, "philosophers in the Yale department sought to carve out a distinctive disciplinary niche by defining themselves as resistors of technicism and torchbearers for more traditional forms of philosophical inquiry, especially ethics, metaphysics, and the philosophy of religion."[71] Yale's approach to philosophy was therefore more pluralist and less single-minded than Harvard's, encouraging "dialogue among advocates of different approaches who all took seriously philosophy's historic mission."[72] Rorty applied to and was accepted by both schools, although only Yale promised a full, "free-ride" scholarship. The difference in offers from the two institutions likely had much to do with the fact that Rorty's knowledge in the history of philosophy and his classical training was a better fit for Yale's profile. Also, given his parents' limited means, his eventual decision to attend Yale over Harvard likely had as much to do with the size of Yale's award, as it did with his own perception of his fit with the department.

At Yale, Rorty worked under the supervision of Paul Weiss, who, according to Bruce Kuklick was "a metaphysician of the grand style."[73] Like Hartshorne, Weiss was also a student of Whitehead at Harvard, although, as Gross notes, "Weiss was less prone than Hartshorne to championing Whitehead's views."[74] What is more, Weiss and Hartshorne worked closely together at Harvard editing the papers of Charles Sanders Pierce. Both of Rorty's graduate supervisors, then, had an appreciation for pragmatism as well as sympathy for metaphysical reflection, especially of the Whiteheadian variety. Weiss's metaphysical reflections took up Whitehead's problem concerning the reconciliation of process and permanence. In distinguishing his approach from Whitehead's, "Weiss claimed that being is always and intrinsically incomplete, oriented as it is toward the future it will become."[75] For his dissertation, Rorty again picked up the theme of potentiality, this time exploring its treatment in three historically unique philosophical systems: Aristotelian, seventeenth-century rationalism (Spinoza, Descartes, and Locke), and logical empiricism. Gross explains Rorty's rationale for continuing to write on this topic as follows: "The reason for writing on potentiality was that, as Rorty saw it, the efforts of the logical empiricists to deal with this notion had been largely unsuccessful; greater traction on the problem could only be had through dialogue with other schools."[76] The 600-page dissertation Rorty finally composed does not argue for a return to previous philosophical systems, but instead recommends that modern, technically oriented philosophy take the theme of potentiality seriously, a topic Rorty's mentors taught him to think of as "an inescapable philosophical category."[77]

It is fascinating to learn that Rorty, who in *Philosophy and the Mirror of Nature* would mount a scathing criticism of what he took to be philosophy's obsession with "permanent neutral frameworks," devoted so much of his intellectual energy in graduate school to the study of metaphysics. Yet perhaps this is not so odd, for the precise metaphysical theme he seized upon, potentiality, is the very place where the metaphysical tradition tries to come to terms with the realities of creativity, freedom, spontaneity, and novelty, themes that receive a prominent place throughout Rorty's *corpus*. Gross suggests that in following this theme Rorty was taking up the following challenge Hartshorne issued in his 1950 essay "Whitehead's Metaphysics": "A difficult concept in Whitehead is that of the

Creativity, or the ultimate ground, or substantial activity. Is this a sort of God beyond God? I have some doubt whether all his utterances on this topic can be reconciled."[78] While Rorty may not have considered it his task to perform the required reconciliation, it would seem that his metaphysical interests in graduate school were still continuous with his search for an overarching intellectual framework for understanding reality that would not leave out his fragile and fleeting wild orchids.

PROFESSIONAL LIFE: BEFORE AND AFTER *PHILOSOPHY AND THE MIRROR OF NATURE*

Rorty received his PhD from Yale in 1956, at only 25 years of age. Upon completion of the degree, he was drafted into the US Army, where he worked for 2 years in the computer section of the Signal Corps. Gross reports that Rorty found his military service to be emotionally trying, and Rorty himself looks back with regret that he did not do more to avoid it: "I was drafted into the army because I stupidly didn't delay my dissertation until past my twenty-sixth birthday. I have no idea why I was that dumb."[79] Once discharged from the military, Rorty was keen to make up for lost time. He received an instructorship position at Wellesley College in 1958, which turned into an assistant professorship in 1960.

While at Wellesley, he seems to have taken to heart Hook's advice to "publish early and often." Gross desribes Rorty's ambitious research agenda during this time as divided into two main streams.[80] The first stream, following the path set out in his doctoral dissertation, concentrated on playing the role of translator between analytic and nonanalytic approaches to philosophy. As we have seen, Rorty's graduate training prepared him well for this task; although Rorty pursued the metaphysical theme of potentiality throughout his graduate studies, he did not do so in ignorance of the technical approach of analytic philosophy, especially at the doctoral level. His attempts at brokering the difference between analytic and nonanalytic approaches would continue at Wellesley, where both his familiarity with and appreciation for analytic philosophy would deepen.

Rorty's growing appreciation for analytic philosophy can perhaps be best understood once we consider the second research stream Gross mentions, which involves Rorty's attempt "to make a case for pragmatism's centrality for the analytic project."[81] Rorty was one of the first philosophers to highlight pragmatist themes in the work of such contemporary analytic philosophers as W. V. O. Quine and Wilfrid Sellars. These two thinkers in particular did much to challenge the basic assumptions of the logical positivist program, while thereby not eschewing the technical methods of so-called analytic or "linguistic" philosophy.[82] This period also marks the time when the influence of the posthumous publications of the later Wittgenstein, especially the *Philosophical Investigations*, was beginning to assert itself in North American analytic philosophy. Rorty saw this development as an opportunity to make a case for an emerging sympathy between elements of classical pragmatism and the latest developments in analytic thought. In a 1961 article, Rorty argued for the continued relevance of Pierce's pragmatism for current analytic debates, suggesting that "Pierce's thought envisaged, and repudiated in advance, the stages in the development of empiricism which logical positivism represented, and . . . came to rest in a group of insights and a philosophical mood much like those we find in the *Philosophical Investigations* and in the writings of philosophers influenced by the later Wittgenstein."[83]

Rather than consider the details of Rorty's position vis-a-vis analytic philosophy at this point, I here simply call on the reader to notice the fact that, from the earliest stages of his professional career, and indeed even stretching back into his graduate studies, he remained engaged with pragmatist philosophy, even if he did not yet explicitly align himself with this tradition, as he would later. His early professional work, then, can be seen as a development of his efforts in graduate school to point to places where pragmatist philosophy could help address the problems confronted by contemporary analytic philosophers. Nor was Rorty alone in this type of engagement. The common assumption that analytic philosophers of the 1950s and 1960s ignored or failed to take account of the earlier contributions of pragmatist philosophers is simply mistaken. Gross points to such figures as Quine, Morton White, and Sellars as Rorty's precursors in the effort to establish a conversation between the classical pragmatists and contemporary analytic philosophy. Because Rorty's early professional research contributions can be seen as a continuation of these efforts, it would be wrong to conclude, as several commentators have done, that his interest in pragmatism arose only after he made a definitive break with analytic philosophy in the 1970s. To the contrary, says Gross, "his earliest work is characterized by a desire to harness pragmatist insights in the service of a revised conception of the analytic project."[84]

While Rorty's efforts at this early stage of his professional career were continuous with the philosophical pluralism he evinced in his graduate studies, one nevertheless detects a drift toward a deeper engagement with analytic philosophy at this time, a development not completely explained as an organic evolution of the philosophical problems he had been addressing up to this point. As Gross notes, there came a certain time when Rorty jettisoned the metaphysical aspirations he entertained at Chicago, and began to consider himself more as a linguistic philosopher than as a critic of the analytic tradition. Gross makes a strong case for the fact that Rorty's career ambitions played a major role in this transition. Rorty himself, in the "Intellectual Autobiography" he composed for the volume of the *Library of Living Philosophers* dedicated to his work, claimed that, already at Yale, he sensed that the analytic philosophy of Carnap and Quine might well be "the wave of the future," and so he felt some pressure to become part of that wave, even if he still had a distaste for its more reductive and positivistic versions. This pressure would only intensify once he landed a prestigious appointment at Princeton: "My first years at Princeton I was desperately trying to learn what was going on in analytic philosophy," he confesses. "Most of my colleagues had been at Harvard, and you had to know what they were talking about at Harvard in order to be with it."[85]

Of course, Rorty's transition into analytic philosophy cannot be explained in terms of sheer opportunism either. Although he was definitely an ambitious professional scholar, a thinker of Rorty's integrity could only respond to the professional pressure he felt to practice a certain mode of philosophy by finding a figure in that world whose work he could engage authentically. Gross hypothesizes that, in the philosophy of Wilfrid Sellars, Rorty found just such a figure. His encounter with Sellars's philosophy allowed him to make a more fulsome shift into the analytic fold, providing "the symbolic materials necessary for him to begin telling a coherent story" about his transition into it.[86] Sellars, then, provided the gateway through which Rorty could authentically respond to the professional pressure he felt to move further in the direction of a full immersion into the world of analytic philosophy. As Gross notes, although Sellars' influence alone did not turn him into an analytic philosopher, his engagement with Sellars allowed him to pursue a philosophical program that could be recognized as important at the highest levels of a discipline that was becoming increasingly dominated by analytic philosophy, without thereby dropping his other concerns: "Sellars, along with Wittgenstein, Quine, White, and others, provided Rorty with a model he could follow that did not require him to abandon the other philosophical commitments—to the reality of vagueness, the richness of intellectual history, and the valorization of intersubjectivity—he had previously held dear."[87] That said, Gross still believes that "conformity to disciplinary status structures" was the major factor driving Rorty to embrace analytic philosophy, an embrace that, as later developments would show, fit rather awkwardly with his deeper sense of intellectual identity.[88]

Rorty was at Wellesley for only 3 years before he landed the aforementioned position at Princeton. He remained at Princeton from 1961 to 1982, receiving tenure there in 1965, and becoming full professor in 1970. By that time, his CV could boast credit as editor of an important anthology surveying the field of contemporary analytic philosophy, *The Linguistic Turn* (for which Rorty also composed a substantive introduction), as well as many journal publications, including an innovative and well-received article in *The Review of Metaphysics* addressing current analytic debates in the philosophy of mind, entitled "Mind-Body Identity, Privacy, and Categories." With the publication of this latter article, in 1965, Gross concludes that "Rorty's transition from Whiteheadian Metaphysician and McKeonesque historian of philosophy to mainstream analytic philosopher was complete."[89]

The story of Rorty's post-tenure career at Princeton, however, is one of increasing disenchantment with the state of the art in analytic philosophy, especially with what he came to regard as its excessive narrowness and professionalism. Although, as Gross suggests, Rorty continued to work in a "modified analytic mode" throughout his career, his basic philosophical orientation did shift in the years leading up to the publication of *Philosophy and the Mirror of Nature* in 1979. During that time, he became more interested in such continental figures as Jürgen Habermas and Jacques Derrida (and, by way of Derrida, Martin Heidegger). He also renewed his interest in engaging broad, interdisciplinary studies by participating in discussions with members of Princeton's Institute of

Advanced Study, including Quentin Skinner, Thomas Kuhn, and Clifford Geertz (Kuhn's work would become especially influential on Rorty's thought). Finally, from the early 1980s on, he increasingly came to identify himself as an antifoundationalist pragmatist in the Deweyan or Jamesean mold, and no longer as an analytic philosopher.

While there are too many steps on the road from Rorty's embrace of mainstream analytic philosophy to his thorough disenchantment with its dominant preoccupations to mention here, a couple of key episodes might serve to highlight the nature of his growing dissatisfaction. The first has to do with his objection to the "presentism" or "ahistoricism" of the analytic movement. In a 1974 letter to the classicist Michael Frede, whom Rorty hoped would become a colleague at Princeton, Rorty expressed the following opinion of Princeton's philosophy department: "I find it a bit terrifying that we keep turning out PhDs who quite seriously conceive of philosophy as a discipline in which one does not read anything written before 1970, except for the purposes of passing odd examinations. I think that a genre of philosophy is coming into existence in which, to be sure, it will be unnecessary to read further back than four years or so. But I would like our students to know that there are also other genres of philosophy."[90]

Rorty's second major source of dissatisfaction with analytic philosophy had to do with its cultural relevance, or lack thereof. This concern can perhaps be traced back to his parents' strong moral conviction that intellectual work ought to remain responsive to social need. Recall Winifred's worry that life in the university would tempt Rorty to evade such a responsibility. James shared his wife's concern, as illustrated in the following response to one of his son's published analytic papers ("Pragmatism, Categories, and Language," published in *Philosophical Review* in 1961): "I realise belatedly that philosophy is concerned not so much with *what* to belief [*sic*], but *how* to believe or doubt or think—at least that this is the chief present preoccupation of philosophers, the epistemological problem as I find it called, having looked it up in the Oxford dictionary for the twentieth time." As Gross, notes, anyone who knew Rorty's father would perceive the subtle dig present in these comments: "If philosophy is not about what to believe, if someone who is well educated has to consult a reference source twenty times to understand it, of what use is it to life?"[91] Rorty was close to his parents, and surely comments like these must have remained in the back of his mind throughout this period of academic professionalization, perhaps even playing a major role in his disenchantment with analytic philosophy and his reembrace of pragmatism. At any rate, this perceived cultural irrelevance would become a major problem for someone coming to increasingly identify himself as a pragmatist philosopher, a philosopher for whom the worth of an idea is to be measured according to its usefulness in addressing particular human problems. As Gross notes: "The problem, from the perspective of pragmatism, was not just that [the analyst's] emphasis on precision and finality led them to employ technical methods that made their work impenetrable by others but also that there was little relationship between the issues they were taking up and those of real concern to the rest of the world."[92]

Rorty's growing dissatisfaction with analytic philosophy put him at odds with many of his colleagues in Princeton's philosophy department. While there is little evidence of outright hostility or acrimony, Rorty's post-tenure moves surely isolated him within his department. This sense of isolation led to an increasing desire to find new employment, preferably a position outside a philosophy department altogether; due to the dominance of analytic philosophy throughout the profession, he had little confidence that he would be any less isolated in the philosophy departments of other leading universities. Rorty's fame ensured that, once he put feelers out, many attractive offers came his way. As Gross tells the story, he bided his time until just the right kind of opportunity arose. The stars would align for him in 1982, when, with a lucrative MacArthur Foundation "genius grant" in hand, he took up a university professorship as Kenan Professor of the Humanities at the University of Virginia, a position that would allow him to become "a sort of all-round intellectual, or man of letters. . . ."[93] He would remain there until 1998, when he took up a position as Professor of Comparative Literature at Stanford University, where he became Professor Emeritus after retiring in 2005. He died of pancreatic cancer at his home in Palo Alto, California, on Friday, June 8, 2007.

Philosophy and the Mirror of Nature, then, marks a turning point in Rorty's career as a professional philosopher, even if we can locate sources for that turning point at several places in Rorty's past. In this book, he felt that he had adequately expressed his dissatisfaction with the state of the art in analytic philosophy, as well as pointed to an alternative, more "edifying" model of intellectual discussion for philosophy to pursue. In "Trotsky and the Wild Orchids" he describes what he took to be the book's personal accomplishments: "I had gotten back on good terms with Dewey; I had articulated my historicist anti-Platonism; I had finally figured out what I thought about the direction and value of current movements in analytic philosophy; I had sorted out most of the philosophers whom I had read." In spite of these not inconsiderable achievements, however, he confesses that the book did not do much for the "adolescent ambitions" that got him started reading philosophy in the first place. According to him, the topics it treated, such as the mind-body problem and Kuhnian philosophy of science, "were pretty remote from both Trotsky and the wild orchids." Upon its publication, he says, "I was no closer to the single vision which 30 years back, I had gone to college to get."[94]

Much of the story of the next 25 years of Rorty's intellectual life can be understood in terms of his response to this supposed failure, and the twists and turns of that story will occupy us for much of the remainder of this book. We will see how Rorty would come to consider the original quest itself as something of a mistake, a problem that he thought could be cured, not by hitting upon the right solution, but instead by dissolving the problem perceived to lie at the heart of the question itself: the need to integrate one's private and idiosyncratic desires and fascinations with one's public and social responsibilities. Yet here we are already jumping too far ahead; in the next chapter, we will look more closely at Rorty's extended argument against epistemologically focused analytic philosophy in *Philosophy and the Mirror of Nature*, including the motivations that led him to reembrace the pragmatism of his parents and their intellectual cohorts.

CHAPTER 2

THE PHILOSOPHICAL THERAPIST: RORTY'S CRITIQUE OF "PHILOSOPHY-AS-EPISTEMOLOGY"

CHANGING THE SUBJECT: RORTY'S THERAPEUTIC INTENTION

There is a famous quote from Ludwig Wittgenstein that reads: "The real discovery is the one that makes me capable of stopping doing philosophy when I want to."[1] At first blush, this quote sounds quite odd: Why *start* doing philosophy in the first place, when success (the *real* discovery) is measured by one's ability to stop? Why go through the ordeal at all? Yet, if we linger over this quote awhile, nuances emerge, and we start to pick up more than just the hint of vague paradox. For starters, Wittgenstein's use of the word "capable" hints that he finds himself *incapable* of stopping, yet his use of the word "want" indicates that he would like to. What kind of peculiar situation is this? Wittgenstein later compares it to the condition of a fly trapped inside a bottle, repeatedly banging its head against the invisible barrier in a vain attempt to escape. Wittgenstein's aim for philosophy, then, is "to shew the fly the way out of the fly-bottle."[2] The real philosophical discovery is the discovery of the elusive opening, the discovery that allows the fly to escape, and so finally cease banging its head against the glass.

§133 of Wittgenstein's *Philosophical Investigations*, where this quote about the desire to cease philosophizing emerges, is the *locus classicus* for understanding philosophical activity as a form of intellectual therapy, and that is why I raise it at this point in my exposition of Rorty. In full, §133 reads:

> It is not our aim to refine or complete the system of rules for the use of our words in unheard-of ways.

> For the clarity that we are aiming at is indeed *complete* clarity. But this simply means that the philosophical problems should *completely* disappear.
>
> The real discovery is the one that makes me capable of stopping doing philosophy when I want to.—The one that gives philosophy peace, so that it is no longer tormented by questions which bring *itself* into question.—Instead, we now demonstrate a method, by examples; and the series of examples can be broken off.—Problems are solved (difficulties eliminated), not a *single* problem.
>
> There is not *a* philosophical method, though there are indeed methods, like different therapies.[3]

The nonsystematic, therapeutic approach to philosophy that Wittgenstein here outlines provides a key to understanding much of what Rorty attempts to achieve in his *magnum opus*, *Philosophy and the Mirror of Nature*. One can profitably read a large portion of that book (certainly the first two parts) as an updated attempt to show the fly the way out of the bottle. (The third and final part is, on Rorty's own admission, a relatively underdeveloped exploration of how we flies might make best use of the open air beyond these glassy confines.[4]) Rorty is therefore in broad agreement with Wittgenstein that many of the key problems that occupy contemporary Western philosophy are little more than fruitless head-banging exercises. As opposed to directly addressing or attempting to solve these problems, Rorty thinks we are better off putting them aside. Instead of seeking their theoretical resolution, we should undertake their therapeutic dissolution.[5]

Of course, it will be hard to show this purported fly the way out of the bottle if it does not mind, but rather enjoys, all the buzzing around, and if, furthermore, it does not agree that it is in any sort of bottle at all. To say the least, then, not all philosophers would agree with Rorty (or Wittgenstein) that vast stretches of their intellectual activity amount to little more than the repetition of symptoms (heads banging against glass) masking a deeper—undetected and therefore unaddressed—malaise (being trapped in a bottle). Indeed, it is predictable and understandable that many of them would take offense to just such a suggestion (a state of affairs that helps explain why *Philosophy and the Mirror of Nature* rubbed so many of Rorty's analytic peers the wrong way). Before accepting any therapeutic approach to philosophical puzzles, then, one must first diagnose the need for it, or concur with such a diagnosis, and the problem is that many if not most philosophers fail to recognize anything "pathological" about their endeavours at all.[6]

The difference in philosophical approach I am here outlining is the difference between seeing most if not all of the philosophical problems that occupy professional philosophers (especially in the Anglo-American philosophical establishment) as real problems that are capable of genuine solution, or, alternatively, simply seeing most of them (at least some of the more dominant ones) as pseudo-problems, the historical result of acquired philosophical baggage that we can now do without. Do we need everything in these suitcases? Rorty thinks we can put much of this luggage down, without thereby missing anything we really need. He can only make this claim, however, because he has thoroughly inspected the baggage himself.[7] The philosophical detail he provides in the first two parts of *Philosophy and the Mirror of Nature* makes the reader privy to that thorough inspection. The result, as we shall see, is Rorty's recommendation to drop much of this luggage, and thereby stop asking certain sorts of questions and stop speaking in certain kinds of ways. In making these recommendations, however, he hopes we will become able to ask different sorts of questions and start speaking in different kinds of ways (and here he moves beyond a strictly therapeutic approach). In his therapeutic persona, then, Rorty seeks to liberate philosophers from certain inherited fixations, so that they may be free to explore more fruitful intellectual paths. Philosophical therapy is a necessary step in this transformative process, even if it is not a sufficient one.

Yet given the profundity of the transformation Rorty envisions (and which we will explore in detail below), it is somewhat perplexing to hear him frequently adopt a rather casual rhetorical tone when arguing for it. This tone is evident, for example, in his extensive use of the language of "setting aside" and "dropping."[8] Such language seems to suggest that undertaking the kind of radical change he envisions amounts to little more than nonchalantly letting go of one view and blithely picking up another. Yet this nonchalance does not seem to comport well with the seeming radicalism of his philosophical challenge. His recommendations seem to ring with the insouciance of one who was never struck with any philosophical ailment in the first place, someone who is thus cheerfully able to assure his worried philosophical colleagues that little is lost and much is gained through the dissolution of traditional philosophical problems. "Come on in, the water is warm," one can almost hear him say.

While Rorty's apparent insouciance might throw us off the trail, I suggest that it would be a mistake to conclude from such a rhetorical posture that he fails to recognize the profundity of the shift for which his philosophical therapy calls. In fact, there is a way to understand such rhetoric as embodying a recognition of that very profundity; the change which Rorty recommends is of such a revolutionary nature that it must be framed as the adoption of a new paradigm or vocabulary, one that necessitates "dropping" or "setting aside" the older vocabulary, including many if not most of its lingering problems. Furthermore, while a good many readers may find this rhetorical posture alienating, I think Rorty in fact intended it to be encouraging. He wanted to give his readers the sense that the change he hoped they would make, while indeed profound, is at the same time not akin to a scary, rug-pulling gesture. After making it, he thinks, much remains the same as it did before, even if one's orientation in the midst of these unchanged (though, of course, not invariant) things has radically altered.

So even though the familiar facts of ordinary existence do not change through this transformation (i.e. the transformation does not cause them to change), we ourselves change, and this has consequences for our understanding of the world; it allows us to relate to things differently, to see all things new. So when later, in *Consequences of Pragmatism*, Rorty will talk about "The World Well Lost," he is not talking about a world that we now possess but for some reason must throw away or do without. Rather, he is speaking about a world we never did have and never could get. The baggage he would have us drop or "lose," then, has to do with the problems surrounding our philosophical attempts to demonstrate a path to the secure access of such a world.[9] At the end of the day, he questions the desire for certainty that leads us to construe the human mind as something that is able to achieve privileged, incorrigible access to a mind-independent, invariant reality, and thus serve as a permanent anchor for human knowledge. As we shall see, he views the desire to secure such anchorage to be damaging, and any claims to have in fact secured it as illusory. His philosophical therapy is intended to help those who remain beguiled by this philosophical picture to see that they can do without it.

Rorty's awareness of the profundity of the change for which his therapeutic approach calls will become clearer once we achieve a firmer grasp of what he finds particularly objectionable about dominant trends in Western, Anglo-American philosophy. Which philosophical views and problems in particular did he hope his peers would come to understand as futile distractions best left behind? I will provide a broad answer to this question in the next section. With that framework in place, we will be in a better position to understand the philosophical details involved in Rorty's recommendation that Western philosophy undertake such a wholesale makeover to its self-image.

WHAT'S THE MALADY? RORTY'S DIAGNOSIS OF PHILOSOPHY-AS-EPISTEMOLOGY IN *PHILOSOPHY AND THE MIRROR OF NATURE*

The philosophical problems Rorty attempts to treat in *Philosophy and the Mirror of Nature* fall roughly into two categories: dualism in the philosophy of mind (the "mind-body" problem), and, flowing from this problem set, "representationalism" in epistemology (or the theory of knowledge). Representationalism, as Rorty understands it, is the philosophical position that defines true knowledge as an accurate mirroring relationship between the immaterial mental contents of the mind and the material or physical elements of a mind-independent world, and includes the idea that we have an inner faculty telling us when such a match takes place. As I have already mentioned, behind these two problem complexes, Rorty also detects the operation of a quest for certainty that he, in line with his heroes Wittgenstein, Heidegger, and Dewey, ultimately considers to be detrimental and dehumanizing. Throughout the history of Western philosophy he perceives a desire to secure human knowledge to what he calls a "permanent framework" for all possible inquiry, a desire inspired by the conviction that we can only be assured of our knowledge if we can find a way to secure it to such an invariant foundation.[10] According to Rorty, this philosophical foundationalism encourages an ahistoricist intellectual orientation or frame of mind, one that values necessity over contingency, permanence over change, and incorrigibility over fallibility. According to Rorty, these metaphysical priorities have trickled down into ordinary language, shaping the common sense of the West.[11]

Yet in failing to appreciate the inescapability of contingency, change, and fallibility, Rorty contends that we have lost sight of an important aspect of our humanity. He considers the foundationalist refusal of fallibilism to be a pernicious form of philosophical hubris, and in defense of a more humane modesty he would have us consider the possibility that the apparent obviousness of this foundationalist understanding of knowledge does not imply its correctness; rather, the seeming obviousness of this way of thinking about knowledge might simply be a sign that a historically contingent vocabulary has become hardened, like a layer of sediment. According to Rorty, this sedimented understanding of human knowledge can itself be loosened, and therefore we can be liberated from what otherwise might seem to be an intractable aspect of our way of thinking about knowledge. Because he ultimately judges this historical legacy to be deeply problematic in today's context, he thinks it is important for us to establish a freer relationship with it; he thinks Western culture would be much improved if it became liberated from these intellectual fetters, and the desire for such liberation motivates much of the book. To this end, *Philosophy and the Mirror of Nature* offers a kind of genealogy of the dominant Western way of defining knowledge, a genealogy, as we have seen, with therapeutic intent. That is, by illuminating the heritage of a certain Western understanding of knowledge, Rorty hopes to persuade his reader of its historical contingency as opposed to its ahistorical necessity.[12]

Rorty wastes no time underlining these (rather ambitious) therapeutic intentions, offering the following statement of intent at the beginning of the book:

> The aim of the book is to undermine the reader's confidence in 'the mind' as something about which one should have a philosophical view, in 'knowledge' as something about which there ought to be a 'theory' and which has 'foundations', and in 'philosophy' as it has been conceived since Kant. Thus the reader in search of a new theory on any of the subjects discussed will be disappointed. Although I discuss 'solutions to the mind-body problem' this is not in order to propose one but to illustrate why I do not think there is a problem. Again, although I discuss 'theories of reference' I do not offer one, but offer only suggestions

about why the search for such a theory is misguided. The book, like the writings of the philosophers I most admire, is therapeutic rather than constructive.[13]

As the above quote clearly demonstrates, Rorty intends to employ therapeutic methods in order to break up what he considers to be sedimented thought patterns. In much the same way as Wittgenstein, he thinks his fellow philosophers have become captivated by a "picture," and that to become free from such captivity they must somehow be able to step outside of the frame that surrounds it.[14]

Such stepping out, however, is a difficult purchase, for the picture itself is deeply rooted in our tacit assumptions. As Wittgenstein describes this tricky situation: "A picture held us captive. And we could not get outside it, for it lay in our language and language seemed to repeat it to us inexorably."[15] The difficulty here involves our inability to see the picture *as* a picture, that is, not grasping the fact that the perspective it affords is not the only possible one. As we have seen, Rorty also wishes to jog his reader out of tacitly accepting as necessary a particular philosophical picture that is actually contingent. The "diagnostic narrative" he offers in *Philosophy and the Mirror of Nature* is intended precisely to allow his reader to see this picture as one that is both contingent and therefore optional.[16]

But what ideas or themes in particular does he think go into this picture's composition? He answers that question as follows:

> The picture which holds traditional philosophy captive is that of the mind as a great mirror, containing various representations—some accurate, some not—and capable of being studied by pure, nonempirical methods. Without the notion of the mind as mirror, the notion of knowledge as accuracy of representation would not have suggested itself. Without this latter notion, the strategy common to Descartes and Kant—getting more accurate representations by inspecting, repairing, and polishing the mirror, so to speak—would not have made sense.[17]

Notice the therapeutic rhetoric at work in this paragraph, especially the word "without" (a very important word for Rorty, appearing in the title of many of his philosophical papers). Rorty's use of the word "without" portrays his desire to illuminate (not to mention eliminate) the causes that lead to what he thinks are "symptomatic" (or problematic) construals of knowledge and human intellect; "without" these causes, the symptoms themselves will also disappear.

Ultimately, however, Rorty's diagnostic narrative traces the origin of our intellectual malaise to deeper historical sources than such Enlightenment figures as Descartes and Kant, arguing that it reaches all the way back to the cradle of Western philosophy (and civilization) itself. For him, the representationalist epistemologies these modern thinkers introduce are simply updated historical versions of the perennial philosophical attempt "to eternalize the normal discourse of the day." So while, as we shall soon discover, Rorty thinks that the philosophy of the modern period represents a historically unique "style of reasoning," its self-image continues to be dominated by the desire for eternalization.[18] In the final analysis, Rorty objects to the modern picture of the mind as a mirror of nature because he is suspicious of any attempt to "eternalize the normal discourse of the day," whether ancient or modern. According to him, it is precisely such an attempt, and the fact that we are too-often tempted to undertake it, that causes us to be held captive by a contingent historical picture as though it were permanent and necessary, and not a picture at all. And once a picture holds us captive, we become incapable of stepping outside of it, and the problems it creates will seem to demand (for Rorty, impossible) solution, blocking the path to their therapeutic dissolution.

Before exploring Rorty's particular arguments against the modern conception of the human mind as a mirror of nature, then, I first wish to explore briefly his concern with what he takes to be philosophers' perennial attempts to "eternalize the normal discourse of the day." What in particular does he think is wrong with such attempts? The phrase "eternalize the normal discourse of the day" is a mouthful, as it should be, because it contains a highly condensed formulation of one of Rorty's most important critical themes (and as such, it will make its appearance in several places throughout this book). In this phrase, Rorty invokes Thomas Kuhn's distinction between "normal" and "abnormal" science, and extends that distinction to cover the entire range of human discursive practice, whether we are speaking about the natural sciences, the social sciences, the humanities, the professions, etc. "Normal" discourse denotes the debate and discussion that takes place within a settled intellectual paradigm, in which all the interlocutors more or less agree with each other on what the problems are, which methods are best suited to go about solving them, and which vocabulary is the best one to use in describing them. "Abnormal" discourse, in contrast, takes place in the absence of such consensus; abnormal discourse occurs in the wake of a once-dominant paradigm that is now crumbling under the weight of its inability to synthesize or incorporate new, anomalous discoveries and information. For Kuhn, the existence of "abnormal" science, or the historical alternation between periods dominated by normal and abnormal science, points to the historical nature of scientific inquiry. We can, he thinks, extrapolate from our awareness of such historical alternation to posit the future recurrence of such alternation. That is, what we now take to be "normal" science might itself become unsettled by new discoveries; currently reigning scientific paradigms may (nay, will) themselves one day crumble, as others have in the past. Rorty shares Kuhn's nonlinear, historicist understanding of scientific "progress," and thinks that Kuhn's insights can be extended to cover the development of human discursive practice as a whole.[19]

We are now getting closer to the reason why Rorty thinks it is problematic to "eternalize" the "normal" discourse of the day. For Rorty, to "eternalize" something is to fail to take into account the historical circumstances surrounding its emergence, including the way in which that history shapes what has emerged. It is to understand today's normal discourse ahistorically, as something that just dropped out of the sky, fully formed. What is more, such "eternalizing" also serves to cement normal discourse, thus impairing our ability to imagine alternatives to it. As a consequence, eternalizing also hampers our ability to engage in or even recognize "abnormal" discourse, especially when such discourse might in fact be just what the doctor ordered. In worrying about our attempts to eternalize normal discourse, Rorty is not disparaging such discourse, nor is he simply expressing an eclectic preference for novelty and change over against permanence and stability. Rather, he is seeking to draw our attention to, and simultaneously protect, the space of possibility, a space that becomes neglected or crowded out once a culture has eternalized what is after all historically contingent normal discourse.

As described, Rorty's Kuhnian historicism chimes with his therapeutic intensions; on his view, contemporary Western philosophy has inherited a previous era's normal discourse (one whose historical emergence can itself be seen as an "abnormal" or revolutionary response to a previous era's "normal" discourse). With hindsight, we can understand today's normal discourse as originating in an understandable response to a particular historical moment (a moment that included such issues as the intellectual struggle between the emerging natural sciences and the metaphysics of the schools, the need to make a case for religious tolerance in the wake of the wars of religion, etc.). With these historical struggles more or less resolved, Rorty encourages us to view the lingering philosophical problems that have managed to survive them as vestiges whose continuing usefulness we now have reason to doubt. A big part of the story he tells in *Philosophy and the Mirror of Nature* concerns the way in which the modern self-image of philosophy as a foundational discipline and superjudge of all areas of human culture has emerged from (and outlived) particular historical attempts to deal with particular historical problems.[20]

Rorty's particular hope for his diagnostic narrative is that a dose of philosophical therapy can help us break with our "truth habit" (if I may use such a curt phrase to label Rorty's extended critique of representationalist epistemology). This is another way of saying that Rorty thinks we may be living in an "abnormal" or revolutionary (in the Kuhnian sense) time, a time when the answers provided by today's "normal" discourse no longer suffice. While he cannot be certain that our historical moment is characterized by such Kuhnian abnormality, his hunch is that this analysis of our situation gives us a better grasp of our time in thought.[21] So while Rorty stops short of offering bold predictions concerning the immanence of a paradigm shift, he does think that such a shift is called for, and it is something he encourages. The attempt to eternalize the normal discourse of the day, then, is "self-deceptive" for Rorty because it ignores the historically contingent character of all normal discourse, and in so doing it also prevents us from remaining open to new possibilities—those helpful alternatives that are discovered through or spun out of abnormal discourse.

With this broad framework of Rorty's therapeutic diagnosis now in hand, it is time to explore in finer detail his specific arguments against the peculiarly modern attempt to eternalize the normal discourse of the day. As mentioned above, Rorty mainly objects to modern philosophy's dualism and representationalism. He would thus have his philosophical audience reconsider their tacit acceptance of a Cartesian understanding of the mind as a separate, interior, mental space, a space that must somehow be coordinated, through a representational mirroring relationship, with an exterior, independent, material world. Rorty hopes his therapeutic attempt to disabuse us of this picture will clear the way for an alternative, roughly Sellarsian, understanding of thought and knowledge that he dubs "epistemological behaviorism" (a position that is not to be confused with physically reductionistic variants of psychological behaviorism).[22] In Rorty's words, to be behaviorist in the sense he intends "is not to offer reductionist analyses, but to refuse to attempt a certain sort of explanation. . . ."[23] But what sort of explanation does he refuse to attempt? I now turn to a closer examination of the deceptively simple answer Rorty gives to this question.

PHILOSOPHY FROM DESCARTES TO KANT: PROBLEMATIZING DUALISM AND REPRESENTATIONALISM

The sort of explanation Rorty refuses to attempt, and urges us not to attempt, is implicated in what he considers to be the foundationalist legacy of the Western philosophical tradition, particularly as it comes to paradigmatic expression in the modern period. Rorty's primary target, then, is the intellectual identity that emerges over the course of the seventeenth and eighteenth centuries, especially in the philosophical developments leading from Descartes (1596–1650) to Kant (1724–1804). During this period, Rorty sees the emergence of a conception of philosophy as the superjudge or final arbiter of all areas of human culture—a nonempirical, "armchair" discipline that is somehow able to identify the invariant foundations upon which all human knowledge must finally rest.

Rorty's interest in exploring this portion of intellectual history, as I have already indicated, is genealogical and therapeutic. He wishes to uncover and criticize the aforementioned sense of philosophical self-identity, because it, along with its attendant problems, would continue to beguile philosophers in the twentieth century. For this reason, his diagnostic narrative seeks not only to tell us how this sense of identity came to be historically, it also seeks to describe its subsequent career, including, as mentioned, the way it would come to dominate the self-image of twentieth-century Anglo-American philosophy. In this latter part of the story, philosophers like Sellars and Quine become the heroes, deconstructing this inherited self-image, and thereby showing philosophers how to escape from the bottle in which they find themselves trapped. Rorty views himself as continuing the work thinkers like Sellars and Quine started.

Of course, in telling this story, Rorty does not think there is an unbroken progression between the image Kant gave "the philosopher" in the eighteenth century and the self-image of such twentieth-century rationalists as Bertrand Russell and A. J. Ayer (for no historically sensitive philosopher would simply skip over the nineteenth century, and the impact of such thinkers as Hegel, Kierkegaard, and Nietzsche). Yet he does see these twentieth-century philosophers as the inheritors and renovators of a certain image of the philosopher as cultural overseer that was codified during the neo-Kantian revival of the late nineteenth century, and that is why it is important for him to tell a story about the path he sees philosophy taking from Descartes to Kant.[24] Rorty thus provides his reader with his own telling of the Descartes-Locke-Kant progression in modern Western philosophy, a terrain that will be roughly familiar to anyone who has taken an introductory philosophical survey course of this historical period. As we shall see, however, Rorty's genealogical and therapeutic intentions give his telling of the story a unique twist as compared to standard textbook accounts. The story Rorty tells is full of rich detail and nuance, and while I cannot do justice to that detail and nuance here, I will attempt to mark the major highlights and milestones of the story he tells about this crucial period of intellectual history.

Our story begins with Descartes, whose epistemological innovations represent nothing less for Rorty than "the invention of the mind" (the title of Chapter I of *Philosophy and the Mirror of Nature*). According to Rorty, the particularly important epistemological innovation Descartes introduces is the idea of mental "representation," a concept that he thinks has no precise equivalent in Aristotle's "hylomorphic" conception of knowledge. On the latter conception, says Rorty, "knowledge is not the possession of accurate *representations* of an object but rather the subject's becoming *identical* with the object." For example, on the Aristotelian interpretation, when one comes to know a frog or a star "[t]he substantial forms of frogness and starness get right into the Aristotelian intellect, and are there in just the same way they are in the frogs and the stars—*not* in the way in which frogs and stars are reflected in mirrors." Descartes' insertion of a mental space of representation between the knowing subject and the object known obviates the possibility of such Aristotelian hylomorphism. For Aristotle, the question of the fidelity between our perceptions and the things we perceive, or our knowings and the things we know (if they truly are perceivings and knowings), could not arise because his notion of hylomorphic participation does not allow for the idea of a mentalistic gap between the two. Descartes' insertion of a mental space between subject and object, on the other hand, sets up precisely this problem. With the introduction of this third term, philosophers would come to feel the need to posit the working of an "Inner Eye" that surveys these representations, "hoping to find some mark which will testify to their fidelity."[25]

Rorty goes on to suggest that Cartesian epistemological anxiety, or the newfound historical currency of the question concerning how "anything which is mental represents anything which is not mental," has become so central to our modern understanding of what it means to "think philosophically" that we are surprised to learn that neither Plato nor Aristotle were ever troubled by it. This is not to say that "the Greeks" (as Rorty refers to them) lacked a concept of mind, or even a concept of mind as separable from the body, but rather to say that the Greek mind-body distinction differs in kind from the distinction Descartes and his heirs made. The Greeks mapped their mind-body conception onto their distinction between the universal, eternal, and unchanging, on the one hand, and the particular, the temporal and the changing, on the other. This invidious distinction had no place for those peculiarly modern mental entities like sensations and feelings, which are themselves nothing physical, but rather ghostlike apparitions appearing before the eye of the mind. For somewhat obvious reasons, the Greeks placed the senses firmly on the body side of the divide.[26] But the senses are not the same thing as "sensations" in the modern philosophical sense, as the latter were introduced precisely to allow philosophers to speak of interior states of consciousness or mental events without thereby committing themselves to saying anything positive about the nature or existence of something in the external physical world. The idea of a "sensation of the colour red" or of being "appeared to redly" as a separate, interior state or event, ontologically distinct from anything in the external world, could simply not arise in Aristotle's hylomorphic account.[27]

Rorty thus suggests that in Descartes we see a transition from an understanding of "mind-as reason" to an understanding of "mind-as-consciousness." The Greek conception of "mind-as-reason" seeks to identify that aspect of human persons that is able to grasp universals (the mind, albeit "as-reason"), and to distinguish it from that aspect which takes care of sensation and motion (the body). Descartes' innovation requires a new mind-body distinction, one between "what is consciousness and what is not consciousness." According to Rorty, the modern distinction is more radical than the ancient one; it is no longer simply a "faculty" distinction between different capacities of one and the same being: "It was more like a distinction between two worlds than like a distinction between two sides, or even parts, of a human being." What is more, because Descartes' mind-body distinction is so radically different from that of the Greeks, he must also begin a new search for the feature that designates the mental *qua* mental: "Once mind is no longer synonymous with reason, then something other than our grasp of universal truths must serve as the mark of mind." Descartes' ultimate answer to that question is precisely what will distinguish modern dualism from the ancient version.[28]

Yet what motivates this new search for the mark of the mental? Another way of putting this question is to wonder why the old mark of the mind lost its currency or ceased to be compelling. Why, that is, did a philosopher like Descartes come to see the need to insert a third term between subject and object, thereby creating an epistemological problem where previously none existed? Part of the answer has to do with the very radicality of the modern mind-body distinction as compared to the ancient one. On this distinction, bodies are thought of as material in a most mechanistic, corpuscularian sense. In support of this contention, Rorty cites A. G. A. Balz, who suggests that, while Descartes would have liked to attribute imagination, sense, and feeling to the body, his acceptance of a corpuscularian mechanics prevented him from doing so: ". . . if the pain, caused by the knife, is not a property of the knife as a constellation of modes of matter, it cannot be a property of that constellation of modes of matter that is the human body. So perforce pain and all the remainder of our immediate experience must be dumped into the soul substance."[29] Descartes is thus set upon his revolutionary path because of a perceived need to provide new foundations for immediate experience in light of the fact that the corpuscularian mechanics of the ascending natural sciences had so thoroughly disturbed the former, largely Aristotelian ground. The cultural acceptance of a mechanics that considers the human body as nothing but a "constellation of modes of matter" will have trouble framing the "immediate experience" of imagination, sense, and feeling in terms of physical embodiment. The body thus conceived is just too stupid to be capable of providing for such experience. Another, nonphysical factor must be found to account for it.

Rorty astutely notices that the transition from mind-as-reason to mind-as-consciousness inflates our understanding of the mind (and thus deflates our understanding of the body), expanding the category of the mental to include more than simply the workings of reason, traditionally understood. Descartes must therefore identify a mark or criterion that will unite this diverse array of states of consciousness. Rorty notices, however, that Descartes provides no "explicit doctrine" to answer this question. At the same time he locates a "badly argued" hunch in Descartes, according to which indubitability emerges as the new mark of the mental, the one thing that unites the diverse array of conscious inner states and events: "The hunch in question here was, I think, that the indubitably known mathematical truths . . . and the indubitable momentary states of consciousness had something in common—something permitting them to be packaged inside of one substance."[30] Rorty argues that Descartes discovers the answer to his quest for the mark of the mental inside of his own question: the feature that mathematical truths share with momentary states of consciousness is precisely their indubitability:

> If I am right in thinking that Descartes' badly argued hunch, the one which made him able to see pains and thoughts as modes of a single substance, was that indubitability was the common factor they shared with nothing physical, then we can see him as working his way around toward a view in which indubitability is no longer the mark of eternality, but rather of something for which the Greeks had no name—consciousness. Whereas previous philosophers had more or less followed Plato in thinking that only the eternal was known with certainty, Descartes was substituting 'clear and distinct perception'—that is, the sort of unconfused knowledge gained by going through a process of

analysis—for 'indubitability' as a mark of eternal truths. *This left indubitability free to serve as a criterion of the mental.*[31]

In this rather dense passage, Rorty is saying that, whereas the Greeks considered indubitability to be the mark of eternality, Descartes instead considered indubitability to be the mark of this new thing called consciousness. So, as opposed to the mark of eternal truths being indubitability (as it was for the Greeks), for Descartes the mark of eternal truth becomes clear and distinct perception. In replacing indubitability with clarity and distinctness as the mark of the *eternal*, Descartes frees indubitability to serve as the criterion of the *mental*, or consciousness.

Rorty considers Descartes' understanding of mind as consciousness, with indubitability as its mark, to be a rather fateful shift in intellectual outlook, and he also gives this shift a different interpretation than one commonly found in other standard accounts:

> The Cartesian change from mind-as-reason to mind-as-inner-arena was not the triumph of the prideful individual subject freed from scholastic shackles so much as the triumph of the quest for certainty over the quest for wisdom. From that time forward, the way was open for philosophers either to attain the rigor of the mathematician or the mathematical physicist, or to explain the appearance of rigor in these fields, rather than to help people attain peace of mind. Science, rather than living, became philosophy's subject, and epistemology its center.[32]

In this passage, Rorty adroitly detects a reversal of priorities. The Greeks valued certainty because they understood it to be a mark of the eternal, and as such an indicator that one is following the path of wisdom, a path that values the enduring over the fleeting. The moderns, on the other hand, seem to value eternality (*qua* clarity and distinctness) only insofar as it leads to certainty, thus giving the achievement of certainty a teleological value that the Greeks themselves apparently did not attach to it. The result is that in the modern period epistemology becomes central in a way that it had never been before, and the philosopher-*qua*-epistemologist (not *qua* lover of wisdom) ascends to the throne of the overseer of all cultural endeavour.

As Rorty's narrative continues, Locke makes his entrance as a key player in the further development of Descartes' intellectual revolution. In particular, Rorty sees Locke's conception of the "idea" moving into the space opened up by Cartesian consciousness (which, to recall, collects such diverse items as imagining, feeling, and sensing under the wide umbrella of "thinking" or *penser*). In the wake of Descartes' recently established mentalistic vocabulary, Locke's "idea," although an old word, would come to name something new under the sun: "Once Descartes had entrenched this way of speaking it was possible for Locke to use 'idea' in a way which has no Greek equivalent at all, as meaning 'whatsoever is the object of the understanding when a man thinks' or 'every immediate object of the mind in thinking'."[33] According to Ian Hacking, Locke's distinctive intellectual contribution would inaugurate "the heyday of ideas," a time in which the "idea"—because of its capacity to form the interface "between what [Locke and his contemporaries] conceived of as the world and their Cartesian egos"—ascends to the status of primary unit or instance of knowledge.[34]

Rorty notes an additional curiosity in the Lockean conception of the "idea," one he thinks ultimately amounts to a fateful confusion: this is the quasi-causal role Locke understands it to play in the justification of knowledge. Locke is wont to describe ideas as impressions formed on the blank wax tablet of our minds. Rorty catches a faint whiff of Aristotelian hylomorphism in this way of describing human knowledge acquisition, insofar as the impression so formed shares something (although something formal, and not substantial) with whatever it is that *forms* the impression. That is, the impression bears witness to an immediate causal relationship between the impresser and the impressee (the shape of the impression on the tablet being formally the same as that which shaped it). Yet how literally does Locke intend us to understand his image of the *tabula rasa*? Rorty thinks Locke waffles here, because at the end of the day he remains too Cartesian to be satisfied with the veridicality of impressions in and of themselves. The Cartesian question concerning how we might *know* that these subjective impressions are faithful to their objects still concerns Locke in a way it never would have Aristotle. So, while Locke's "idea idea" allows him to give an account of knowledge justification in quasi-causal terms, for Locke such an account remains insufficient on its own: "It is as if the *tabula rasa* were perpetually under the gaze of the unblinking Eye of the Mind—nothing, as Descartes said, being nearer to the mind than itself. If the metaphor *is* unpacked in this way, however, it becomes obvious that the imprinting is of less interest than the observation of the imprint—all the knowing gets done, so to speak, by the Eye which observes the imprinted tablet, rather than the tablet itself."[35]

Rorty tells us that Locke's inability to stick to his causal guns here does not signify a failure of nerve, so much as it shows him trading on an ambiguity that is itself productive for his philosophy. The ambiguity in question concerns the status of the Lockean idea: is it simply a "quasi-object in inner space" still needing to be epistemologically confirmed by the mind's Eye, or does its presence to mind certify "the knowledge that such an object was there"? Because Locke finally understands sense impressions (i.e. ideas) in a Cartesian way, that is, as *representations*, he cannot in the end avail himself of something akin to Aristotle's hylomorphic understanding of the *identity* of the mind with the object known (when it knows). Rorty thus argues that Locke needs something he otherwise denies himself: "a faculty which *judged* the representations rather than merely had them. . . ." Locke's empiricism has no room for such a faculty, however, because for him to make such room "would have intruded a ghost into the quasi-machine whose operation he hoped to describe." Locke thus ends up "balancing awkwardly between knowledge-as-identity-with-object and knowledge-as-true-judgment-about object," says Rorty, and this tightrope finally will not hold.[36]

Rorty ultimately finds Locke's epistemological predicament untenable because it represents a confusion of reasons with causes. His notion of an immaterial tablet "splits the difference between simple physiological fact and speculative metaphor" and thus strives to reconstrue the social practice of knowledge justification in quasi-physiological terms.[37] Because this attempt ultimately fails, Locke must constantly shuffle between a metaphorical and more literal construal of his image of the *tabula rasa*. In this way, his account of knowledge introduces a confusion "between a mechanistic account of the operation of our mind and the 'grounding' of our claims to knowledge."[38] For Rorty, these are two distinct things. A "mechanistic account of the operation of mind" simply involves the natural scientific attempt to *explain* the proper functioning of a certain aspect of biological organisms like ourselves. The effort to "ground our claims to knowledge," on the other hand, involves the social practice of exchanging reasons in order to justify what we believe before our peers in the court of public opinion. Rorty understands Locke's confusion of reasons with causes, or justification with explanation, as at bottom an ignorance of this important distinction. Invoking Sellars, Rorty claims that Locke's confusion of explanation with justification commits a mistake similar to that of the so-called naturalistic fallacy in ethics (deriving an "ought" from an "is," or an ethical conclusion from a natural fact); it is an attempt to analyze epistemic facts (reasons) completely into non-epistemic facts (causes), or to confuse a causal account of how one comes to have a belief with the justification one might have for that belief.[39] (Rorty's criticism of Locke's confusion of explanation with justification is one of the more important criticisms that he makes of modern philosophy, and we will have cause to return to it later when we examine Rorty's reading of Sellars.)

So for Rorty the shuffle in Locke's treatment of knowledge is not simply between the physiological brain and Aristotelian *nous* (mind-as-reason) but "between knowledge as something which, being the simple *having* of an idea, can take place without judgment, and knowledge as that which results from forming justified judgments."[40] Rorty construes this particular shuffle as a shuffle between "knowledge of" (simply *having* an idea) and "knowledge that" (*judging* the fidelity of a representation). Locke's "idea idea" prevents him from thinking about knowledge as knowledge-that, or as the product of an act of judgment. Instead, in line with his quasi-causal conception of "impression," he thinks of knowledge as knowledge of, something you simply get once the wax tablet of your mind has been dented by an object in the world. Yet, as Rorty argues, because Locke's notion of idea waffles between that of an impression identical to its object and that of a representation whose fidelity to said object remains to be judged by the mind's Eye (and because Locke leans more heavily toward the latter, Cartesian construal), Locke's account requires, yet lacks, an understanding of judgment, of our ability to acquire "knowledge that."

Here, of course, is where Kant enters the scene. As Kant would notice, empirical accounts of human knowledge such as those of Locke or Hume neglect to account adequately for the role human judgment plays in its acquisition. Locke's epistemological shuffle thus ignores the "synthesis" involved in any instance of knowledge, the fact that human cognition is the product of "intuitions" (roughly, Humean presentations to sense) getting together with "concepts" (Kant's categories) to form knowledge. Kant attempts to provide what he thinks is missing in empiricist (and also rationalist) accounts of knowledge with his argument for the foundational role played by what he calls "synthetic a priori judgement"—the capacity that ensures that the sensory manifold presented to our awareness is always already and necessarily (i.e. a priori) interpreted, connected, and unified (i.e. *synthetic*) through the innate, universal concepts or categories humans bring to any experience. In Kantian terms, Locke's image of the *tabula rasa* is all intuition and no concept, and as Kant reminds us, "intuitions without concepts are blind."[41]

Rorty considers Kant's "Copernican revolution" in philosophy—through which he reinterprets what used to be considered "outside" the mind as a product of what takes place "inside" of it—to be somewhat of a step in the right direction, yet only insofar as it represents a significant move away from Locke's modeling of knowledge on perception ("knowledge of") and toward the possibility of modeling knowledge on predication ("knowledge that"). Rorty maintains, however, that Kant remains caught up in the Cartesian problematic, to the extent that his Copernican reversal is still an attempt to answer the Cartesian question of how we get from the inside to the outside. By simply reversing the direction (from outside to inside), Rorty does not think Kant sufficiently shifts the terms of the problematic. So on Rorty's account, Kant has one leg stuck in the Cartesian fly-bottle, and therefore has not succeeded in escaping from it.[42]

Similar to his reading of Descartes, Rorty provides his reader with a breathtaking reading of Kant, dismantling the argument of *The Critique of Pure Reason* in a mere eight, swashbuckling pages. Rorty concludes that Kant takes only a half step in the direction of understanding knowledge as predication, or "knowledge that," because he thinks Kant's notion of synthesis, while ostensibly incorporating an act of judgment, still remains an odd, hybrid species of "knowledge of." For Rorty, a person forms a predicative judgment when they come to believe a sentence to be true, an activity that takes place completely within the social space of exchanging reasons. Kant's synthetic a priori judgment is a different animal: "For a Kantian transcendental ego to come to believe a sentence to be true is for it to relate representations (*Vorstellungen*) to one another: two radically distinct sorts of representations, concepts on the one hand and intuitions on the other."[43] Here Rorty construes both concepts and intuitions as representations, something "in mind," and that is why he thinks Kant ultimately fails to escape the Cartesian paradigm. Kantian synthesis remains a peculiar version of "knowledge of" because it still seeks to get behind reasons to causes, to transcend the social space of reason exchange and anchor human knowledge to something structural and invariant.

After Kant, says Rorty, philosophy is left with a bifurcated picture of knowledge, or "cognitive experience," according to which it is understood as the combination of an "immediate" or "given" component (intuition), and a formal, constructive, or interpretive one (concept). Underlying this duality, Rorty argues, remains the modern philosophical desire to substitute reasons with causes that we saw in Locke, giving philosophy its modern image as the nonempirical discipline that locates and isolates these peculiar causes:

> Thought is only *philosophical* if, like Kant's, it looks for causes of, rather than merely reasons for, claims to empirical knowledge .... Philosophical thinking of the sort which finds this duality [between what is given and what is interpreted] inescapable is supposed to do more than tell us that normally we have knowledge when we have justified true belief, referring us to common sense and common practice for details about what counts as justification. It is supposed to *explain how knowledge is possible*, and to do that in some a priori way which both goes beyond common sense and yet avoids any need to mess about with neurons, or rats, or questionnaires.[44]

As we shall see, Rorty the pragmatist does not think much, if anything, can be added to the definition of knowledge as justified true belief, and he thinks that there is no court of appeal outside the bounds of common sense and common practice (talk about neurons, rats, and questionnaires) to tell us what counts as justification. The search for a more compelling form of justification than the one provided in "the logical space of giving reasons" inevitably leads us to confuse causes for reasons (and in Kant's case, synthesis for predication).[45]

So the sort of explanation Rorty refuses to attempt, and encourages his reader not to attempt, is the foundationalist one that he finds running from Descartes through Kant. He summarizes his position by claiming that we can think of knowledge in two ways, one which he prefers and the other which he eschews. He would prefer it if we would think of knowledge as a relation to propositions, and thereby of justification as "a relation between the propositions in question and other propositions from which the former may be inferred." If we thought of knowledge in this way, says Rorty, we would see no need "to end the potentially infinite regress of propositions-in-defense-of-other propositions." This social practice will come to its own natural, albeit provisional and temporary, end "once everyone, or the majority, or the wise, are satisfied." Yet the philosophers we have been examining do not construe knowledge in this pragmatic, social justificatory way. Instead of regarding knowledge as a relation to propositions, their way involves thinking of knowledge "as privileged relations to the objects those propositions are about." If we think of knowledge in this second way, says Rorty, "we will want to get behind reasons to causes, beyond argument to compulsion from the object known, to a situation in which argument would be not just silly but impossible, for anyone gripped by the object in the required way will be *unable* to doubt or to see an alternative."[46] Philosophers who understand knowledge in this second way are never satisfied when Rorty thinks they should be. That is, they refuse to consider any "merely human" form of justification to be sufficient. For his part, Rorty cannot see why they should feel the need for a higher standard of satisfaction than the pragmatic one which he thinks is the only one that does any real work.

Although Rorty does not consider the historical development that culminates in the modern "theory of knowledge" to be linear, he nevertheless understands this development to form a thread that extends from the seventeenth century through the neo-Kantian consensus of the nineteenth century and into twentieth-century analytic philosophy. He gives this development the following summary description: "The theory of knowledge will be the search for that which compels the mind to belief as soon as it is unveiled. Philosophy-as-epistemology will be the search for the immutable structures within which knowledge, life, and culture must be contained—structures set by the privileged representations which it studies. The neo-Kantian consensus thus appears as the end-product of an original wish to substitute *confrontation* for *conversation* as the determinant of our belief."[47] In the end, Rorty objects to this conception of philosophy because for him it represents an attempt to preclude or circumvent the social practice of knowledge justification (conversation) via the production of a dubious philosophical trump card that is somehow able to put an end to any further discussion (confrontation). But for Rorty, any such card will always be counterfeit.

In the next part of the story, Rorty asks what knowledge might look like if we simply gave up the philosophical desire to get behind reasons to causes, and instead considered it our collective human lot to remain in the space of reasons (for Rorty does not believe this space can be transcended). This response forms the aforementioned "deceptively simple" answer Rorty gives to the question concerning what sort of explanation of knowledge we ought to refuse to attempt. As we shall see in the next section, Rorty's epistemological behaviorism (or pragmatism) is more than the simple refusal to insert a mentalistic third term "between the impact of the environment on human beings and their reports about it" (although it includes that), but more importantly a refusal to use such a mentalistic third term *to explain the reliability of such reports.*[48] Rorty primarily objects to the idea that such reliability stands in need of an explanation that only philosophers can supply through a demonstration of privileged epistemological access to a permanent, neutral framework for all possible inquiry. A closer examination of Rorty's epistemological behaviorism will give us a better grasp of what is at stake in his refusal of this sort of explanation of knowledge.

WHAT'S THE THERAPY? SELLARS, QUINE, AND EPISTEMOLOGICAL BEHAVIORISM

In forthright, fallibilistic fashion, Rorty refuses to define the aforementioned reliability in terms of an absolute certainty achieved through privileged epistemological access to something incorrigible and indubitable, because an acceptance of such an unattainable standard would force us to conclude that none of our knowledge is reliable, or even knowledge. The Cartesian notion that nothing is closer, or more certain, to the mind than itself introduces the possibility of "veil of ideas" skepticism, or anxiety concerning how such "inner" certainty might possibly hook up with "outer" reality. Epistemological behaviorism is Rorty's response to this legacy. It is a therapeutic response, insofar as it is an attempt to preclude the possibility of these sorts of epistemological problems from arising in the first place, or showing how they can be dissolved once they have.

As we saw in the previous section, Rorty thinks Kant's Copernican revolution, while a step forward, ultimately fails to escape this Cartesian fly-bottle. Kant's understanding of knowledge as the synthesis of intuition and concept entrenched a distinction between what is given (intuition) and what is added by the mind (concept). Yet what Kant thinks the mind adds is also a species of "given" on Rorty's account; it remains a species of "representation" insofar as it is a permanent structural feature of all possible awareness, cognition, or knowledge—a mental given that we bring to any and all experience. Rorty now wants to tell a story about how these two different sorts of representations would come to fall into disrepute in the latter days of the analytic movement, and he relies heavily on the work of Sellars and Quine to make his case. Rorty thinks the work of these two philosophers successfully undermines the philosophical attempt to get behind reasons to causes, an attempt he attributes to both Locke and Kant. Rorty urges us to steer clear of that path, and finally become content with our lot, which is to remain in the space of reasons. Doing so, he suggests, will allow us to understand knowledge solely in terms of the social practices involved in its justification. For reasons we shall explore, Rorty thinks this would be a salutary development.

So Rorty criticizes both the Cartesian conception of mind as an inner arena as well as the Kantian conception of knowledge as the synthesis of two kinds of representations within that inner arena. Before exploring Rorty's use of Sellars and Quine to criticize the latter conception of knowledge, however, it is important to delve a little deeper into his critique of the former understanding of mind. In the end we will see how Rorty understands the work of Sellars and Quine to undermine both the Cartesian conception of mind as well as the Kantian conception of knowledge.

The analytic critique of the Cartesian construal of mind finds its roots in Gilbert Ryle's seminal work, *The Concept of Mind* (1949). This book directly confronts Cartesian dualism, attacking the idea that there is an ontological distinction between body and mind, according to which the body, like the rest of the natural or material world, is understood as a complex, yet unthinking, machine, and the mind is thought of as an immaterial substance governing the body and accounting for human intelligence. (It was Ryle who coined the phrase "ghost in the machine" in order to characterize the Cartesian anthropology he rejects.) In *The Concept of Mind*, he argues that there is no ontological distinction, or gap, between the workings of the mind and the body, for they are one and the same. We can account for the distinctiveness of our mental vocabulary simply by understanding it as one of several different ways of describing human action, and so we need posit no immaterial mind stuff as an objective reference for such language. Instead, Ryle interprets such mental concepts as "knowing" and "believing" as "dispositional concepts," concepts that describe certain tendencies, or propensities to act in a certain way under certain conditions.[49]

Needless to say, Rorty is sympathetic to Ryle's desire to do without Descartes' ghost. At the same time, he smells a problem. Most analytic philosophers of mind, he notes, are happy to redescribe much of our mental vocabulary in the dispositional manner Ryle recommends. But there is a class of mental terms that resist such redescription, terms that appear to name events as opposed to describing traits, propensities, or dispositions. In this class belongs such mental terms as "raw feels," "mental images," and "thoughts," basically those experiences that comprise our inescapable sense of having an "inner mental life." Physical "pain" is a perfect example of an item in this class. There is something counterintuitive and reductionistic about thinking of such pain in purely materialist terms, for the simple reason that my experience of your pain is different from your experience of your pain. I can observe your pain behavior, hear your anguished cries, understand your reports about your injury, and even examine and diagnose it; but for all that I cannot *feel* your pain. This fact seems to lead to the inescapable conclusion that, between the injurious impact of the environment on your body, and the subsequent reports, visible signs, and actions that accompany the manifestation of your injury, there exists something else, something private, hidden, unobservable and therefore incommunicable to me. Rorty's challenge (similar to Sellars' challenge in *Empiricism and the Philosophy of Mind*) will be to account satisfactorily for such inner experience, and in general our intuitive sense of having an inner mental life, without explaining it in terms of the existence of a private, immaterial mental substance.

Rorty takes up this challenge by arguing that the Cartesian leap of positing an immaterial mental substance in order to explain the fact that we seem to have privileged access to our own pains (say) is unnecessary. In order to see this, he asks his reader to distinguish between the claim that "we have privileged access to our own pains" and the claim that "we know which mental states we are in purely by virtue of their special felt qualities." Rorty takes the former claim to be relatively straightforward and unproblematic, while the latter claim in his opinion imports all sorts of unnecessary philosophical baggage: "The former claim merely says that there is no better way of finding out whether somebody is in pain than by asking him, and that nothing can overrule his own sincere report. The latter says that the mechanism which makes this privilege possible is his inspection of the 'phenomenological properties' of his own mental states." The unnecessary leap here, says Rorty, is to smuggle in the idea of mental introspection—to explain one's privileged access to one's own pain in terms of an Inner Eye surveying an occurrent mental state. Once again, this leap involves thinking of the privileged access in question in terms of perception, in terms of the way we see and pick out objects in physical space: "To get from the first claim to the second we need the Cartesian model of self-knowledge as analogous to observation—the image of the Inner Eye—and the notion that stomach cramps, for example, are not Naturally Given in the way in which the feelings produced by stomach cramps are."[50]

This unwarranted leap, says Rorty, confuses two senses of "knowledge": the first sense is what the prelinguistic infant "knows" when it experiences pain, and the second is what a language-user knows when she knows what pain is. Rorty compares the first sense of knowledge to a plant's knowledge of the direction of the sun, or an amoeba's knowledge of the temperature of the water; it is a form of behavioral discrimination. The second sense has to do with learning how to use a word properly, and therefore does not rely on anything private or privileged. We teach children to associate typical cases of overt pain behavior with words like "toothache," and therefore help them learn about the behavioral and environmental context in which this word and other associated words are used. In the second sense, then, once one knows how to use the word "pain" properly in a variety of contexts, one knows all one needs to know about what pains are. The former sort of knowledge (or awareness), then, becomes simply understood as one occasion or causal antecedent for the use of such words; it does not thereby form the indubitable epistemological foundation for the second sort of knowledge (knowing what the word means or how to use it). To think otherwise is once again to repeat the mistake of confusing reasons with causes, and also to persist in the Cartesian error of attempting to ground knowledge on the supposed indubitability of a process of interior introspection.[51]

So Rorty's objection to "raw feels" such as pain is not that he thinks there is no such thing as a raw feel, or my privileged access to my own pain, but rather the more subtle point that this privileged access "is a causal condition for knowledge but not a *ground* for knowledge."[52] That is, in order to use the word "pain," in order to know what a pain is, we do not need an Inner Eye to locate an essence in some "Naturally Given" private, incommunicable state, which can then be labeled with that word. We do not even need to have pain. This word, and our understanding of its meaning, is part of a larger, communal language game, one into which children are initiated as they learn a language. The private experience is simply the causal antecedent that initiates the particular language game in question (e.g. the offering of a first-person report), or the infant's learning of how to participate in it. In the sense Rorty intends, our knowledge of what pain is takes place completely within what Sellars calls the "logical space of reasons," and so it is a publicly discussible item on all fours with the more everyday tables and chairs that we can simply point to (which is not the same thing as pointing to an interior or private mental state that no one else can see).

Rorty insists that the only "ground" or justification for such knowledge (of what pain is, for example) is one's mastery of a certain area of human language use, or one's membership in a linguistic community, and not the indubitable existence of a private, mentally introspected state of consciousness. Rorty describes this position as a type of "holism," and locates its paradigmatic expression within analytic philosophy in the work of Sellars and Quine. Rorty contrasts this holism with the "atomism" or "reductionism" he finds embedded in the traditional epistemological understanding of justification. In the latter case, justification is understood in terms of a representational relationship between idea or word, on the one hand, and object, on the other (e.g. "pain" and the private mental state that it purportedly names), and therefore tends to reduce and atomize knowledge in terms of its supposed constituent parts (ideas, words, sense data, intuitions, concepts, etc.). On this understanding of justification, one loses all the rich nuance that accrues to our knowledge of "pain" when one instead thinks of the justification for its use in less confrontational, more conversational, terms. According to Rorty's conversational sense of justification, pain becomes a matter of everything we say about it, a matter of all the ways in which we use the word and play the language games that are associated with it. As James Tartaglia summarizes the position, philosophical holism follows a general Hegelian line of thought according to which "any attempt to split conscious experience into atomistic elements—such as Kantian intuitions and concepts—[is] to make an artificial and falsifying abstraction from an essentially unified whole."[53]

According to Rorty, the holistic positions of Sellars and Quine represent two different versions of the same basic argument. The holism they share "is a product of their commitment to the thesis that justification is not a matter of a special relation between ideas (or words) and objects, but of conversation, of social practice."[54] Adopting this holistic position as his own, Rorty informs his reader that it rests upon one crucial premise: "that we understand knowledge when we understand the social justification of belief, and thus have no need to view it as accuracy of representation."[55] Quine and Sellars help Rorty establish this premise insofar as their work undermines two key distinctions that twentieth-century analytic philosophy has taken over from Kant: the intuition-concept distinction, and the analytic-synthetic distinction. According to Rorty, Sellars' attack on the "Myth of the Given" takes care of the former, while Quine's attack on "analyticity" undermines the latter.

Yet the immediate target of Sellars' attack on "the myth of the given" is not Kant's distinction, but rather "sense-data empiricism," or the idea that our knowledge rests on a preconceptual basis of "given" sense data. According to the empiricist position Sellars critiques in *Empiricism and the Philosophy of Mind*, we have knowledge of these sense contents simply by virtue of having had various sensations. Sense-data empiricism thus emphasizes the foundational role played by what Rorty calls "knowledge of" in his discussion of Locke. This purported knowledge is "given," "immediate"—simply the result of our cognitive apparatus being affected by various stimuli coming to it from the surrounding environment. In criticizing this position, Sellars actually encourages analytic philosophy to make a Kantian turn, and reject the idea of direct epistemological access to unconceptualized, or given, sense data. (So—and this is somewhat confusing—although Rorty thinks Sellars' argument ultimately undermines the Kantian distinction between concept and intuition, here he recognizes that Sellars' critique can be understood as a quasi-Kantian turn within analytic philosophy.)[56]

Sellars therefore disagrees fundamentally with empiricists like Locke, Berkeley, and Hume, who, he says, "all take for granted that the human mind has an innate ability to be aware of certain determinate sorts . . . *simply by virtue of having sensations and images.*"[57] Sellars disagrees, insisting that all "awareness" is a conceptual, or linguistic, affair. In saying this, he even means to include "awareness of such sorts, resemblances, and facts as pertain to so-called immediate experience. . . ."[58] That is, "the process of acquiring the use of language" is not built upon and does not presuppose some form of preconceptual or prelinguistic awareness. On the contrary, our *awareness* of our immediate experience presupposes that we have successfully undergone the process of acquiring the use of language.

Rorty summarizes Sellars' position as follows: "Having a sense-impression is, by itself, an example neither of knowledge nor of conscious experience."[59] This is because for both Rorty and Sellars all knowledge and conscious experience is a linguistic affair, a predicative species of "knowledge that," or a product of judgment that depends for its possibility upon our successful acculturation into a particular linguistic community. Our knowledge is therefore subject to and a product of social justificatory norms. As Sellars famously summarizes: "The essential point is that in characterizing an episode or a state as that of *knowing*, we are not giving an empirical description of that episode or state; we are placing it in the logical space of reasons, of justifying and being able to justify what one says."[60] One's conscious awareness of seeing a red triangle involves more than simply having a physical sense impression of something red and triangular (which is the causal precondition of such experience); one must also possess, understand, and so be able to use the concepts "red" and "triangle," as well as a complicated network of interrelated concepts like "shape," "colour," "object," etc. Finally, the act of claiming to *know* that the object before one is a red triangle is an act that places this claim in the court of public justification, the place Sellars calls "the logical space of reasons."

In claiming that all awareness is a linguistic affair, and that knowledge is a product of the public justification of predicative claims, Sellars' Kantian turn rounds a bend that Rorty thinks Kant himself did not follow. For Sellars, the linguistic or conceptual is not "transcendental" in Kant's sense (i.e. a condition for the possibility of experience that is not a part of experience itself). According to Rorty, "Sellars, like the later Wittgenstein but unlike Kant, identified the possession of a concept with the mastery of the use of a word."[61] While Sellars agrees with Kant that we have no epistemological access to preconceived intuitions or sensory presentations, he does not think we must understand our concepts as permanent, built-in structural categories that presort and synthesize the sensory manifold that constantly bombards our Cartesian mental arenas. On Sellars' account, Kant's Copernican revolution ultimately replaces one candidate for the status of "given" with another, and he intends his argument against the myth of the given to reject *all* philosophical candidates for immediacy or givenness.[62] Concepts, for Sellars, are therefore nothing more or less than the norm-governed yet mutable items that our ordinary language use shows them to be.

For Rorty, the upshot of accepting Sellars' critique of the myth of the given is to accept that "knowledge is inseparable from a social practice—the practice of justifying one's assertions to one's fellow-humans. It is not presupposed by this practice, but comes into being along with it." Once one accepts the idea that there are no objects with which one is "directly acquainted" or that are "immediately before the mind," no candidates for immediacy or givenness, we must also refrain from privileging sensory reports as "reports of the immediately given." Rorty, following Sellars, insists that "such reports are no less mediated by language, and thus by social practice, than reports that there are cows or electrons in the neighbourhood."[63] Finally, for Rorty, Sellars' critique implies that we come to understand rationality itself quite differently than traditional philosophy has tended to. On a Sellarsian approach, rationality becomes no longer understood as a matter of "obedience to standards . . . which epistemologists hope to codify." Instead, says Rorty, it becomes a matter "of give-and-take participation in a cooperative social project."[64]

As mentioned earlier, Rorty understands the upshot of Quine's critique of analyticity to be much the same as Sellars' critique of the myth of the given. Rorty's argument relies primarily upon the position Quine puts forward in his essay "Two Dogmas of Empiricism."

There Quine questions analytic philosophy's analytic-synthetic distinction, which tries to set up a hard distinction between matters of meaning (the analytic) and matters of fact (the synthetic). Unlike matters of fact, matters of meaning are analytic because they are true solely by virtue of the definition or meaning of the terms they employ. Unlike matters of meaning, matters of fact are synthetic because they rely upon experience for their justification. A paradigmatic example of an analytic statement is "all bachelors are unmarried men," which is true because the definition of bachelor is "unmarried man." "All bachelors are between the ages of 20–25," on the other hand, would be considered a synthetic statement, because in order to find out if it is true we have to check. Through a complex, primarily negative path of argumentation, Quine finally rejects this bifurcation of language into analytic statements whose definitions supposedly structure experience (telling us what a bachelor is so that we can go out and find one) and synthetic statements through which we, among other things, make reports of our experience (like performing a survey that disconfirms the statement that all bachelors are between the ages of 20–25). Instead of this bifurcated understanding of knowledge, Quine puts forward a holistic alternative according to which our statements "face the tribunal of sense experience not individually but only as a corporate body."[65] On this picture, the analytic-synthetic distinction is recast in terms of a practical distinction between more and less central beliefs, those beliefs whose adjustment it is at present difficult to imagine, and those beliefs whose potential adjustment is a simple, unproblematic matter. Quine's holistic position here chimes nicely with Sellars' view that "empirical knowledge, like its sophisticated extention, science, is rational, not because it has a *foundation* but because it is a self-correcting enterprise which can put *any* claim in jeopardy, though not *all* at once."[66]

For Rorty, an important consequence of Quine's holistic view of language is the freedom it creates with respect to the justification and adjustment of our beliefs. Recalcitrant experience, on this picture, does not *confront* us in such a way as to dictate which of our particular beliefs must be adjusted in the face of it. The choice of which beliefs to adjust in the face of recalcitrant experience is always ours, and so according to this position reality does not dictate in any absolute sense how it *must* be described. While we are unable to wish such recalcitrance away, the adjustments we make in response to it remain a social matter of our corporate freedom and shared responsibility. That is, we have leeway in this process, for, in responding to such experience, we can choose from a range of possible adjustments to the total field of interconnected beliefs associated with it.[67]

Taken together, Rorty thinks Quine and Sellars demonstrate the futility of any philosophical attempt to found knowledge upon a permanent, metaphysical framework, and thereby take knowledge out of the social domain. Neither the immediate awareness of sense data, or the analytic necessity of an experience-structuring part of our language can perform this function, because neither of these things exist in the way that Western philosophers have described them. Immediate sensations are not some kind of foundational knowledge or conscious awareness, and analyticity is simply a faulty explanation of the centrality of those beliefs we could not imagine, at this historical moment, doing without. Advocates of these candidates for epistemological foundation think they have discovered a metaphysical escape hatch that allows them to transcend the social space of justification. For Rorty, this would be to repeat Descartes' mistake of turning inward rather than outward in his attempt to understand those things he wanted to understand ("the superiority of the new science to Aristotle, the relations between this science and mathematics, common sense, theology, and mortality"). Yet to understand these things or anything else, for that matter, Rorty says we need to turn outward "toward the social context of justification rather than to the relations between inner representations."

Rorty finally understands the image of the mind as mirror of nature to be the modern Western philosophical tradition's answer to the supposed need for a permanent metaphysical framework. The conclusion he draws from his reading of Sellars and Quine is that there are no privileged representations in this mirror, because there is no mirror. If Sellars and Quine are right, then this philosophical image "will no longer answer to the need for a touchstone for choice between justified and unjustified claims upon our belief. Unless some other such framework can be found, the abandonment of the image of the Mirror leads us to abandon the notion of philosophy as a discipline which adjudicates the claims of science and religion, mathematics and poetry, reason and sentiment, allocating an appropriate place to each."[68]

PHILOSOPHY AS CULTURAL CONVERSATION: ALLOCATING AN APPROPRIATE PLACE TO EACH

We now have before us the nub of Rory's therapeutic case, put forward in response to the intractable problems he finds inherent in philosophy-as-epistemology. As I suggested in the second part of this chapter, a big part of his motivation for putting forward this case is to create wider scope for our intellectual imagination. In the third and final part of *Philosophy and the Mirror of Nature*, simply entitled "Philosophy," Rorty takes a significant stab at responding to the question concerning what philosophy might become once it has been liberated from its epistemological preoccupations. We will have cause to return to particular passages in part III in subsequent chapters, as we trace the origins of Rorty's later work back to several evocative comments he makes there. Suffice it to say for now that once philosophy is liberated from its fly-bottle, Rorty thinks it becomes free to embrace a more conversational mode of justification and inquiry. In a "post-philosophical" culture, philosophy becomes one more voice in the conversation of humankind, a voice without any special privilege, but one that can still do its unique part to edify and enrich that very conversation.[69]

In part III of *Philosophy and the Mirror of Nature*, then, Rorty seeks to show a path whereby philosophy might return to addressing real world concerns, a path whereby philosophers might once again concern themselves with life and wisdom as opposed to certainty, abstraction, and professional specialization. Echoing his parents' concern about the increasing social irrelevance of the modern American academy, Rorty decides that it is more important for philosophers to join the larger cultural conversation about what to believe than it is for them to restrict themselves to talking only about how to believe. Participating in this conversation is an important part of what Rorty calls "cultural politics," a term he says "covers, among other things, arguments about what words to use."[70] In the next chapter, I will explore the Rortyan persona of the "cultural politician," the thinker who seeks to participate in normatively inflected "talk about what we should be talking about." It is perhaps when speaking in this voice that one most clearly hears Rorty articulate his social hope (not to be confused with expectation), for it is in this voice that he advances his vision for "what will help create a better world." Rorty also thinks the question concerning what will help create a better world should determine the question concerning what we should be talking about.[71] To have a voice in this discussion, he says, one must leave the philosophical sidelines and go "all in." In like spirit, Rorty risks advancing his own ungrounded yet trusted vision of what will make life better. To an exploration of that vision I now turn.

CHAPTER 3

THE LIBERAL IRONIST: RORTY'S CULTURAL POLITICS

PUTTING AWAY CHILDISH THINGS

Recall Rorty's impression in "Trotsky and the Wild Orchids" that, although writing *Philosophy and the Mirror of Nature* resolved many of his philosophical concerns and preoccupations, it did not do much to address his adolescent intellectual ambitions, the ones that inspired him to pursue the study of philosophy in the first place. Specifically, Rorty says, writing *Philosophy and the Mirror of Nature* did little to address his original desire to achieve a "single vision," one that would bring his social concern for general human welfare into line with the idiosyncratic desires and fascinations that strongly urged him to become the poet of his own life. Was there a philosophical position that would allow him to synthesize his esteem for social responsibility with his desire to achieve personal authenticity and autonomy?

Rorty would return to face this question in the 1980s, in the context of the increased intellectual breathing space afforded him by his new position as Kenan Professor of Humanities at the University of Virginia. As I mentioned at the end of Chapter 1, he ends up giving a negative answer to this question, concluding that there is no theoretical standpoint from which to unify these divergent imperatives. He therefore abandons the possibility of achieving a theoretical perspective that would unify his public concern for social justice with his private desire for personal authenticity and autonomy. But the story does not end there, with Rorty simply throwing his hands in the air. For in giving a negative answer to his adolescent question, he fashions a unique position with respect to the relationship between these two imperatives, one that invokes the liberal private–public distinction in order to make room for both Nietzschean self-overcoming and liberal democratic efforts to widen the scope of human freedom, equality, and solidarity.

Part of Rorty's job in developing this position involves the airing of his liberal political views, and as these views gradually emerge in articles published throughout the 1980s, his comments draw a wide variety of critical responses from thinkers on both sides of the political spectrum.[1] When taken together with his metaphilosophical observation that philosophy in particular (not to mention "theory" in general) is not as politically efficacious as many of its practitioners imagine it to be, many Left-leaning critics come to form the impression that the political position he articulates tends toward political quietism, if not conservatism.[2] Meanwhile, thinkers on the Right chide him for poisoning the minds of the youth with a cynical and nihilistic brand of historicist relativism.[3] While not surprised by the criticism he receives from those on the Right, Rorty is surprised by the negative reaction he receives from the Left, and he makes several attempts at clarification in order to defend himself from such charges.[4]

In this chapter, I will unpack Rorty's political philosophy, in an effort to highlight the holistic position in which it plays a part (which to recall involves the articulation of a perspective that seeks to balance and hold in tandem two different and nonsynthesizable imperatives, one private and one public). Because Rorty comes to articulate his version of political liberalism as part and parcel of this larger attempt to work through and move beyond his original adolescent quest for a "single vision," it is best to avoid reading him as a political philosopher in the specialist sense, as, say, someone like John Rawls. This is not to suggest that Rorty fails to make an important contribution to discussions of political liberalism, but simply to place his contribution to that discourse in the context of its personal motivation. In saying this, I agree with Rorty's contention that awareness of such motivation can do much to prevent readers from misinterpreting his position. In "Trotsky and the Wild Orchids" Rorty denies that his position on political matters is intentionally frivolous, or that he will say anything to get a gasp. There, as we saw, he tells his reader that "even if my views about the relation of philosophy and politics are odd, they were not adopted for frivolous reasons."[5] Rorty's idiosyncratic views on the relationship between philosophy and politics come to make much more sense when read in the context of such "nonfrivolous" reasons.

The first, and perhaps most important, nonfrivolous reason involves Rorty's conclusion that he must give up his adolescent desire to accede to an intellectual position from which he might hold reality and justice in a single vision. For reasons we will explore below, he thinks that the two imperatives signaled by the words "reality" and "justice" cannot be synthesized, nor need they be in order for us to continue to value them both. For this reason, he also urges his fellow academics and citizens to forego the intellectual desire to achieve this elusive synthesis. Our pursuit of such "synoptic visions" has come at too high a cost, says Rorty. In chasing after them, he says, we risk "losing the sense of finitude, and the tolerance, which result from realizing how very many synoptic visions there have been, and how little argument can do to help you choose among them." He goes on to describe the desire he himself once felt for such a synoptic vision as a form of "intellectual snobbery" from which he is grateful to have been delivered. The main trouble with this pursuit, he says, "is that you might succeed, and your success might let you imagine that you have something more to rely on than the tolerance and decency of your fellow human beings." The democratic community of the future that Rorty envisions is a community where no one imagines that. Instead, it is "a community in which everybody thinks that it is human solidarity, rather than knowledge of something not merely human, that really matters." He regards the actually existing political communities that strive to approximate this ideal democratic community to be "the greatest achievement of our species."[6]

In the book *Democracy and Education*, Rorty's primary philosophical hero, John Dewey, also struggles to find the best way to hold private and public exigencies together, and his effort is instructive for our attempt to understand Rorty's position. In chapter 22, "The Individual and the World," Dewey argues that the modernist philosophy of the Enlightenment perverts rather than transcribes what he takes to be the historical development of a "legitimate intellectual individualism." For Dewey, this legitimate intellectual individualism allows inquiry to operate at an arm's length from received traditions and other sources of communal authority (although he also recognizes that no individual can act competently in complete separation from these enabling factors, either). For

Dewey, this legitimate intellectual individualism forms the "pivot" around which social progress and innovation turns. Progress and innovation are thus piecemeal, retail affairs, always occurring against the background of more stable and (for the time being) unquestioned certainties. Yet over time the accumulation of such changes can indeed amount to revolutionary change. For Dewey, the modern period represents just such a time of (ultimately) radical change, one that completely transforms the way humans think about themselves and their place in the world. Unfortunately, the philosophers of this period miss the lesson this legitimate form of intellectual individualism carries, and instead translate it into a moral and social individualism, one that conceives of the mind and the self as existing in complete, splendid isolation from both other selves and the "objective" world it would hope to know. For Dewey, this is a vicious individualism that sits at the antipode to an equally vicious form of blind conformity to habit and received tradition. In so radically isolating the mind, Dewey argues, this conception of self neglects the "ties that bind" one to one's fellow humans. An appropriate intellectual individualism would, in contrast, use the intellectual independence gained from traditional sources of authority to *deepen* one's connection with both the natural world and one's fellow humans.[7]

While Rorty does not give exactly the same answer as Dewey to the question of the mutual influence of the individual and the social, he seems to be asking a similar question. Like Dewey, he also seeks to find a way to cherish and use "legitimate intellectual individualism," as well as to strengthen the moral and ethical ties that bind. The question remains whether, like Dewey, Rorty finds a mutually reinforcing interconnection between an appropriate form of individualism and a concomitant social concern, or whether he makes such a radical distinction between these imperatives that they simply come to rest alongside each other, but otherwise have very little to do with one another. Dewey, for his part, worries about the consequences of making too radical a separation between the private and the public, the individual and the social:

> When the social quality of individualized mental operations is denied, it becomes a problem to find connections which will unite an individual with his fellows. Moral individualism is set up by the conscious separation of different centers of life. It has

its roots in the notion that the consciousness of each person is wholly private, a self-inclosed continent, intrinsically independent of the ideas, wishes, purposes of everybody else. But when men act, they act in a common and public world. This is the problem to which the theory of isolated and independent conscious minds gave rise: Given the feelings, ideas, desires, which have nothing to do with one another, how can actions proceeding from them be controlled in a social or public interest? Given an egoistic consciousness, how can action which has regard for others take place?[8]

Several of Rorty's critics on the Left consider his political position to be excessively individualist, and therefore insufficiently concerned with "action which has a regard for others." As if to answer this charge, Rorty, not unlike Dewey, points out the public importance of maintaining wide scope for individual inquiry and imagination. In an essay on Derrida written during this period, he suggests that "[m]any responsibilities begin in dreams, and many transfigurations of the tradition begin in private fantasies." Furthermore, as if to counter the idea that he considers private concerns as somehow ultimate, at the very end of "Trotsky and the Wild Orchids" he concludes that, when compared to the historical achievement of authentic democratic community, even his private intellectual obsessions seem little more than "optional, orchidaceous extras."[9]

Needless to say, one can marshal evidence from Rorty's writings to support both sides of this question, and I will not here make up the reader's mind. In what follows, I will simply unpack the subtleties of Rorty's political philosophy in order to give readers the tools required to make their own decision. To accomplish this, I will explore three separate themes by means of which Rorty articulates his political liberalism, the themes that form the title of his 1989 book, *Contingency, Irony, and Solidarity*. An exploration of these themes will round out Rorty's portrayal of "the liberal ironist," his archetype of the model democratic citizen—someone who thinks cruelty is the worst thing humans do, someone who, moreover, maintains that commitment even while recognizing its historical contingency, all the while worrying about what sort of new person she or he might yet be able to become. Freedom emerges as a theme of central importance in Rorty's portrayal of the liberal ironist, to such an extent that Rorty would have us substitute it for truth as our ultimate normative guide. Because Rorty's prioritization of freedom over truth provides the context for his discussion of contingency, irony, and solidarity, I will first introduce his arguments for that priority, and then proceed to explore the latter three themes in turn.

SUBSTITUTING FREEDOM FOR TRUTH: FROM THEORY TO NARRATIVE

The position Rorty puts forward in *Contingency, Irony, and Solidarity* expands upon the description of the human condition he provides in *Philosophy and the Mirror of Nature*. In *Philosophy and the Mirror of Nature*, as we have seen, Rorty rejects the Western philosophical conception of mind as something that can supply or otherwise access an immutable foundation for knowledge, thereby securing it to a neutral and ahistorical ontological framework. For Rorty, there is no such mind; humans do not possess the capacity to passively and neutrally mirror mind-independent nature. We do not share any sort of deep, underlying cognitive essence, a little piece of *logos* that is identical with *ontos*, or reality as it is "in itself," something that would thereby allow us to escape Plato's cave, or cross Plato's dividing line between appearance and Reality with a capital R. Because he fundamentally rejects this philosophical anthropology, he describes our human condition as a matter of coping or getting along without recourse to any such transcendent framework: "I urge that, rather than trying to climb out of our own minds—trying to rise above the historical contingencies that filled our minds with the words and beliefs they presently contain—we make a virtue of necessity and rest content with playing off parts of our minds against other parts. For us antirepresentationalists, this is just to say that we should not try to do the impossible: we should not look for skyhooks, but only for toeholds."[10] Just as human inquiry always remains within the immanent (and contingent) space of reason exchange, so also the human condition in general cannot transcend the vagaries of time and circumstance, try as we might. Accepting contingency, then, means recognizing one's time in thought as the upshot of historical happenstance; in Rorty's words, it is a position "sufficiently historicist and nominalist to have abandoned the idea that [one's] central beliefs and desires refer back to something beyond the reach of time and chance."[11]

Yet Rorty's embrace of contingency amounts to more than simply the consistent outworking of his critique of Western philosophy's understanding of knowledge. As an "embrace," and not merely a logical extension of his epistemological position, it also forms an active and productive philosophical orientation. *Qua* embrace, it is not just a "letting go" of an old way of seeing human existence, it is also a "taking up" of a new alternative, one he thinks has much to recommend it. For Rorty, as we shall see, the historical contingency that inescapably shapes the human condition is not merely something to be *accepted*, but also something to be *appropriated*. As opposed to the philosophical attempt to escape this contingency, he thinks that actively embracing it will liberate human existence, imaginatively opening our intellects to genuinely novel possibilities that the course of history has, haphazardly, made available to our present moment.

Still, it is true to say that the first step in Rorty's recommendation to embrace historical contingency involves a form of "letting go"—specifically, letting go of the desire and effort to secure human existence to "something beyond the reach of time and chance." The Western philosophical tradition has proposed several candidates for this "something," and in the introduction to *Contingency, Irony, and Solidarity*, Rorty focuses on one particular candidate—the idea of a "common human nature." He selects this candidate because he sees it as the locus of the Western philosophical attempt to achieve the aforementioned single vision; in order to synthesize the private and the public, the individual and the social, this tradition has held that we must, and in fact do, find something common, something universal and unchanging, at the basis of every self. We require this purported common human nature in order to be able to transcend our peculiarities and idiosyncrasies and see the world whole. At the same time, it provides a ground for human solidarity that we cannot secure by ourselves, without recourse to the self-transcendence this common essence supposedly makes possible. As the traditional philosophical story goes, this common nature is what will finally secure our connection to the external world and to each other, uniting reality and justice in a single vision. Once desirous of this vision himself, Rorty now comes to reject the idea that forms its lynchpin—the existence of a common human nature or essence; for him, this idea amounts to little more than the dangerous presumption of a metaphysical guarantee or backup to our deepest, albeit historically contingent, longings—when no such guarantee is or can ever be made available to us.

Extending a historicist development he sees inaugurated in the philosophy of Hegel, Rorty rejects this insistence upon the existence of a common human nature, an insistence that he describes with the adjectives "metaphysical" and "theological." On Rorty's reading, metaphysics and theology share the aforementioned ambition of transcendence, and thus both reject the historicism that he would have his readers embrace. Historicists like him, he says, deny "that there is such a thing as 'human nature' or the 'deepest level of the self'." Instead, they "insist that socialization goes all the way down—that there is nothing 'beneath' socialization or prior to history which is definatory of the human." This historicist turn, he goes on to claim, has gradually helped to free us from theology and metaphysics, activities that he describes as involving "the temptation to look for an escape from time and chance." By eschewing the possibility of such an escape, he claims, our increased willingness to become historicist "has helped us substitute Freedom for Truth as the goal of thinking and of social progress."[12]

But why does Rorty think it is desirable to substitute Freedom for Truth as the goal of thinking and social progress? While this key question of Rorty interpretation eludes the provision of a short and simple answer, his very way of framing the issue reveals his suspicion that there is something enslaving or prematurely restricting, something *unfree*, involved in taking Truth (understood in the "metaphysical" or "theological" sense he gives it) to be the ultimate goal of inquiry. It may be instructive here, once again, to note the way in which Rorty's position on Truth both aligns with and departs from that of his philosophical hero, Dewey. Save for the fact that Rorty appears to give the word "Truth" to the ancient philosophical tradition he rejects, his position is quite close to the one Dewey puts forward in *Reconstruction in Philosophy*. In this book, Dewey devotes a significant amount of space to articulating and arguing for a conception of truth that better fits his open and experimentalist approach to human inquiry. On Dewey's account, truth is a label we use to name those paths of inquiry upon which we have experienced reliable guidance in our intellectual attempts to resolve the particular problems or perplexities that led us to embark upon those paths in the first place:

> If ideas, meanings, conceptions, notions, theories, systems are instrumental to an active reorganization of the given environment, to a removal of some specific trouble and perplexity, then the test of their validity and value lies in accomplishing this work. If they succeed in their office, they are reliable, sound, valid, good, true . . . . Confirmation, corroboration, verification lie in works, consequences . . . . That which guides us truly is true—demonstrated capacity for such guidance is precisely what is meant by truth.[13]

Like Dewey, Rorty also cherishes those paths of inquiry that actively reorganize a given environment in the service of removing some specific trouble or perplexity people commonly experience. He therefore applauds the willingness of pragmatists like Dewey and William James to index truth to social (as opposed to private or idiosyncratic) utility. In his words: "Attributions of reality or truth are . . . compliments we pay to entities or beliefs that have won their spurs, paid their way, proved themselves useful, and therefore been incorporated into accepted social practices."[14]

Rorty wants us to substitute Freedom for Truth because he agrees that what Dewey describes as "an inheritance from the classic tradition" has saddled us with a conception of truth that fosters a dogmatic conservatism that unnecessarily binds those who accept it, making them unreceptive to new directions and novel possibilities. According to Dewey, to the extent that this classic inheritance divides reality into two realms, "a higher one of perfect being and a lower one of seeming, phenomenal, deficient reality," it conceives of truth and falsity "as fixed, readymade static properties of things themselves."[15] The culprit here, for Dewey as for Rorty, is this understanding of truth and falsity as fixed, static, and readymade, simply waiting to be mirrored by our otherwise passive intellects. For Dewey, a society that understands truth in terms of such passive mirroring is simply avoiding the responsibility to work through the uneasiness and fear that accompanies the ever-changing dynamics of human social life:

> A society that chiefly esteems order, that finds growth painful and change disturbing, inevitably seeks for a fixed body of

superior truths upon which it may depend. It looks backward, to something already in existence, for the source and sanction of truth. It falls back upon what is antecedent, prior, original, a priori, for assurance. The thought of looking ahead, toward the eventual, toward consequences, creates uneasiness and fear. It disturbs the sense of rest that is attached to the ideas of fixed Truth already in existence.[16]

Both Dewey and Rorty consider this sense of rest to be misleading and dangerous; neither of them can make sense of the idea that we are somehow able to anchor ourselves to something so fixed and final, and they both consider the belief that we have succeeded in doing so to be detrimental to both our responsibility and our motivation to address the various, shifting problems humanity faces.

Yet Rorty's and Dewey's critical responses to this ancient understanding of truth are not exactly the same. Whereas Dewey's response involves asking his readers to reconceive their understanding of truth, Rorty's involves asking them to substitute Freedom (with a capital "F") for Truth. To many readers, this makes Rorty sound as though he is giving up on truth. While, with Dewey, he certainly gives up on the "classic inheritance" (what he calls the "metaphysical" or "theological" understanding of Truth), it is not so clear that he also gives up on Dewey's alternative, pragmatic understanding of truth, even if he no longer uses that word to name what both of them are attempting to describe. As we have seen, Rorty does endorse the pragmatist position whereby truth becomes a compliment or name for those beliefs and entities that have earned their spurs and continue to pay their way (in a public, communal context). Having said that, it remains fair to say that Rorty is more deflationary than Dewey with respect to truth, less concerned to find a way to keep using the word in a general sense: "To say that we should drop the idea of truth as out there waiting to be discovered is not to say that we have discovered that, out there, there is no truth. It is to say that our purposes would be served best by ceasing to see truth as a deep matter, as a topic of philosophical interest, or 'true' as a term which repays 'analysis'."[17] While we may use the word "true" in a variety of particular ways in many different situations, Rorty does not think that anything usefully general can be said about that variety.

Notwithstanding this subtle difference over the worth of salvaging a general sense for the word "truth," there can be no question that Rorty affirms the larger concern lying behind Dewey's attempt to articulate an alternative, pragmatist conception of truth—the concern to keep inquiry responsive to the problems we experience, and open to the leads we encounter along the various historical paths we take toward achieving their resolution. For Rorty, as for Dewey, this is a process that may come to a provisional, but never a final, end. That is why, I think, Rorty would have us substitute Freedom for Truth, instead of simply redefining the latter term. For him, our acceptance of Truth as the goal of inquiry encourages us to think we can achieve or have achieved a finality that can never be ours, while the valorization of Freedom keeps us ever on our toes, constantly open to possible alternative responses to newly emerging situations.

In the end, Rorty thinks we must drop the pursuit of Truth, understood as the *theoretical* attempt to acquire a single vision, because, as we have seen, he thinks "there is no way to step outside the various vocabularies we have employed and find a metavocabulary which takes account of *all possible* vocabularies." For this reason, he recommends "a general turn against theory toward narrative." We always find ourselves as characters in the middle of a story we ourselves are narrating to one another, and from this position we continue to fashion and refashion possible endings that temporarily and provisionally define our hope and our striving, and thereby guide our current efforts. So, instead of striving for a single vision, says Rorty, or for a theory that claims to put everything in its place and to know how everything pans out, "[a] historicist and nominalist culture of the sort I envisage would settle instead for narratives which connect the present with the past, on the one hand, and with utopian futures, on the other. More important, it would regard the realization of utopias, and the envisaging of still further utopias, as an endless process—an endless, proliferating realization of Freedom, rather than a convergence toward an already existing Truth."[18] So, in the final analysis, Rorty would substitute Freedom for Truth because he wants us to recognize that the story we are living remains unfinished. Such a realization, he thinks, will free us to imagine and to choose between and strive toward a proliferation of different possible, but always temporary and provisional, endings.

CONTINGENCY: LANGUAGE, PERSONS, AND COMMUNITIES WITHOUT SKYHOOKS

As we have seen, Rorty's prioritization of freedom includes both the recognition and the appropriation of the contingency of human life. He divides his exploration of contingency into three parts: the contingency of language, the contingency of the self, and the contingency of community. Throughout, he urges his reader to stop searching for something timeless, necessary, or essential about any of these three things, something that would provide a skyhook by which one might escape time and chance; in doing so, he emphasizes our collective freedom, within certain constraints, to reimagine or reinvent any of these three features of human existence.[19]

In consistency with his overall philosophical perspective, Rorty's recognition of the contingency of language also flows from his rejection of the possibility of achieving a single theoretical vision; in this case, the impossibility of discovering a metavocabulary that would commensurate any and all possible vocabularies. For Rorty, there could only be such a metavocabulary if, at bottom, there was only one correct way of speaking about the world. And there could only be one such correct way, he says, if human language was nothing more than a representing *medium*. The philosophy of Donald Davidson becomes particularly important for the development of Rorty's position here because in Rorty's opinion Davidson, more than any other philosopher, "breaks *completely* with the notion of language as something which can be adequate or inadequate to the world or to the self."[20]

The picture that Davidson's philosophy helps Rorty escape is the traditional subject–object picture that we have already seen him criticize in *Philosophy and the Mirror of Nature*, a picture that posits a radical demarcation between self and world. This picture also interposes language, or the sentential attitudes expressed in a "network of beliefs and desires," between "the essential core of the self" on one side, and mind-independent Reality on the other: "In this picture," says Rorty, "the network is the product of an interaction between the two, alternately expressing the one and representing the other."[21] Following Davidson, Rorty objects primarily to the idea that we can make such a radical demarcation between self and world, subject and object. Without the need or ability to precisely locate this border, questions about whether or not the language we use adequately expresses our core Self, on the one hand, or accurately represents objective reality, on the other, will not need to be settled, for they will no longer arise.[22]

The specific position Rorty and Davidson share, and which makes Rorty think of Davidson as a philosophical ally, is also one we have already come across in *Philosophy and the Mirror of Nature*; namely, the importance of distinguishing between reasons and causes, including the refusal to grant our causal relationship with the world any justificatory status. For Davidson, the only thing that can justify a belief is another belief. He can therefore dispense with the notion that a belief's correspondence with mind-independent reality does some sort of epistemic or justificatory work, that such correspondence can make a belief true. So, while Davidson admits that the world indeed causes us to have beliefs, and that there might even be a way to make sense of the idea of objectively getting that world right, he maintains that this causal chain does not perform any justificatory role; it cannot choose for us which beliefs we *must* adopt in responding to it.[23]

Following up on what he sees as some important consequences of Davidson's position, Rorty wants us to realize that we have more freedom concerning what we might come to believe than the traditional philosophical subject–object picture would have us think. In making this case, he, like Davidson, does not deny that the world is, in some important sense, "out there." What he denies is the idea that *truth* is "out there." He continues: "To say that the world is out there, that it is not our creation, is to say, with common sense, that most things in space and time are the effects of causes which do not include human mental states. To say that truth is not out there is simply to say that where there are no sentences there is no truth, that sentences are elements of human languages, and that human languages are human creations."[24]

Causally speaking, we are always already, and inescapably, caught up in a world not of our own making. Rorty thus agrees with the philosophical realist that "there is such a thing as brute physical resistance." Yet unlike the realist, he denies that we can transfer this "nonlingusitic brutality" to facts, which are components of our descriptions and explanations, and so have no existence prior to language: "When the die hits the blank, something causal happens, but as many *facts* are brought into the world as there are languages for describing that causal transaction." Facts, Rorty says, are hybrid entities; the causes of their assertibility include "both physical stimuli and our antecedent choice of response to such stimuli." Rorty here claims to agree with Davidson that sheer causation is not under any description, although explanation is. Rorty thus distinguishes between facts, which are integral linguistic components of our explanations-descriptions, and causes, which are not: "To say that we must have respect for facts is just to say that we must, if we are to play a language game, play by the rules. To say that we must have respect for unmediated causal forces is pointless. It is like saying that the blank must have respect for the impressed die. The blank has no choice, nor do we."[25]

Rorty thinks that the modern philosophical tradition, with its insistence on the "hardness" and "directness" of sense data, misses the cultural space in which we *do* have a choice and so may therefore exercise some spontaneity in our describing and explaining activity (not to mention other sorts of nonscientific activity):

> The philosophical tradition has yearned for a way of approximating the total passivity of the blank. It has seen language as interposed, like a cushion, between us and the world. It has regretted that the diversity of language games, of interpretive communities, permits us so much variation in the way in which we respond to causal pressures. It would like us to be machines for cranking out true statements in 'direct' response to the pressures of reality upon our organs.

Rorty suggests that pragmatists like him want to replace "this masochistic talk about hardness and directness" with metaphors of "linguistic behavior as tool-using" and "language as a way of grabbing hold of causal forces and making them do what we want, altering ourselves and our environment to suit our aspirations." Simply because, like the blank, we have no choice about the causal nexus in which we are caught up (we cannot make it other than it is by simply redescribing it, or by wishing it away), this does not mean that, like the blank, we have no choice in how we might respond to these causal pressures. *Pace* Locke, we are never simply and only stamped. For Rorty, language gives us the power of variable response; it does not gives us an ability to transcend or escape this causal nexus, to be sure, but that does not mean we are powerless to appropriate it and attempt to bend it in the direction we would have it go, even as we ourselves remain subject to its pressures, like fish are subject to water. "The pragmatist," Rorty concludes, "thus exalts spontaneity at the cost of receptivity, as his realist opponent did the reverse."[26]

For Rorty, language cannot be a medium of representation, because to understand language that way would be to accept the idea that the world "out there," with its causal pressures, dictates which sole language we must use in speaking about it. Several philosophers have been tempted to read Rorty's rejection of the idea that language forms such a medium of representation between self and world as tantamount to a form of subjectivism that denies any alterity or otherness to the world, a position according to which the world simply becomes whatever we arbitrarily choose to make of it.[27] As I have been suggesting, however, reading a radical subjectivism and constructivism into Rorty's views would miss the main point of his Davidsonian antirepresentationalism. In Davidson, Rorty finds a peer who, like him, would rather circumvent than answer the question of how a radically separated subject and object can be brought together. Like Davidson, he does so by denying the philosophical presumption of their prior separation and isolation. In a few influential essays, Davidson, in rather Wittgensteinian fashion, instead depicts human language as an inextricably interfused dimension of the human form of life.[28] In these essays, Davidson refuses to draw a sharp border between our linguistic competence and the more general knowledge our everyday comportment exhibits. For him, knowing a language is thus part and parcel of "knowing our way around the world generally."[29] Furthermore, Davidson argues that once we reject the dualism of (subjective) interpretive scheme and (objective) uninterpreted content, rather than losing the world (i.e. the "content"), we get it back:

> In giving up dependence on the concept of an uninterpreted reality, something outside all schemes and science, we do not relinquish the notion of objective truth—quite the contrary. Given the dogma of a dualism of scheme and reality, we get conceptual relativity, and truth relative to a scheme. Without the dogma, this kind of relativity goes by the board. Of course truth-of sentences remains relative to language, but that is as objective as can be. In giving up the dualism of scheme and world, we do not give up the world, but reestablish unmediated touch with the

familiar objects whose antics make our sentences and opinions true or false.[30]

While this last sentence may seem puzzling for its apparent non-Sellarsian acceptance of "unmediated touch" with the world, notice that "unmediated" does not necessarily mean the same thing as "immediate" or "given" does for Sellars. For Davidson, truth-of sentences remains relative to language. What he objects to is the idea of language as *transparently* mediating, or representing (yet somehow, strangely, "immediately"), an otherwise inaccessible outer reality. Our "touch" with the world is not mediated in that sense, even if, as Sellars tells us, and Rorty accepts, "all awareness is a linguistic affair."[31]

In the final analysis, Rorty insists on the contingency of language because he cannot credit the idea of a metavocabulary that contains all possible others, a language interposed like a transparent veil between ourselves and the world that would thereby allow us to escape contingency, and represent to ourselves "the way the world is anyway." As I noted earlier, all he thinks we ever possess are "the historical contingencies that filled our minds with the words and beliefs they presently contain." And while these contingencies do not, per impossibile, provide an escape hatch from time and chance, they do, in spite of that "limitation," provide us with quite a bit; they provide us with a rich panoply of dynamic, constantly evolving language games, metaphors, narratives, and vocabularies from which we may fashion new responses to the brute causal pressures that continue to impact us. Rorty therefore opposes a reductionism that laments and seeks to eliminate this variety, for without that variety our interactions with our surroundings would be greatly impoverished.

For this reason, Rorty encourages his reader to understand language, not as a medium, or as a jigsaw puzzle that cuts reality at its joints, but as a toolbox. On his view of intellectual history, when such luminaries as Galileo, Hegel, or Yeats develop radically new vocabularies for speaking about their subjects, they are not giving a more accurate representation of the antecedently real; instead, they are equipping themselves with "tools for doing things which could not have been envisaged before these tools were available."[32] Likewise, in encouraging his readers to understand language use as analogous to tool use, Rorty means to highlight "the contrast between the attempt to represent or express something that was already there and the attempt to make something that had never been dreamed of before."[33] Freedom to pursue the latter path only becomes possible, he says, once we recognize, and then appropriate, the contingency of language.

This emphasis on the importance and possibility of creating space for the radically new also figures prominently in Rorty's discussions of the contingency of the self and the contingency of community. In underlining the contingency of the self, Rorty intends to highlight the potential for self-creation he sees in human life, and which he thinks the Western philosophical tradition largely ignores. In making this case for self-creation, he draws attention to the perennial "quarrel" between poetry and philosophy in Western intellectual history, which he describes in terms of "the tension between an effort to achieve self-creation by the recognition of contingency and an effort to achieve universality by the transcendence of contingency."[34] Rorty sees this tension typifying philosophy from the nineteenth century onward, largely due to the influence of Romanticism: "The same tension has pervaded philosophy since Hegel's time, and particularly since Nietzsche. The important philosophers of our own century are those who have tried to follow through on the Romantic poets by breaking with Plato and seeing freedom as the recognition of contingency."[35] Once we understand the historical developments that made us what we are as contingent rather than necessary, we will recognize that the course of history is not predetermined, and that together we have the power, again not without limits, to change it. On the personal level, we are free to compose and enact a different script than the one history seems to have written for us.

Rorty singles out Nietzsche and Freud as the two thinkers who do most to help us recognize the contingency of the self, and therefore show us the freedom we have to embark upon paths of self-transformation. Nietzsche does this by suggesting that the boundary to cross is not the boundary between appearance and reality, but rather the boundary between the old and the new. Unlike the Western philosophical tradition that, says Rorty "thinks of a human life as a triumph just insofar as it breaks out of the world of time, appearance, and idiosyncratic opinion," Nietzsche "thinks a human life triumphant just insofar as it escapes from inherited descriptions of the contingencies of its existence and finds new descriptions."[36] Freud helps along our crossing of this latter boundary by highlighting the formative role played by our contingent personal obsessions and idiosyncrasies, helping us appreciate how these contingent intrusions can lead to the development of metaphors that may be taken up both personally and publicly. Freud thus links contingency, personal idiosyncrasy, and the power of redescription to draw a picture of our freedom to change both ourselves and perhaps even our societies.[37]

Rorty invokes the work of Nietzsche and Freud to highlight the power of redescription, a power he considers a crucial feature of the freedom we might appropriate from our recognition of contingency. Rorty thinks that the power of redescription that he sees coming together near the end of the nineteenth century (contingently, of course) exhibits a newly emerging playfulness that allows us to entertain alternative descriptions alongside others simultaneously, thereby making something new possible. He considers this playfulness to be the product of a shared ability among thinkers of this era to appreciate "the power of redescribing, the power of language to make new and different things possible and important—an appreciation which becomes possible only when one's aim becomes an expanding repertoire of alternative descriptions rather than The One Right Description."[38]

This newly acquired power of redescription is not absolute, however, because it too must remain subject to the brute causal pressures mentioned above. Although Rorty insists that we acquire the ability of playful redescription through a "de-divinization" of both the Self and the World (i.e. no longer understanding them to have a language of their own that we must somehow get right), he recognizes that the world's causal pressure still places limits on our redescribing activity. Both the Self and the World, he says, have the power to kill us: "The world can blindly and inarticulately crush us; mute despair, intense mental pain, can cause us to blot ourselves out." Here we face nonlinguistic pressures over which we remain powerless, and whose power over us we must simply recognize:

> For our relation to the world, to brute power and naked pain, is not the sort of relation we have to persons. Faced with the nonhuman, the non-linguistic, we no longer have an ability to overcome contingency and pain by appropriation and transformation, but only the ability to *recognize* contingency and pain.

> The final victory of poetry in its ancient quarrel with philosophy—the final victory of metaphors of self-creation over metaphors of discovery—would consist in our becoming reconciled to the thought that this is the only sort of power over the world which we can hope to have. For that would be the final abjuration of the notion that truth, and not just power and pain, is to be found 'out there'.[39]

Only power and pain, other names for the world's causal pressure, are out there. They may cause our end, even as they cannot dictate to us how they must be described.

For Rorty, the contingent selves we happen to be, who speak contingent languages, also live in contingent communities. Not only is our sense of "I" historically contingent, so too is our sense of "we," whether we care to admit this to ourselves or not. Focusing on his own liberal political community, Rorty takes issue with those among him who continue to hold the "Enlightenment hope" that this culture as a whole can be "scientized," as opposed to merely "poeticized." That is, he objects to those who seek for, or wish to establish, ahistorical philosophical foundations for their sense of liberal community, metaphysically underwriting their desire for a community that equalizes all people's freedom to pursue their own personal version of his wild orchids. We need, Rorty says, "to substitute the hope that chances for fulfilment of idiosyncratic fantasies will be equalized for the hope that everyone will replace 'passion' or fantasy with reason."[40] Rorty goes on to claim that recognizing the contingency of liberal community, or any community for that matter, means getting along without such philosophical foundations, and not being disturbed by the lack of them. In this mood, the specters of "relativism" and "irrationalism" which haunt the philosophical foundationalist dissolve for want of a point of contrast. The ongoing political justification of a liberal society thereby becomes for Rorty simply a matter of historical comparison of its moral vision with those found in other historical attempts at social organization, or those envisaged through utopian projection.

Recognizing the contingency of one's political community entails accepting the fact that one always engages in such attempts at justification from some specific somewhere, and that there is no neutral ground from which to compare one's society to other alternatives on offer (no metaphysical escape hatch from time and fortune).

This also means that any particular community's sense of morality is also historically contingent. Yet, again, Rorty does not think that admitting this contingency relativizes morality in any vicious sense, by say, reducing it to a matter of individualistic prudence: "We can keep the notion of 'morality' just insofar as we can cease to think of morality as the voice of the divine part of ourselves and instead think of it as the voice of ourselves as members of a community, speakers of a common language." Our historically contingent community membership is all that is required to keep our sense of morality from slipping into a vicious form of relativism. In putting things this way, Rorty claims to share Sellars' view that any particular community's sense of morality consists of "we-intentions." Morality and immorality are first understood (and learned), at the most basic level, as those things that "we" do or don't do. Recognizing the contingency of his political community the way he does, Rorty sees no escape from such use of we-intentions *as a starting point*. Our sense of morality then becomes a matter of historical narration and future speculation ("what might we become?"), as opposed to the search for eternal, universal rules or principles.[41]

Rorty concludes his discussion of contingency by offering the following summary of his understanding of the ideal community: "To sum up, the citizens of my liberal utopia would be people who had a sense of the contingency of their language of moral deliberation, and thus of their consciences, and thus of their community. They would be liberal ironists—... people who combined commitment with a sense of the contingency of their own commitment."[42] Rorty's vision of a political community that embraces contingency, a community that indeed understands freedom as the recognition of contingency, eventually ushers in his vision of the ideal citizen of such a community, the liberal ironist. I now turn to a closer examination of this Rortyan type.

IRONY

An ironist, says Rorty, is someone who is able to combine a deep sense of commitment with a simultaneous awareness of the contingency of that commitment. That is, the ironist's awareness of contingency does not necessarily serve to undermine his sense of commitment, but only introduces a sense of fallibility to it. An ironist may remain committed to a particular cause even unto death, yet because he is an ironist his doubts about the suitability of that commitment will accompany him all the way to this bitter end. An ironist, says Rorty, is able to devote himself to such a cause or perspective, while also realizing that, because of its contingency, there are other languages he could speak and other communities he might belong to. Yet his acute sensitivity to the very existence of these alternatives introduces worry in the midst of his commitment, worry that might even encourage him to consider altering this commitment radically. The ironist is someone who pursues personal authenticity with the tools of a contingent cultural inheritance that for him has become precisely an issue. He is someone who is sensitive to what Charles Taylor calls the "cross pressures" applied by the existence of alternative commitments, and may even explore such alternatives in his private efforts to remake himself.[43]

Rorty introduces two important notions in order to unpack and qualify his understanding of irony as the combination of commitment with an awareness of the contingency of that commitment. These are the liberal private–public distinction, and what he calls a "final vocabulary." Rorty gives the label "final vocabulary" to those basic words one uses to justify one's life, one's actions, and beliefs. They are the words one uses to articulate both one's deepest self-doubts and highest hopes. This vocabulary is "final" for Rorty simply because there is nothing beyond it that one might invoke to support it. As Rorty explains, "[i]t is 'final' in the sense that if doubt is cast on the worth of these words, their user has no noncircular argumentative recourse. Those words are as far as he can go with language; beyond them there is only helpless passivity or a resort to force."[44] A final vocabulary has a public side, insofar as it is something that we inherit through socialization, through our initiation into the communities to which we belong, and a private side, insofar as we can harbour doubts with respect to it, and reimagine ourselves in contrast to it, eventually even remaking it. The ironist, for Rorty, is someone whose life has become preoccupied with the latter effort, someone who is committed to reinventing herself by creating her own final vocabulary.

"The ironist," Rorty says, "spends her time worrying about the possibility that she has been initiated into the wrong tribe, taught to play the wrong language game. . . . But she cannot give a criterion of wrongness."[45] She cannot give such a criterion, of course, because she cannot step completely outside of her final vocabulary—either the one she inherited or the one she is developing in critical response to that inheritance—and see whether it corresponds to something antecedently and independently real. The ironist therefore does not invoke context-transcending criteria when endorsing her own, emergent final vocabulary; instead, she views appeals to such purportedly objective criteria as nothing more than "the platitudes which contextually define the terms of a final vocabulary currently in use."[46] For this reason, the ironist will describe her efforts at self-transformation differently than would her foil, the metaphysician: "Her description of what she is doing when she looks for a better final vocabulary than the one she is currently using is dominated by metaphors of making rather than finding, of diversification and novelty rather than convergence to the antecedently present. She thinks of final vocabularies as poetic achievements rather than as fruits of diligent inquiry according to antecedently formulated criteria."[47]

Rorty sees such ironism come to the fore in the expressivism of the Romantic period as well as through the introduction of the expansive freedoms that emerged during the formation of liberal societies. Because the ironist, the person who works at inventing a new final vocabulary, is a cultural persona that Rorty cherishes, and whose legitimacy he would defend, he remains committed to the liberal model of social and political organization that has managed to make room for this creative figure. For Rorty, liberal societies are preferable to others because, among other things, they make room for ironists, the figures of suspicion who continually question the adequacy of the culture into which they have been socialized. For whatever reason, liberal societies have been able to carve out space for persons who wish to articulate their own sense of alienation from the societies to which they otherwise belong, and this articulation often makes them appear antiliberal. Yet, for Rorty, their very presence is definitive of a liberal society *qua* liberal.

At this point, Rorty's invocation of the liberal private–public distinction comes into play. He introduces this distinction in order to distinguish two forms of responsibility—one that we owe to ourselves and one that we owe to others. As we have seen, he follows Nietzsche in honouring the fact that some of us (especially the intellectuals) feel a responsibility to ourselves, a responsibility to remake our lives in ways that do more than simply act out a previously written script from an inherited final vocabulary. Rorty also insists, however, that our ability to notice the brute pain and suffering of our fellows calls us to a second responsibility, that of addressing the needs of those who, for whatever reason, cry out to us in pain. According to Rorty, irony operates mainly on the level of the former, private responsibility. No society could exist for very long, Rorty thinks, if irony were also a public matter, that is, if a society socialized its youth to entertain radical doubts about their own processes of socialization all the time. Rather, the ironist gesture is marked precisely by one's prescinding, in private, from the vocabulary one otherwise shares with the rest of one's community in public. For this reason, Rorty says, "[i]rony seems a private matter. On my definition, an ironist cannot get along without the contrast between the final vocabulary she inherited and the one she is trying to create for herself. . . . Ironists have to have something to have doubts about, something from which to be alienated."[48] The concern Rorty is expressing here is that, although enculturation into the public (in the sense of shared) "final vocabulary" of a linguistic community is a necessary condition for human existence, and therefore something we are not able (and should not wish) to throw entirely into doubt, this shared vocabulary nevertheless remains open to the effects of novel ways of speaking, ways that he thinks emerge from "private" (in the sense of new and idiosyncratic) attempts to avoid simply speaking from a predefined public script.[49]

Yet the ironist, according to Rorty, is not immediately concerned about the potential public effects of her private attempts at self-creation. In worrying about the vocabulary into which she has been socialized, and trying to create a new one for herself, she must come to terms with the possibility that the final vocabulary she is busy making, and to which she may become deeply attached, may never be shared, might only ever be hers. While most philosophers think that our deepest commitments should be reserved for those things we find to be universal, common to us all, Rorty argues that any idiosyncratic constellation of beliefs and desires can set up "a commandment no less unconditional because it may be intelligible to, at most, only one person."[50] At the same time that Rorty affirms this possibility, however, he also worries about the potentially corrosive public effect it might have.

While Rorty would defend the legitimacy and desirability of the ironism he describes, his invocation of the liberal private–public distinction qualifies it in an important way. By insisting on the privacy of irony, he displays sensitivity to the criticisms of such social theorists as Habermas, who argue that unfettered ironism can harm social solidarity, can weaken the social bond or "glue" that keeps a society together.[51] Rorty affirms the worries of thinkers like Habermas when he notes that ironism, for all its attractions, can also become a source of cruelty:

> Ironism, as I have defined it, results from awareness of the power of redescription. But most people do not want to be redescribed. They want to be taken on their own terms—taken seriously just as they are and just as they talk. The ironist tells them that the language they speak is up for grabs by her and her kind. There is something potentially very cruel about that claim. For the best way to cause people long-lasting pain is to humiliate them by making the things that seemed most important to them look futile, obsolete, and powerless.[52]

As he goes on to say, "[r]edescription often humiliates." For this reason, Rorty thinks that ironism must be seasoned with the adoption of a concomitant public responsibility to minimize and eliminate cruelty. Rorty therefore argues for a position that holds both public and private imperatives in high esteem, while forgoing any attempt at their theoretical synthesis.[53] Expressed in philosophical shorthand, Rorty wants Nietzsche without the elitist sneer toward his fellow compatriots (not to mention Nietzsche's willingness to condone their exploitation), and Habermas without the suspicion that the aesthetic quest for personal autonomy and authenticity necessarily conflicts with the liberal political goals of justice, equality, freedom, and solidarity.[54]

Rorty ends up saying we just don't need the kind of social glue most social philosophers are after, if by that we mean "the discovery of some universally shared essence" or "some form of universal grounding for liberal politics and morality":

> The liberal metaphysician wants our *wish to be kind* to be bolstered by an argument, one which entails a self-redescription which will highlight a common human essence, an essence which is something more than our shared ability to suffer humiliation. The liberal ironist just wants our *chances of being kind*, of avoiding the humiliation of others, to be expanded by redescription.

She thinks that recognition of a common susceptibility to humiliation is the *only* social bond that is needed.[55]

Here, Rorty is questioning the "metaphysical" inclinations of his fellow liberals, but of course not their liberalism per se, which he shares. He wishes such intellectuals would be less metaphysical and more ironic. Yet it is also crucial that the adjective "liberal" still qualify that irony. That is, he is just as suspicious, if not more so, of ironists who are not liberals, ironists like Nietzsche who can be rather callous concerning human suffering.[56]

Rorty's insistence that any celebration of the power of private ironism be joined with a robust public concern for human welfare brings us to his discussion of the key social value of solidarity. As we shall see, Rorty's recognition of contingency and his cherishing of ironism lead him to provide an untraditional interpretation of this important social value as well.

SOLIDARITY

Rorty's treatment of the theme of solidarity plays a key role in his developing position for several reasons. First of all, his recognition and embrace of contingency denies the existence of the universal and atemporal ground that many philosophers think is necessary for securing human solidarity. He must therefore explain how his denial of these grounds does not preclude an alternative way of construing the possibility or desirability of achieving solidarity. Second, as we have just seen, his embrace of irony, if unqualified in a liberal direction, has the potential to introduce a selfish individualism that could be corrosive of solidarity. In sketching the figure of the *liberal* ironist, Rorty seeks to address these concerns.

While dropping the demand for a theory which would commensurate public and private imperatives, the liberal ironist, says Rorty, still wishes to treat "the demands of self-creation and of human solidarity as equally valid. . . ." The liberal ironist must view these demands as equally valid because, *qua* liberal, he must abjure suffering and cruelty, and also desire and seek out their elimination. In saying this, Rorty takes his definition of "liberal" from Judith Shklar, who describes liberals as "the people who think that cruelty is the worst thing we do." So, although a liberal ironist will be sufficiently historicist and nominalist to recognize the contingency of her most central beliefs and desires, so long as she calls herself a liberal she will include among these ungroundable beliefs and desires her own hope "that suffering will be diminished, that the humiliation of human beings by other human beings may cease."[57]

Practically speaking, solidarity for the liberal ironist is no different than it is for the liberal metaphysician; both use the word to describe the social bond that keeps a society together through fellow feeling and a sense of shared purpose, a bond that keeps it from fragmenting into millions of tiny, different pieces. The only difference between the liberal ironist and the liberal metaphysician lies in the way they account for solidarity. Unlike the liberal metaphysician, says Rorty, the liberal ironist does not see the need to ground solidarity in the theoretical notion of a common human essence. In fact, he does not think the metaphysical invocation of such theoretical entities as a common human essence does any real moral or political work: "The real work has been done by . . . the societies which developed the moralities and institutions in struggle and pain. All the Platonic or Kantian philosopher does is to take the finished first-level product, jack it up a few levels of abstraction, invent a metaphysical or epistemological or semantical vocabulary into which to translate it, and announce that he has *grounded* it."[58] The task Rorty thus sets for himself is to explain how liberal societies might continue to pursue increased levels of solidarity without requiring recourse to the notion of something like a universal human essence. In true ironist fashion, Rorty thinks it is more helpful in this effort to understand human solidarity as an achievement as opposed to a discovery, something that is made rather than found. His denial of the existence of a common human essence, then, does not lead him to give up on solidarity, but instead to appreciate the fragility of its achievement, and thus to cherish it all the more.

Rorty argues that all we require in order to achieve solidarity is the *recognition* of a common human susceptibility to pain and humiliation. Yet this is more than simply registering the bare fact that another person is in pain. This recognition has to *matter*. Presumably in slaveholding societies slaveholders are able to notice when their slaves are in pain, but that doesn't seem to matter. The slave's pain doesn't matter because, as far as the slaveholder is concerned, the slave is not "one of us," and so he may be treated without moral concern. What is missing in this scenario is the slaveholder's recognition of the moral relevance of the slave's susceptibility to pain and humiliation, a susceptibility the slaveholder shares. Someone is a liberal ironist, according to Rorty, just insofar as they recognize this common susceptibility to be a sufficient condition for considering someone to be included within the range of any morally relevant "we."

Yet it is precisely this kind of recognition that often goes missing in our societies, even those that profess to be liberal. For Rorty, this problem confronts both the liberal metaphysician as well as the liberal ironist. Yet each responds to the problem in opposing ways. Whereas the liberal metaphysician is counting on the existence of something that escapes contingency, something that will *make* us recognize this common human susceptibility, the liberal ironist must live without any such guarantee (a guarantee he considers false, at any rate, and therefore only capable of providing an equally false sense of security). The liberal metaphysician emphasizes the importance of theory in confronting the problem of moral recognition, hoping that such disciplines as theology, science, or philosophy, those "charged with penetrating behind the many private appearances to the one general common reality," would be able to secure solidarity, and thus help "to eliminate cruelty." Obviously, as a liberal ironist, Rorty does not share the metaphysician's confidence in theory. Instead, he places his hope in "literature," precisely that area of culture which the metaphysician restricts to the private realm. Within an ironist culture, he says, it is the disciplines which specialize in "thick descriptions of the private and idiosyncratic" which are assigned the job of augmenting our limited sense of solidarity. "In particular, novels and ethnographies which sensitize one to the pain of those who do not speak our language must do the job which demonstrations of a common human nature were supposed to do. Solidarity has to be constructed out of little pieces, rather than found already waiting, in the form of an ur-language which all of us recognize when we hear it."[59]

In an effort to practice what he preaches, Rorty delves into literary criticism in order to demonstrate the efficacy of literature to bolster and enlarge a liberal's sense of social solidarity. The first two chapters of part III of *Contingency, Irony, and Solidarity* explore the work of two authors that at first glance might appear to be strange bedfellows—Vladimir Nabokov and George Orwell. For all their apparent differences, however, Rorty believes that both authors provide unique insights into the human ability to be cruel, thereby educating the liberal temperament concerning forms of cruelty of which it had been unaware. Unlike such books as *Les Misérables* and *Uncle Tom's Cabin*, books that help us see the cruel effects of certain social practices and institutions upon others, the works of Nabokov and Orwell, says Rorty, "help us see the effects of our private idiosyncracies upon others."[60] These novels are especially helpful to the liberal ironist, because they sensitize such a person to the very real possibility that their private, ironic quest for personal authenticity and autonomy may become a source of cruelty that harms social solidarity. In differing ways, says Rorty, both Nabokov and Orwell, "warn the liberal ironist intellectual against temptations to be cruel. Both of them dramatize the tension between private irony and liberal hope."[61]

Rorty's sensitivity to the potential for cruelty latent in the ironism he would otherwise defend leads him to draw a moral from Nabokov's *Lolita* that Nabokov himself may not have drawn. (Rorty begins his discussion of Nabokov by exploring Nabokov's claim that *Lolita* "has no moral in tow.") According to Rorty, Nabokov too struggles with the tension between balancing the private pursuit of aesthetic bliss with the necessity, at certain crucial moments, of tearing oneself away from that pursuit in order to avoid cruelty and serve the cause of social solidarity. In unpacking the way Nabokov treats this problem, Rorty draws the reader's attention to a repeated worry Nabokov expresses through his work, the worry that one's pursuit of aesthetic autonomy or private bliss can blind one to cruelty. According to Rorty, while Nabokov may have wanted to synthesize kindness and tenderness (aversion to cruelty) with the achievement of artistic ecstasy, he highlights the difficulty of achieving this synthesis by composing characters who are capable of the latter but not the former.[62] The paradigm case is *Lolita*'s Humbert Humbert. In the character of Humbert, says Rorty, Nabokov describes a particular sort of monster, "the monster of incuriosity," a monster that he thinks had not been thought up before. The portrayal of this particular monster therefore forms "Nabokov's contribution to our knowledge of human possibilities."[63] Humbert reveals his lack of a form of ethical curiosity, or sensitivity to narratives not his own, when he sits in the chair of the Barber of Kasbeam, remaining inattentive to the barber's story about the death of his son. It's a small moment, one sentence, which a reader might also miss, and so be guilty of the same indecent incuriosity:

"The reader, suddenly revealed to himself as, if not hypocritical, at least cruelly incurious, recognizes his *semblable*, his brother, in Humbert. . . ."[64] Once this realization is made, says Rorty, *Lolita* suddenly does have a moral in tow:

> But the moral is not to keep one's hands off little girls but to notice what one is doing, and in particular to notice what people are saying. For it might turn out, it very often does turn out, that people are trying to tell you that they are suffering. Just insofar as one is preoccupied with building up one's private kind of sexual bliss, like Humbert, or one's private aesthetic bliss, like the reader of *Lolita* who missed the sentence about the barber the first time around, people are likely to suffer still more.[65]

Novels like *Lolita* help along the liberal cause of achieving solidarity, Rorty claims, not through theoretical argument about common essences, but through thick descriptions of particular situations that sensitize us to, and thus help us avoid, particular forms of cruelty.

Orwell's writing, especially a novel like *1984*, would seem to be harder to enlist in the service of Rorty's way of describing the social efficacy of literature. For if nothing else, surely this novel stands as a defense of the traditional, metaphysical notion of truth, of the social and political importance of distinguishing between appearance and reality, of telling it like it is. In likening Orwell to Nabokov, Rorty nevertheless grabs the bull by the horns: ". . . the kind of thing Orwell and Nabokov did—sensitizing an audience to cases of cruelty and humiliation—is not usefully thought of as a matter of stripping away appearance and revealing reality. It is better thought of as a redescription of what may happen or has been happening—to be compared, not with reality, but with alternative descriptions of the same events."[66] Instead of suggesting the importance of maintaining a metaphysical understanding of truth, thinks Rorty, Orwell instead offers his reader a chilling redescription of what may happen to liberal societies in the future, based on the hints he finds around him in the present.

Rorty focuses much of his analysis on the character of O'Brien, Winston's torturer. Rorty suggests that O'Brien is the true subject of the last third of *1984*, claiming that this part of the book is about torturing as opposed to being tortured. What is truly terrifying about *1984*, Rorty says, is that we recognize the monstrous character of

O'Brien as no far-fetched dystopian projection, but rather a figure whose possibility, thanks to the twentieth century's political events, is not difficult to imagine: "Orwell managed, by skillful reminders of, and extrapolations from, what happened to real people in real places—things that nowadays we know are still happening—to convince us that O'Brien is a plausible character type of a possible future society, one in which the intellectuals had accepted the fact that liberal hopes had no chance of realization."[67]

For Rorty, Orwell's work serves to remind liberal society just how far it has fallen from its ideal. The grand political visions of the Left and the Right, communism and capitalism, have failed to bring about the equality and freedom they originally promised. Yet rather than reading Orwell as fatalistic concerning the inevitability of an oncoming totalitarianism, Rorty instead reads him as someone who is frankly pessimistic. There is a difference between these two orientations because the pessimist is not someone without hope, or without a vision for how things might be. The pessimist is simply one who admits to being at a loss as to which practicable steps we might take in order to achieve that vision, and informs his society that everyone needs to go back to the drawing board. This is an assessment of liberal society that Rorty shares: "I do not think that we liberals *can* now imagine a future of 'human dignity, freedom and peace'. That is, we cannot tell ourselves a story about how to get from the actual present to such a future. We can picture various socioeconomic setups which would be preferable to the present one. But we have no clear sense of how to get from the actual world to these theoretically possible worlds, and thus no clear idea of what to work for."[68] According to Rorty, 40 years of further experience have only served to confirm Orwell's pessimistic description of our political situation. "This bad news remains the great intransigent fact of contemporary political speculation, the one that blocks all the liberal scenarios."[69]

Rorty therefore reads Orwell's cautionary tale as a tale about freedom rather than truth. For Rorty, Winston's diary entry—"Freedom is the freedom to say that two plus two equals four. If that is granted, all else follows"—is not so much about the importance of being able to say what is true, but rather about the freedom to say what you think to be true:

> [I]t does not matter whether "two plus two is four" is true, much less whether this truth is "subjective" or "corresponds to reality."

All that matters is that if you do believe it, you can say it without getting hurt. In other words, what matters is your ability to talk to other people about what seems to you true, not what is in fact true. If we take care of freedom truth can take care of itself. If we are ironic enough about our own final vocabularies, and curious enough about everyone else's, we do not have to worry about whether we are in direct contact with moral reality, or whether we are blinded by ideology, or whether we are being weakly "relativistic."[70]

Rorty worries less about the fact that contemporary societies the world over have lost or are losing touch with Truth, than he does about the fact that they are busy closing down on human freedom, blocking all the liberal scenarios, and thereby becoming increasingly capable of cruelty.

Rorty shares what he takes to be Orwell's pessimism because Orwell, according to him, also recognizes the contingency of this current state of affairs: "Orwell helps us see that it *just happened* that rule in Europe passed into the hands of people who pitied the humiliated and dreamed of human equality, and that it may *just happen* that the world will wind up being ruled by people who lack any such sentiments or ideas. Socialization, to repeat, goes all the way down, and who gets to do the socializing is often a matter of who manages to kill whom first."[71] This recognition of contingency is important, says Rorty, because it helps us appreciate the fragile achievement of whatever levels of solidarity humans have been able to achieve. In line with this sensitivity, Rorty hopes, but does not expect, that something like the liberal vision for human dignity, freedom, and peace will survive into the future. For him, the historically contingent achievement of human solidarity is not to be taken for granted because there is no guarantee that it will remain in place if we cease to care for it. In summarizing his understanding of solidarity, Rorty suggests that we read the slogan "We have obligations to human beings simply as such," not as a metaphysical claim about a shared, universal essence, but rather as an ethical call to maintain and *enhance* the solidarity we have historically achieved: "We should stay on the lookout for marginalized people—people whom we still instinctively think of as 'they' rather than 'us'. We should try to notice our similarities with them. The right way to construe the slogan is as urging us to *create* a more expansive sense of solidarity than we presently have."[72] By helping us to notice another person's susceptibility to pain and humiliation, writers like Orwell and Nabokov heighten our ethical sensitivity, and thereby help us to overcome the differences that keep us ignorant of this underlying similarity.

OCCUPY WALL STREET: WHAT WOULD RORTY DO?

Perhaps a look at a contemporary political event might help round out our understanding of Rorty's political perspective. As I write these words, people across the globe, most notably in Manhattan, are occupying their respective city's financial districts, protesting the crony capitalism they conclude has led the world to the brink of financial collapse, while at the same time further lining the pockets of the wealthiest 1 percent of the population and decreasing the economic chances of almost everyone else. How might Rorty have responded to these protests? Would he have been sympathetic, critical, or a mixture of both? Of course it is difficult to answer such a speculative question, but an editorial in *The New Republic* on the Occupy Wall Street protests is noteworthy for articulating a political perspective that is very reminiscent of Rorty's. To start, the editors agree that, in Wall Street, the occupiers have chosen a deserving target: "Wall Street *should* be protested. Its resistance to needed regulations that would stabilize the U.S. economy is shameful. And, insofar as it has long opposed appropriate levels of government spending and taxation, it has helped to create a society that does a deeply flawed job of providing for its most vulnerable, educating its young, and guaranteeing economic opportunity for all."[73] Rorty often expresses similar reservations about the effects of government deregulation, and regrets the erosion of the social safety nets once tended to by a more caring polity.[74]

But Rorty remains a liberal, not a radical. His political philosophy eschews revolutionary politics and instead embraces reformist politics. He considers the latter approach, while perhaps less sexy, to be much more effective. Such reformism, of course, means that Rorty has to make his peace with capitalism. As the editors at *The New Republic* assert: "One of the core differences between liberals and radicals is that liberals are capitalists. They believe in a capitalism that is democratically regulated—that seeks to level an unfair economic playing field so that all citizens have the freedom to make what they want of their lives." While it might be too much to say that Rorty "believes in" capitalism (he was a "Left-wing" American patriot, after all), so long as the radicals and revolutionaries he encounters fail to supply the nitty gritty details of a viable alternative, his advice is still to stick with, and work at reforming, existing economic and political structures. As he says in *Achieving our Country*: "I think that the left should get back into the business of piecemeal reform within the framework of a market economy."[75]

Interestingly, the editors of *The New Republic* also discuss certain remarks made by Slavoj Žižek, the Left-wing theorist *du jour*, in a speech to Occupy Wall Street protesters. In response to the criticism that the protesters are "dreamers," Žižek draws his audience's attention to the official Chinese policy of censoring all artworks depicting alternative reality or time travel. He goes on to claim that such state censorship is a "good sign," one that indicates that the Chinese people have not lost their capacity to dream. Then, in his typically perverse fashion, he claims that the lack of such censorship in the United States, rather than being an indication of the higher degree of freedom enjoyed by its citizens, is actually a portentous omen of the American people's inability to dream of alternatives, an imaginative capacity that has been so eroded that "the ruling system" (capitalism) does not even worry enough about it to attempt to suppress it. The editors of the *New Republic* find this statement particularly offensive, and I'm quite sure Rorty would not have been a big fan of it either. He would have most likely considered it to be a particularly exaggerated species of *Ideologiekritik*, an academic discourse devoted to "unmasking" the "bourgeois ideology" of "late capitalism"—a discourse that Rorty thinks "has long been overworked and has by now turned into self-parody." He gives this discourse the satirical label "Leftspeak," which he borrows from Frederick Crews, and goes on to describe it as "a dreadful, pompous, useless mishmash of Marx, Adorno, Derrida, Foucault, and Lacan. It has resulted in articles that offer unmaskings of the presuppositions of earlier unmaskings of still earlier unmaskings."[76] Rorty would have no doubt considered Žižek to be the latest in a long train of pompous would-be unmaskers.

In criticizing "Leftspeak," Rorty reiterates a deeply held metaphilosophical position with respect to the political efficacy of theory. Indeed, much of his *Achieving Our Country* is devoted to a critique of the academic Left for abandoning the reformist politics of the nonacademic Left in favor of the theoretical purity of the ivory tower. Or, as he bluntly puts the point in a rejoinder to his friend Richard Bernstein: "When one thinks of the fate of democracy and of socialism as largely a matter of who shoots whom first, or whose agents co-opt which revolution first, one's sense of the importance of the theorist in politics diminishes."[77] Rorty appreciates ground-level reformist politics over ivory-tower purist politics, because he is sensitive to the dynamics of power, the slow pace of real change, and to the fact that total revolution more often than not leads to utter chaos and further violence and injustice. When you are fighting thugs, fine tuning one's critical theory is of little help.

In "Trotsky and the Wild Orchids," Rorty provides yet another memorable quip regarding the disappointment that Left-wing theorists express when they hear him espouse what they take to be a rather run-of-the-mill version of liberal politics: "Some postmodernists who initially took my enthusiasm for Derrida to mean that I must be on their political side decided, after discovering my politics were pretty much those of Hubert Humphrey, that I must have sold out."[78] Rorty's choice of Humphrey in this quip is instructive, I believe, as Humphrey was a reformist liberal, one who, moreover, played a crucial role in uniting the Democratic Party behind the cause of civil rights at the 1948 Democratic National Convention. Humphrey was a politician who fought to expand Americans' sense of solidarity. As Vice President to Lyndon Johnston, however, he became associated with Johnston's policies during the Vietnam War, thereby garnering the mistrust of an emerging radical Left who felt that American involvement in Vietnam tainted the moral virtue of that country beyond repair. Although grateful for the efforts of this New Left in ending the war in Vietnam, Rorty disagrees with their assessment that the United States, as a political community, has moved beyond reformist repair.

While it is too early to judge with finality regarding the direction of the Occupy Wall Street protests, insofar as the protesters persist in espousing politically vague "Leftspeak" (and I am not saying that all of them do), Rorty would have remained skeptical about their program. His political reflections are constantly critical of those who see no hope for America outside of a total (and perhaps even violent) revolution. The best chance for meaningful social change, he thinks, is through gradual democratic reform.[79]

I like to think that beyond sympathizing with his reformist politics, Rorty had another reason for championing a politician like Humphrey. For, like Rorty, and even Dewey, Humphrey had a keen sense of the importance and difficulty of achieving a balance between individualism and community, freedom and solidarity. In a speech he made in 1966, he posed the problem of constructing such a balance in a way that chimes well with Rorty's position: "The great challenge which faces us is to assure that, in our society of bigness, we do not strangle the voice of creativity, that the rules of the game do not come to overshadow its purpose, that the grand orchestration of society leaves ample room for the man who marches to the music of another drummer."[80] Here Humphrey sounds an important American political theme, one we have also seen both Dewey and Rorty champion. For Rorty, it is fair to say that whatever "the grand orchestration of society" turns out to be, the success of such orchestration ought to be determined according to the space it creates for a plurality of different drummers and drumbeats. In contrast, when Truth becomes our only social goal, Rorty thinks that society will only have room for one kind of drummer, and only one very dull beat. For this reason, he recommends we substitute Freedom for Truth, and thereby give up what he describes as the "theological" or "metaphysical" quest to discover Reality's "one right description."

As we will see in the next chapter, Rorty carries this deep-seated suspicion of the theological or metaphysical desire for Truth into his interpretation and criticism of Western religious culture. At the same time, however, he does not entirely fail to appreciate the inspirational and critical power of certain forms of religious insight, including their ability to provide present hope for a future that somehow escapes the dark times we currently inhabit. At the same time, however, Rorty does not hold out much hope that these more edifying forms of religious comportment will win the day over their fundamentalist and theocratic rivals, and so he ultimately maintains that mainstream religious culture is, much more often than not, a threat to the health of democratic societies. Let us now turn to a consideration of Rorty's understanding of this powerful cultural force, religion.

CHAPTER 4

THE ANTICLERICAL PROPHET: RORTY AND RELIGION

REVISITING RORTY'S ATHEISM: COMPLICATING THE PICTURE

Rorty's outspoken atheism is a well-known feature of his overall philosophical perspective. If nothing else, his philosophy presents a thoroughgoing articulation of humanistic self-reliance, a position that leaves little if any room for God or God-substitutes. With Dewey, Rorty completely rejects religious supernaturalism. As we saw in the previous chapter, he lumps theology and metaphysics together as inhuman attempts to transcend a "merely" human perspective; for him such ambitions of transcendence represent nothing more than the impossible wish to achieve a "God's eye view" independent of human interests and subjectivity. He considers such attempts to grasp a "skyhook" to be self-defeating, for the skyhook turns out to be an illusion; instead, he argues that we should rest content with the immanent, contingent "toeholds" that are all we have to support us as together we negotiate life's cliffs and crags.

Rorty's atheism is also an extension of his version of pragmatism. That is, he understands his atheism to be a natural corollary of his pragmatist embrace of contingency, which we explored in the previous chapter. Recall the distinction Rorty makes in *Contingency, Irony, and Solidarity* between metaphysics and irony—between the quest to secure mind-independent foundations for our beliefs, and the willingness to forego such support and instead remain content with our power to redescribe, from within, the particular constellation of historically contingent beliefs (or "final vocabulary") we inherit through our acculturation into a particular community.

Because Rorty can see no way of escaping this historical contingency, he recommends going with irony and redescription over metaphysics and foundationalism; and because he also proceeds to map his metaphysics/irony distinction onto a religious/secular distinction, his preference for irony entails a rejection of religion as he understands it. In recommending irony over metaphysics, he therefore understands himself to be promoting the further secularization of Western liberal society. For Rorty, religious life patterns (especially Western monotheisms) represent little more than variations on a singular metaphysical theme, and as such he considers them to be outdated: "The difference between a search for foundations and an attempt at redescription," he says, "is emblematic of the difference between the culture of liberalism and older forms of cultural life."[1]

According to Rorty, the emergent liberal culture of the West is one that is proving itself capable of doing without such metaphysical support. In making this claim, he prophetically points toward the possibility of a future liberal culture that would be willing to embrace secularization completely, and so do without any ambition of transcendence whatsoever. He portrays this ideal in the following terms:

> [I]n its ideal form, the culture of liberalism would be one which was enlightened, secular, through and through. It would be one in which no trace of divinity remained, either in the form of a divinized world or a divinized self. Such a culture would have no room for the notion that there are nonhuman forces to which human beings should be responsible. It would drop, or drastically reinterpret, not only the idea of holiness but those of 'devotion to truth' and of 'fulfillment of the deepest needs of the spirit'.[2]

It would indeed be difficult to compose a more complete rejection of any and all notions of divinity, including whatever other "nonhuman forces" modern humankind has, according to Rorty, substituted for more traditional religious conceptions of the divine (such as a divinized Self or a divinized World).

Rorty rejects the idea that humans are responsible to nonhuman forces, in whatever way these may be construed, because he thinks that humans are only responsible to, or required to answer, those with whom they can speak.[3] For him, this position excludes both God and the mind-independent World as potential conversation partners. Because on his account neither of these speaks a language, we cannot hold a conversation with them, and so it is impossible for us to answer, or be response-able to them. As it turns out, says Rorty, we only have each other to rely on, and it is dangerous to pretend that we may avail ourselves of something more than the tolerance and decency of our fellow human beings, some nonhuman power, to come to our aid when the chips are down. Such a pretension is dangerous because it may lead us to neglect the important task of tending to and growing the levels of human solidarity that we have so far been able to achieve, to the point of even shirking our responsibilities to our fellow humans and ourselves, the only real responsibilities we have anyway.[4] Our desire to claim the support or backing of some nonhuman power, says Rorty, simply masks an all-too human tendency to deny our freedom as well as our responsibility for assuming that freedom.

When seen in this light, Rorty's rejection of divinity, or the idea that humans are responsible to some nonhuman power, chimes with Dewey's rejection of religious supernaturalism in *A Common Faith*. In this book, Dewey rejects religious supernaturalism in order to encourage in humankind a heightened sense of respect for human freedom and responsibility: "Men have never fully used the powers they possess to advance the good in life," Dewey says, "because they have waited upon some power external to themselves and to nature to do the work they are responsible for doing."[5] Because he agrees with Dewey's assessment, Rorty views human religious culture as, on the whole, detrimental to the health of democratic societies.[6] The democratic community Rorty envisions is a community that does not shirk its responsibility for bettering society by placing that responsibility in the hands of a nonhuman power. According to him, Dewey's imagined ideal democratic community "is a community in which everybody thinks that it is human solidarity, rather than knowledge of something not merely human, that really matters."[7]

Yet in spite of all his suspicions regarding the irresponsible metaphysical tendencies of religious culture, Rorty would, late in his career, come to resist using the label "atheist," at least without further qualification, to describe his philosophical position. He tells us that "only two sorts of philosophers are still tempted to use the word 'atheist' to describe themselves." The first sort, he says, "are those who still think that belief in the divine is an empirical hypothesis and that modern science has given better explanations of the phenomena God was once used to explain." Rorty is not an atheist of this sort, because he rejects the epistemology upon which it is based. Agreeing with an insight contained in both Hume's and Kant's critiques of eighteenth-century natural theology, he holds that "the notion of 'empirical evidence' is irrelevant to talk about God." Yet this point, says Rorty, bears equally against both theism and atheism, insofar as both positions represent attempts to prove something about God on the basis of so-called empirical evidence. Rorty concludes: "Neither those who affirm nor those who deny the existence of God can plausibly claim that they have evidence for their views. Being religious, in the modern West, does not have much to do with the explanation of specific observable phenomena."[8]

Because neither side in this dispute can claim the vindication of empirical evidence, Rorty understands both of these versions of theism and atheism as faiths. Because of his epistemological objections to their implicit foundationalism, Rorty holds to neither faith. Instead, he continues to tell us about a second sort of philosopher who still describes himself or herself as an atheist, a figure with whom he does in fact identify. Philosophers of this type, Rorty says, are "the ones who use 'atheism' as a rough synonym for 'anticlericalism'." He goes on to say that he wishes he would have used this latter term to describe his own view (hence the title of this chapter), instead of the word "atheist," so that he might have avoided the epistemological connotations associated with atheism of the first sort. He prefers what he calls anticlericalism to this version of atheism, he says, because "anticlericalism is a political view, not an epistemological or metaphysical one."[9]

Yet even if Rorty's anticlericalism is epistemologically humbler than the more militant forms of atheism we see today, his judgment remains negative concerning the net social impact of institutional religious culture on democratic society. This is because his anticlericalism entails "the view that ecclesiastical institutions, despite all the good they do—despite all the comfort they provide to those in need or in despair—are dangerous to the health of democratic societies."[10] Notwithstanding this summary and perhaps hasty judgment of institutional religious culture, Rorty's atheism still loses a measure of stridency by placing itself in the messy but egalitarian arena of cultural politics (where we all simply "muddle through," arguing "in the old, familiar, inconclusive ways"), as opposed to the (for him) illusively cut and dried arena of evidentialist verification.[11]

Rorty's atheism also loses some stridency through his willingness to engage in extended dialogues with religious thinkers. These exchanges demonstrate that his position with respect to religion is not simply or only one of outright hostility or blunt dismissal. The story, as we shall see, is more complicated than that, and in these very complications one discovers Rorty's potential willingness to "drastically reinterpret" such religious themes as divinity and holiness. My task in this chapter will be to spell out these complications, not in order to make Rorty sound religious, but instead to describe those thematic areas in which religious thinkers might engage his work more positively, without an immediate allergic reaction. In order to accomplish this task, I will once again walk through several facets of Rorty's rejection of transcendence, or his rejection of the idea of human answerability to nonhuman power. While this examination shows his rejection of transcendence to be quite thorough, it also reveals the presence of a lingering notion of temporal transcendence, a sense of hopeful longing for a healed or redeemed future that has rough parallels with certain recent attempts in Western religious thought to "drastically reinterpret" received understandings of holiness and divinity.

THERAPY OR PROPHECY? RORTY'S CRITIQUE OF THE WESTERN AMBITION OF TRANSCENDENCE

On its face, the very suggestion that Rorty's work retains any appreciation for transcendence seems almost laughable. For Rorty is, as I have already mentioned, that twentieth-century thinker, *par excellence*, who takes up the torch of human self-reliance, who thinks we would be much better off without entertaining any notion of transcendence whatsoever. If nothing else, his work expresses the fervent wish that humankind will one day come to embrace life in a world "without God or his doubles."[12] Although it is true to say that Rorty is highly suspicious of the very notion of transcendence (at least the way that term gets used in various philosophical and religious circles), as I have already suggested, a positive appreciation of this notion does not go completely missing in his work, even if he avoids using that term explicitly, or backs away from it in those very moments where he seems to approach it most closely.

If we are to hear Rorty in his own voice, however, we must first come to a fulsome appreciation of his reasons for being suspicious of the very idea of transcendence, and only then will it become possible to explore any lingering positive appreciation for (or drastic reinterpretation of) that notion in his work. As we have already seen in the previous two chapters, Rorty's reasons for rejecting the idea of transcendence are intimately intertwined with his therapeutic critique of the Western philosophical tradition. Stated bluntly, Rorty thinks transcendence has been bad for us; we need to move past our obsession with it so that we can become better persons, more responsible and interesting democratic citizens. These therapeutic reasons for rejecting transcendence are succinctly formulated in the introduction to his first volume of philosophical papers, *Objectivity, Relativism, and Truth*. There Rorty roots his suspicions of transcendence in the Wittgensteinian conviction that "questions which we should have to climb out of our own minds to answer should not be asked."[13] As we have already seen, Rorty thinks the Western philosophical and theological traditions harmfully preoccupy themselves with precisely these kinds of questions; the differing attempts to answer them signal to Rorty little more than the desire to cross Plato's dividing line between shifting appearance and immutable Reality. Not only is he certain this trick cannot be done, he thinks we should not even wish that it *could* be done. For in the end, as we saw in Chapter 3, he does not think there is a line that needs to be crossed. There is no chasm radically separating the deliverances of our senses and our intersubjective communication about the world, on the one hand, from a reality that is completely independent of these, on the other—a chasm that only a priestly caste of philosophers can show us how to cross. Rorty means to do without this distinction altogether.[14]

Rorty blames this philosophical mind-world dualism for inserting the thin edge of the skeptical wedge that has allowed us to conceive of the possibility that everything we think and believe at any particular time might be out of touch with reality as it is in itself. Because, for Rorty, this intellectual Humpty Dumpty never fell off the wall in the first place, there is no need to marshal all of the king's horses and all of the king's men to put Mr Dumpty together again (a task which they are incapable of performing anyway). Less colourfully put, because Rorty follows Davidson in insisting that we are always in contact with reality, there is no human need, epistemological or otherwise, to establish a representational relationship between what it is that we believe and the supposedly mind-independent things those beliefs are about. "The antirepresentationalist," says Rorty, "is quite willing to grant that our language, like our bodies, has been shaped by the environment we live in. Indeed, he or she insists on the point—the point that our minds or our language could not (as the representationalist skeptic fears) be 'out of touch with reality' any more than our bodies could."[15]

Because, following Davidson (and to a certain extent also Hilary Putnam), Rorty cannot make sense of what it might mean for us to be radically out of touch with reality, he sees no need to adopt what the philosopher Thomas Nagel, in a more positive assessment of such representationalism, calls "the ambition of transcendence."[16] Following Putnam and Davidson, Rorty refuses "to contrast the world with what the world is known as, since such a contrast suggests that we have somehow done what Nagel calls 'climbing out of our own minds'." Rorty here rejects what he describes as a "Cartesian-Kantian" picture, one which, as we saw in the previous two chapters, understands our minds or our language as an "inside" that can be contrasted to something, perhaps even something very different, "outside": "From a Darwinian point of view," he says, "there is simply no way to give sense to the idea of our minds or our language as systematically out of phase with what lies beyond our skins."[17]

Because Rorty accepts Davidson's arguments for the impossibility of such radical mistakenness, he urges us to refrain from answering the philosophical skeptic, the philosopher whose sleep is disturbed by the possibility that our perceptions and conceptions might be totally out of phase with the way the world is anyway. As we saw in Chapter 2, Rorty credits such seventeenth-century thinkers as Descartes and Locke with introducing this form of "veil of ideas" skepticism. For various reasons, these seventeenth-century thinkers considered the task of answering the skeptic to be a pressing intellectual concern, and the philosophical work they put into responding to that problem has left an historical impress that Rorty believes we still suffer from today.[18] According to him, Modern epistemology, with its novel notion of inner mental representations that somehow need to be coordinated with the world outside the mind, introduces a new anxiety about the reliability of our knowledge. According to those who hold to this epistemology, such reliability must be indexed to certainty, and this certainty, so the story goes, can only be established if these purported inner representations can be shown to correspond with outer reality—precisely the trick of climbing out of our own minds that Rorty, *pace* Nagel, thinks is impossible. His rejection of the epistemological quest for objectivity, therefore, stems from his recommendation that we ought to therapeutically dissolve, rather than intellectually resolve, the skeptic's fears. We do not need to acquire an ambition of transcendence, he thinks, in order to have reliable, if fallible, knowledge.

Yet Rorty's critical response to the Western metaphysical ambition of transcendence is not simply or only therapeutic. In a highly astute commentary on Rorty's attack against the modern philosophical quest to secure a skeptic-beating objectivity, Jeffrey Stout notes that, in addition to the therapist, Rorty is also wont to adopt a "prophetic" persona when dealing with the attendant epistemological issues at stake in his critique.[19] The Rorty I have been describing thus far is the "philosophical therapist" we explored in Chapter 2, the one who simply tries to talk us out of asking questions that we would have to climb out of our own minds to answer. This Rorty understands the modern desire for objectivity, a desire that supposedly can only be met if we can pull off the trick of climbing out of (or transcending) our own minds, as a cultural malaise we have acquired, a malaise that requires therapy as opposed to theoretical resolution. In Stout's words, Rorty's therapy "is directed against the compulsion to take sides in an endless and fruitless metaphysical debate between those who define truth as correspondence to reality and those who define it in terms of either idealist metaphysics or sociology."[20] Rorty the therapist thinks that the Western ambition of transcendence can be cured in Wittgensteinian fashion, simply by describing the different ways we actually use the word "true," and thereby disabusing us of the philosophical temptation to locate a common essence—called "correspondence"—for that variety of uses.[21]

But what about the prophetic persona that Stout mentions? As it turns out, appreciating this Rortyan persona is also highly pertinent for understanding his intellectual allergy to the Western ambition of transcendence. In this persona, we discover the Rorty with whom most of his critics are more familiar, the irrepressible quasi-Nietzschean who says such seemingly counterintuitive and supposedly irresponsible things about truth and our knowledge of the world. It is Rorty the prophet who also rejects transcendence in the name of self-reliance, an ideal that is intimately linked to his Deweyan affirmation of human responsibility. In this persona, Rorty characterizes the metaphysical ambition of transcendence as one version among others of our propensity to submit—and in so doing to give away our freedom as well as our responsibility for that freedom—to unanswerable, nonhuman authority. Rorty's embrace of pragmatism can also be understood in this prophetic mode, motivated as it is by his desire for liberation from these authoritarian bonds. As Stout notes, for Rorty "the most interesting and liberating thing in pragmatism is the boldly thorough character of its anthropocentrism."[22] So, in his prophetic mode, Rorty expresses the concern that it will take more than Wittgensteinian or Davidsonian philosophical therapy to disabuse us of our yearning for a form of transcendence that, in his opinion, does nothing but keep people down. Donning the mantle of the prophet, he feels compelled to direct us away from our vain metaphysical pursuit of truth as correspondence and instead points in the direction of a utopian, post-Philosophical future in which human beings have, at long last, "gotten out from under the thought of, and the need for, authority."[23]

For Rorty, it seems, any openness to transcendence courts the danger of becoming such a pernicious form of deference to nonhuman authority, and it is in the name of human dignity that he rejects it. Rorty's antiauthoritarian anthropocentrism is nowhere more evident than when he responds to Stout's attempt, following such fellow pragmatists as Robert Brandom and Mark Johnston, to articulate a "non-narcissistic" version of pragmatism, one that remains thoroughly anthropocentric while at the same time respecting the human interest in objectivity that Stout describes as "our interest in getting things right."[24] As Stout observes, Rorty will have none of Stout's attempt to rescue a workable, pragmatist notion of objectivity; instead of caving into what he here regards as these pragmatists' backsliding, Rorty actually embraces the label of "narcissism" they seek to evade: "I think that the point of . . . pragmatism in general, is precisely to encourage narcissism," Rorty says. In this vein, he offers the following summary of his reasons for embracing rather than avoiding narcissism, reasons that bear directly upon our examination of his negative appraisal of transcendence: "What Stout calls narcissism," Rorty says, "I call 'self-reliance'." He continues:

> As I see it, the whole point of pragmatism is to insist that we human beings are answerable only to one [an]other. We are answerable only to those who answer to us—our conversational partners. We are not responsible either to the atoms or to God, at least not until they start conversing with us. So whereas Stout sees pragmatism as allowing room for a non-metaphysical version of theism, I see theism as a resilient enemy of human self-reliance, and metaphysics as merely a surrogate for the traditional theistic insistence that we humans need to abase ourselves before something non-human.[25]

In this passage, Rorty makes his reasons for rejecting the Western ambition of transcendence manifestly clear; not only does it entangle us in philosophical problems that only some kind of intellectual therapy can dissolve, it also involves us in a form of abasement to unanswerable, nonhuman authority that is beneath human dignity. It is for the sake of preserving such human dignity that Rorty finds pragmatic anthropocentrism to be such an attractive alternative. As anticlerical prophet, he urges his society to move into the vista he thinks this anthropocentrism opens.

RESPONSIBILITY AND THE NEW

As outlined above, Rorty's prophetic persona has primarily two motivations. The first, as I already mentioned, has to do with the fact that he thinks the Western metaphysical desire for transcendence has encouraged people to shirk their own responsibility, and instead give it over to an illusory nonhuman power. The second, related motivation, one whose importance will become evident as we assess Rorty's drastic reinterpretation of certain religious themes, is his conviction that the metaphysical desire for transcendence has, to our detriment, blocked human openness to the new. In fact, Rorty's attack on metaphysical transcendence can be fruitfully read as an attempt to defend the intertwined values of responsibility and openness to novel possibility. Most if not all forms of deference to transcendence, he concludes, exhibit a regrettable human tendency to slavishly bend before a nonhuman, authoritarian power, and in so doing neglect our responsibilities as well as our ability to release new possibilities in our effort to meet these responsibilities. These forms of deference to transcendence instead appeal to antecedently established truth, and thereby remain conservatively closed to new possibilities and the potential alternative consequences of exploring novel paths. Thus, in rejecting deference to metaphysical transcendence, Rorty primarily objects to a form of heteronomy that leaves humans utterly disempowered. We must interpret whatever positive appreciation for transcendence that remains in his thought, then, in light of his desire to defend human responsibility and openness to novel possibility from such a heteronomous threat.

Novelty is intertwined with Rorty's defense of responsibility because for him an integral part of the task of taking up our responsibility involves our freedom to erect *new* theories and vocabularies, a freedom that we give up when we give all our power away to heteronomous, nonhuman authority. Near the end of *Philosophy and the Mirror of Nature*, in a discussion of Jean-Paul Sartre, Rorty detects this evasion of freedom and responsibility in our tendency to confuse *contact* with reality for *dealing* (or "coping") with it. Our contact with reality, he says, is "a causal, non-intentional, non-description relative relation," whereas our dealing with reality involves such description-relative activities as "explaining, predicting, and modifying" reality. The temptation, Rorty says, is to privilege one descriptive vocabulary we use when *dealing* with reality (say the one employed in the physical sciences) by claiming that it alone is capable of mirroring reality as it is in itself, completely independent of human interests. This temptation expresses one more form of the ambition of transcendence, he thinks, insofar as it leads us to entertain "the notion of 'one right way of describing and explaining reality'"—the one that finally allows us to jump out of our own skin and see the world aright. Following Sartre, Rorty sees the desire to possess such a vocabulary as an attempt to "slough off" human responsibility, and even "to attempt to escape from humanity." Such reductionism is nothing other than a poorly concealed urge lurking within the Western ambition of transcendence: "the urge to be rid of one's freedom to erect yet another alternative theory or vocabulary."[26]

Here we finally see how Rorty understands there to be a connection between the refusal of human freedom and responsibility, and what he takes to be a dangerous and impoverishing form of closure against the new. For Rorty, as we just saw, the ambition of transcendence represents little more than "the urge to be rid of one's freedom *to erect yet another alternative theory or vocabulary.*" One hears echoes here of Marx's eleventh thesis on Feuerbach, according to which the need to change the world is given priority over any philosophical representation of the world as we already find it.[27] This echo rings most forcefully when Rorty distinguishes "edifying" from "systematic" philosophy and emphasizes the cultural importance of engaging in (to use Kuhnian terms) "abnormal" as opposed to "normal" discourse:

> Edifying philosophy is not only abnormal but reactive, having sense only as a protest against attempts to close off conversation by proposals for universal commensuration through the hypostatization of some privileged set of descriptions. The danger which edifying discourse tries to avert is that some given vocabulary, some way in which people might come to think of themselves, will deceive them into thinking that from now on all discourse could be, or should be, normal discourse. The resulting freezing-over of culture would be, in the eyes of edifying philosophers, the dehumanization of human beings.[28]

For Rorty there can be nothing worse than this freezing-over of normal discourse that freezes out alternative ways of describing and coping with reality. While there is nothing wrong with normal discourse (understood as inquiry that proceeds in a context in which everyone more or less agrees on what they are working on and what the main problems to be addressed are), problems arise when, due to an ambition of transcendence, we reify one vocabulary by thinking of it as the one that speaks nature's own language.

Rorty gets at the problems inherent in such philosophical reductionism by noticing how, when we so reify the vocabulary of the natural sciences, we raise the specter of a de-humanizing scientism:

> The fear of science, of 'scientism', of 'naturalism', of self-objectivation, of being turned by too much knowledge into a thing rather than a person, is the fear that all discourse will become normal discourse. That is, it is the fear that there will be objectively true or false answers to every question we ask, so that human worth

will consist in knowing truths, and human virtue will be merely justified true belief. This is frightening because it cuts off the possibility of something new under the sun, of human life as poetic rather than merely contemplative.[29]

For Rorty, there is nothing wrong with *some* discourse being "normal" discourse. His fear is rather the temptation to reduce *all* discourse to the normal discourse of the day, and thereby slough off our responsibility to pursue "abnormal" discourse, those paths of exploration and inquiry that keep us open to "the possibility of something new under the sun."

Rorty ultimately rejects the reification of normal discourse because of his conviction, explored in the previous chapter, that things cannot dictate to us how they are to be described. While he thinks it is true that we are not in ultimate control of things, that reality "impinges" in ways (causal ways) that do not depend on our descriptions, he refuses to conclude from this lack of ultimate control over reality that the world somehow controls our descriptions. "The world is out there, but descriptions of the world are not."[30] For Rorty, descriptions are "in here" in the sense of being located within Sellars' "logical space of reasons."[31] They traffic in the arena of ongoing public conversation and inquiry in both normal and abnormal ways. Rorty thinks that we are responsible for maintaining the robustness, variety, and differentiation of that traffic. Indeed, any reduction of it to one "normal" form represents an impoverishment of the conceptual, intellectual, and poetic resources we will have available to us in our attempt to address new problems and meet new situations. He therefore rejects the attempt to control and minimize this traffic, a tendency that our ambition of transcendence—by tempting us to think that the one right way of describing reality is within our grasp—encourages.

So we see that Rorty criticizes transcendence and our desire for it because he views this ambition as leading us to shirk our responsibility, and as concomitantly closing down our openness to the new and the strange. Yet the question remains as to whether or not Rorty's critique of the ambition of transcendence implies that he is done with transcendence once and for all, and that therefore no remaining trace of transcendence remains in his work. The British philosopher Simon Critchley, an astute reader of Rorty as well as an expert in the school of French phenomenology represented by such thinkers as Emmanuel Levinas and Jacques Derrida, has raised the possibility that Rorty's ethical and political philosophy includes a notion of ethical transcendence, or ethical respect for "the Other," similar in kind to the one expressed in the work of Levinas and Derrida.[32] Critchley suggests that Rorty's liberal politics, with its deep protest against suffering and cruelty, retains a deference to something "beyond," and therefore Rorty's rejection of metaphysical transcendence need not entail a rejection of ethical transcendence. In order to test Critchley's intuition, in the next section I will return to an exploration of Rorty's liberal ethics and politics, this time with an eye to discerning its distance from and proximity to Levinas's invocation of the transcendent figure of the "face of the other" (*autrui*).

TRANSCENDENCE AS ETHICAL ALTERITY: ANOTHER PROBLEMATIC GOD SUBSTITUTE?

Before delving into Critchley's take on Rorty, I first need to set the stage by turning to Rorty's brief essay "Postmodern Bourgeois Liberalism." In this essay, Rorty raises doubts about the notion that the institutions and practices of the "surviving democracies" require the support of any form of "traditional Kantian backup." The latter phrase is Rortyan shorthand for those immutable, ahistorical supports or foundations that certain philosophers think liberal societies require if they are to avoid sliding into a debilitating historicism or relativism. As we have seen, Rorty thinks that liberal democracies require no more support than that provided by the solidarity of their members (hence the titles of two other essays in *Objectivity, Relativism, and Truth*: "Solidarity or Objectivity?" and "The Priority of Democracy to Philosophy"). Rorty goes on to explain that, while the label "postmodern bourgeois liberalism" seems oxymoronic, such a perception is only apparent. The label appears oxymoronic for two reasons: (1) many "postmoderns" have self-consciously sought to distance themselves from bourgeois values; (2) it is also hard to disentangle political liberalism from the very *modern* Enlightenment vocabulary in which it originated. By stringing these seemingly ill-fitted terms together, Rorty hopes, he says, "to suggest how such liberals might convince our society that loyalty to itself is morality enough, and that such loyalty no longer needs an ahistorical backup." To this he adds his contention that postmodern bourgeois liberals "should try to clear themselves of charges of irresponsibility by convincing our society that it need be responsible only to its own traditions, and not to the moral law as well."[33] Comments such as these make it clear that Rorty also intends to carry his rejection of any ambition of transcendence into the social and political realms.

Or does he? I raise this question at this point because in "Postmodern Bourgeois Liberalism" Rorty recognizes at least one valid objection to his insistence on the historical contingency of political liberalism. This objection involves the claim that, on Rorty's view, "a child found wandering in the woods, the remnant of a slaughtered nation whose temples have been razed and whose books have been burned, has no share in human dignity."[34] Faced with this objection, Rorty bites the bullet and admits that this is indeed a consequence of his position. Such a child has little more of a share in human dignity than one who has been raised in a pack of wolves. But for Rorty this child's lack of a share in human dignity is simply a result of the fact that, on his account, human dignity is a product of the recognition or inclusion (which includes such things as love, nurturing, educating, etc.) one receives as a member of a particular historical and cultural tradition or community. This dignity is not "innate," but rather something that is conferred, a status. It is a fragile achievement, and Rorty would not have us evade its historically contingent character. Therefore, if there is no community to confer that status, no community to provide that recognition of membership or inclusion (including all the nurturing and support that goes along with it), then this lost child must also go without the dignity that attends such membership.

While Rorty admits that this tragic scenario is in fact a logical consequence of his position, he nevertheless feels it to be an unhappy consequence. This reaction has always interested me. The one philosopher of the twentieth century who would have us stare contingency square in the face is, here, unable simply to say "tough luck." For although it is a consequence of his position that such a child would have no share in human dignity, he adds that "it does not follow that she may be treated like an animal." Why not? For the following reason: "For it is part of the tradition of *our* [postmodern bourgeois liberal] community that the human stranger from whom all dignity has been stripped is to be taken in, to be reclothed with dignity. *This Jewish and Christian element in our tradition is gratefully invoked by freeloading atheists like myself,* who would like to let differences like that between the Kantian and the Hegelian remain 'merely philosophical'."[35] For Rorty, the outcome of the debate between the "Kantian" who thinks that human rights and dignity are the product of some ahistorical human essence, and the "Hegelian" who thinks they are the *sittlich* (in the social-developmental sense intended by Hegel) products of the evolution of a particular historical community, has little relevance to our actual treatment of such a child. What matters is that, for however contingent the reasons, a community has evolved in which a certain ethical strand, one that traces its genealogy back to religious sources, has become a cherished, non-negotiable (for now) element of that community's identity. It is this strand that Rorty gratefully invokes in such a situation, and it is also this strand that allows him, with Judith Shklar, to define a liberal as someone who thinks that "cruelty is the worst thing we do."[36]

Whether or not Rorty's invocation of Judeo-Christian ethics allows him to escape between the horns of this dilemma, this forsaken child still presents an interesting "limit case" to Rorty's immanent or context-bound affirmation of liberalism. For in this child we see the figure that comes closest to the one Levinas describes as "the face of the Other (*autrui*)" in his magnum opus, *Totality and Infinity*.[37] For Levinas, my inability to treat this child like an object is due to the fact that her sheer presence before me amounts to an ethical interruption of my enjoyment of the world. This stranger arouses my desire, not to consume or devour, but rather for goodness. This desire for goodness, says Levinas, "puts an end to power and emprise," and is something that is "positively produced as the possession of a world I can bestow as a gift on the Other."[38] Critchley wonders whether it would be so far fetched to suggest a degree of proximity between the positions of Levinas and Rorty on this score: "Are not Rorty's definition of liberalism and Levinas's definition of ethics essentially doing the same work, namely attempting to locate *a source for moral and political obligation in a sentient disposition toward the other's suffering*? Do they not both agree that cruelty is the worst thing there is, and that, furthermore, this is the only social bond that we need?"[39] In drawing Levinas and Rorty together in this way, Critchley registers the fact that when Rorty confronts the figure of this destitute child his human capacity for generosity is aroused in a way that is very close to the way Levinas describes. Critchley's reading here is also bolstered by the fact that, for this ethical arousal, Rorty explicitly credits the Jewish and Christian heritage woven into the political liberalism of the West.

Critchley's ability to draw the positions of Levinas and Rorty together in this way depends upon determining whether or not Rorty, like Levinas, finds it helpful to posit an ethical command issuing from a precognitive "sentient disposition" (feeling or desire), one that is aroused through a face-to-face encounter with another person. In order to determine this question, we need to look closer at Levinas's understanding of this encounter, and then find out if Rorty's position agrees with it in most of the salient details. As Critchley notes, Levinas conceives ethics "in terms of an ethical relation between persons." This ethical relation is unlike other relations (such as relations to oneself or to objects), in that it cannot be subsumed under intellectual categories. As Critchley puts Levinas's position: "The other person stands in a relation to me that exceeds my cognitive powers, placing me in question and calling me to justify myself. Levinas's philosophical ambition is to subordinate claims to knowledge to claims to justice."[40] According to Critchley, Levinas understands the ethical claim the other makes upon me as something that moves beyond my cognitive powers; it is experienced at the level of sense and affect, that is, prior to any attempt at cognizing the situation:

> Levinas's phenomenological claim . . . is that the deep structure of subjective experience is always already engaged in a relation of responsibility or, better, responsivity to the other. The ethical relation takes place at the level of sensibility, not at the level of consciousness, and thus . . . it is in my pre-reflective sentient disposition towards the other's suffering that a basis for ethics and responsibility can be found. [41]

Does not the "sentient disposition" that Critchley here describes provide a phenomenologically satisfying account of what someone like Rorty might "feel" in the very moment he is confronted with this destitute stranger? Does not Rorty too "feel" an interruptive call in this situation?

While it is fair to say that Rorty would also want us to subordinate claims to knowledge to claims to justice (letting differences like that between the Kantian and the Hegelian remain "merely philosophical"), he nonetheless balks at Critchley's attempt to enlist his philosophy in support of a Levinasian case for ethical transcendence. In a response to Critchley, Rorty suspects that a Levinasian appeal to a "pre-reflective sentient disposition" as a "basis" for ethics is yet one more ambition of transcendence, one more attempt to eff the ineffable. When it comes to understanding ethical obligation, Rorty insists that Levinas and Critchley are in a different line of business than he and Dewey are:

> I am not, as Critchley thinks I might be and probably should be, trying to 'locate a source of moral obligation in the sentient disposition of the self towards the Other's suffering', nor in any other sort of 'universal fact of human nature'. Maybe there is such a sentient disposition, but it is so malleable—so capable of being combined with indifference to the suffering of people of the wrong sorts—that it gives us precious little to rely on. We should just thank our lucky stars that there are quite a lot of people nowadays who are pretty consistently appalled by human beings suffering unnecessarily.[42]

As it turns out, Rorty insists that solidarity or simple loyalty to the contingent tradition of liberalism provides enough support for our sense of ethical obligation, and it is unhelpful to question this support by basing it upon something like a precognitive interruption of ethical transcendence.

In an earlier, and much less friendly exchange between himself and the Derridean philosopher of religion Mark C. Taylor, Rorty expresses the same hesitation with respect to the very idea of ethical transcendence. While Rorty agrees with Taylor that "we need constant doses of Otherness to keep us on our toes, to keep our dialogues from turning monological," he does not want to locate the source of this novelty, this "Otherness," in something bigger than ourselves: "As a good naturalist," he explains, "I take the source of this occasional irruption of Otherness to be simply some curious neural kink, or odd psycho-sexual twist, or genetic mini-mutation. On my view, there is nothing more to Otherness than the random events which produce random effects on our language, and thus on poetry, politics, and philosophy."[43] Given this position, Rorty sees no point in "delving down to the roots of the difference between people who care about others' suffering and those who don't." To him, whether the difference is "all acculturation, or all a matter of the environment of the first few days of infancy, or all in the genes" does not matter.[44] The only thing that matters is that many millions if not billions of people do profess to care, and that is a contingent historical development which we should simply encourage and try to keep going. Nothing transcendent will guarantee that this historical development will continue, and the belief that there is something transcendent could even make us complacent.

So, because of his thoroughgoing naturalism, Rorty refuses even this Levinasian understanding of ethical transcendence. Insisting on the contingency of a liberal culture that happens to encourage people to think that cruelty is the worst thing humans do, he must therefore fall back on the "dumb"—as opposed to "tough"—luck thanks to which this particular set of historical political communities happens to shelter a Judeo-Christian ethical strand.[45] There is nothing more behind the emergence of such a strand, Rorty insists, than "the random occurrence, in the occasional human mind, of new words in which to describe people, or societies, or the universe."[46] Rorty ultimately rejects Levinas's construal of the Other's interruptive presence as a form of transcendence, then, for precisely the same reason that he rejects Nagel's ambition of transcendence in epistemology: "My objection to the Other with a capital O, Language with a capital L, and Différance with a capital D is the same as my objection to Being with a capital B: all such capitalizations tempt us to look outside of time and space, outside of the contingent workings of nature, for salvation." To this objection Rorty adds his contention that those who encourage us to think in terms of such capitals only serve to "re-enslave us to the thought that we are, or can get, under the protection of Something or Somebody Bigger Than Ourselves."[47]

Yet again, we see Rorty's antipathy to transcendence take the form of an insistence that only a thoroughgoing naturalism can preserve human freedom and dignity from authoritarian domination. Even our hypothetical child found wandering in the woods can become such an authoritarian monster, or the occasion for its emergence, if we convince ourselves that we must respond to her need only because something bigger above and behind her commands us to do so.[48] No, Rorty would have our sympathy and responsivity remain much more free and spontaneous, even if that means admitting that the ethical orientation that inculcates such responsivity is merely the product of a happy historical accident.

So is Rorty now finally done with transcendence? With divinity and holiness? Before we can safely come to that conclusion there remains some further textual evidence to examine.

ON KEEPING THE WORD "GOD" IN ONE'S FINAL VOCABULARY

Thus far, we have seen Rorty reject transcendence in metaphysical, epistemological, and ethico-political variants. It would be quite understandable if, due to his sheer consistency on this score, one should conclude that no construal of transcendence plays a positive role in his work at all. Yet there is still reason to complicate the story further at this point. In a comparative exploration of Rorty's debate with Mark C. Taylor, J. Wesley Robbins takes issue with the "seemingly plausible" conclusion that Rorty's version of pragmatism presents us with a straightforward case of aggressive if not narcissistic atheism. To make this case, Robbins locates a "residual theology" in Rorty's exploration of human openness to novelty, specifically in the human capacity for linguistic innovation (which we explored above). He says that Rorty's residual theology can be summarized in one sentence: "the innovative power of human linguistic behavior, in causal interaction with the environment, is all that is left of God." He unpacks this summary as follows:

> Rorty believes that the principal engine of cultural and personal change is the occurrence of differences in linguistic behavior and the new vocabularies that are formed when some of these differences get incorporated into current linguistic practices. He thinks that we would be better off if we were to learn to be more self-reliant than our predecessors by depending on the innovative capacity of our own linguistic behavior for improvement of our social and personal lot rather than looking for salvation to come to us from higher powers.[49]

As we have just seen, Robbins here provides an excellent and concise summary of Rorty's position. While I do not take issue with it, I think it can be extended into an examination of the way that Rorty's "residual theology" leads him to configure time. For it is in this configuration of time that Rorty most closely approaches a sympathetic reading of certain aspects of religious culture.

The first thing to notice in Robbins's concise summary is the central role that the "improvement of our social and personal lot" plays in this residual theology (if one may call it that). The whole point of linguistic innovation, the very reason Rorty cherishes it so much, is because of the key, one might even say "salvific," role it plays in this movement of pragmatic melioration. As Robbins reminds us, "when Rorty calls for self-reliance, it is not because he thinks that humans are little Gods, who originally confer meaning onto words. It is because he thinks that improvements in the effectiveness of human linguistic behavior caused by people talking differently are our best hope in the world for salvation."[50] In this gloss, Robbins mentions the word "hope," and it is precisely this notion of hope that qualifies Rorty's "residual theology" in a way that can be helpfully compared to more "robust" theological perspectives (i.e. ones that are less allergic to the idea of fealty to particular religious traditions).

Our story begins with the essay "Pragmatism without Method," where Rorty affirms John Dewey's attempt to redefine the word "God" as "the active relation between the ideal and the actual." "Hope" is also a good word to use in order to give this "active relation" more specificity; the God who becomes a name for this active relation is a God of hope. Such hope, says Dewey, can become a rallying point for humans in isolation, a reason for them to band together and strive toward the realization of an ideal that calls them out of the actual, an ideal that calls them to disregard the fatalism of the habitual and instead inaugurate the new and the possible. Dewey wishes to keep the word "God" as a name for this union, this active relation, because he thinks that a "religious attitude" can encourage in us "the sense of a connection of man, in the way of both dependence and support, with the enveloping world that the imagination feels is a universe." He continues: "Use of the words 'God' or 'divine' to convey the union of actual with ideal may protect man from a sense of isolation and from consequent despair and defiance."[51] As if to underline the sentiment Dewey here expresses, Rorty, in his discussion of this passage, adds that "Dewey's seemed, and still seems, a good way to keep the term 'God' in one's vocabulary, thus enabling one to keep some of the strands in one's web of belief which, at the time one became a naturalist, one had feared one might have to tease out."[52] Rorty's expressed sentiment concerning Dewey's use of the terms "God" and "divine" encourages one to conclude that, while he may well be allergic to most understandings of transcendence, he does not wish us to be rid of the strand that Dewey keeps using the word "God" to name.[53]

But what is this strand, this "union of ideal and actual" for which Dewey retains the word "God"? For starters, it suggests the opening of a temporal "gap," a space of expectation, longing, or hope for an ideal world that, while *not yet* actual, nevertheless informs our activity in the here and now. Its character of being *not yet* is, I suggest, a form of openness to transcendence; that is, it seeks connection with something that transcends our current situation, albeit in the form of an end or possibility that we can and might, through mutual support and cooperation, achieve together. The specific ideal in mind here centrally concerns human emancipation from sources of oppression and domination, from needless forms of suffering and toward proliferating forms of flourishing.[54] The salient difference between this understanding of transcendence and the metaphysical or supernatural versions that both Dewey and Rorty reject is that, in opposition to these latter construals, neither Dewey nor Rorty understand transcendence as something statically and antecedently existent. The union of ideal and actual in which they place their hope, while indeed something operating in the here and now, retains an integral future dimension, setting its sights by something yet to be achieved. Both thinkers therefore see themselves as taking our ability (and responsibility) to participate in the realization of this emancipatory ideal more seriously than do their more metaphysically inclined counterparts. Peter Dews nicely captures this difference between metaphysical and pragmatist versions of transcendence in his description of Dewey's position: "'Supernaturalist' religion, and the kind of metaphysical thought which [Dewey] regards as its legatee and conceptual refinement, must be viewed, [he] argues, as attempts to short-circuit the effort required to transform the real in the direction of the ideal. Religious and metaphysical dogmas demobilize us, seeking to prove the existence of a transcendent, immutable reality, in which our aspirations are already fulfilled."[55]

When viewed in the light of his agreement with Dewey concerning the importance of maintaining a space of social hope, and the value of religious language (on their reinterpretation) for helping us do so, Rorty seems in the end to be recommending mainly that we take our understanding of religion and transcendence out of metaphysical and epistemic arenas, as opposed to recommending that we do away with everything religious language and culture represents, root and branch.[56] As Dews notes, in the final phase of his work, Rorty still finds it meaningful "to make space for a conception of human emancipation able to house aspirations formerly nurtured by religion."[57]

The theme of temporal transcendence Rorty expresses in "Pragmatism without Method" (first published in 1983) finds a ready companion in his late essay "Anticlericalism and Atheism" (first published in 2002, 5 years before his death), and he picks up this same thread several times throughout the intervening 19 years. Rorty's emphasis on the importance of maintaining social hope—his deep desire for the triumph of goodness—also connects back to his early adolescent sensitivity to the demands of social justice. The sense of hope and expectation Rorty seeks to cultivate in "Pragmatism without Method," then, is carried throughout his work, and so is not, as Dews maintains, a late addition or amendment to his larger body of work. That said, Rorty's summary of his position in "Anticlericalism and Atheism" still stands out for its willingness to approach religious themes and insights quite closely:

> My sense of the holy, insofar as I have one, is bound up with the hope that someday, any millennium now, my remote descendants will live in a global civilization in which love is pretty much the only law. In such a society, communication would be domination-free, class and caste would be unknown, hierarchy would be a matter of temporary pragmatic convenience, and power would be entirely at the disposal of the free agreement of a literate and well-educated electorate.
>
> I have no idea how such a society could come about. It is, one might say, a mystery. This mystery, like that of the Incarnation, concerns the coming into existence of a love that is kind, patient, and endures all things. 1 Corinthians 13 is an equally useful text for both religious people like Vattimo, whose sense of what transcends our present condition is bound up with a feeling of dependence, and for nonreligious people like myself, for whom this sense consists simply in hope for a better human future.[58]

In making what he takes to be this quasi-religious expression of hope against hope, Rorty notes that the sole difference between he and Vattimo rests upon the fact that Vattimo's sense of future expectation is more self-consciously shaped by a *memory* of a particular tradition that gives it flesh, a tradition in which "a feeling of dependence" plays a role that is lacking in Rorty's more anthropocentric account.

While, as we have seen, Rorty gratefully invokes the same memory as Vattimo, he nevertheless does not consider its maintenance or transmission as being all that important. Instead, he tends to view it as a ladder that can now be safely thrown away, as we turn our eyes completely toward the future. Interestingly, he makes this move in the very same sentence in which he *reminds* his readers of an ancient religious text, inadvertently making a case for that text's ongoing relevance, not to mention its continued transmission.[59] All the same, Rorty distinguishes his position from Vattimo's by claiming to be free from a religious feeling of dependence. The reader is then left to wonder what Rorty makes of Dewey's aforementioned affirmation of religion as, at its best, inspiring a sense of connection, "in the way of both *dependence* and support, with the enveloping world that the imagination feels is a universe."[60] For this reason, Dews, for one, does not take Rorty's professed agreement with Dewey's reinterpretation of the word "God" at face value. Instead, he perceives several salient differences between Dewey's position and Rorty's, arguing specifically that, unlike Rorty, Dewey makes more room for a sense of dependence on nonhuman factors. According to Dews, Dewey's point is that "if our remote moral goods are to be more than 'mere rootless ideals, fantasies, utopias', we cannot help believing that 'there are forces in nature and society that generate and support the ideals'."[61] For Dewey, we solidify these ideals when we join our action to them, but it is not as clear that Rorty maintains the same sense of human action as "joining forces" with nonhuman factors, factors upon which we retain a measure of dependence.

In spite of Rorty's stated difference between Vattimo and himself on the matter of retaining a feeling of dependence, strong parallels remain between their positions. These parallels can also be found with respect to the work of other religious thinkers. In both *The God Who May Be* and *Anatheism*, Richard Kearney reconfigures divinity as a form of redemptive possibility that requires both human affirmation and action in order to become real;[62] and, returning once more to Levinas, one finds striking parallels between Rorty's version of temporal transcendence, or social hope, and Levinas's own hopeful understanding of messianic time. In the essay "Difficult Freedom," Levinas offers the following understanding of an ethical life lived in such expectant time:

> One follows the Most High God, above all by drawing near to one's fellow man, and showing concern for 'the widow, the orphan, the stranger and the beggar', an approach that must not be made 'with empty hands'. It is therefore on earth, amongst men, that the spirit's adventure unfolds. . . . My uniqueness lies in the responsibility I display for the other. . . . Man is therefore indispensable to God's plan or, to be more exact, man is nothing other than the divine plans with being. . . . Man can do what he must do; he can master the hostile forces of history by helping bring about a messianic reign, a reign of justice foretold by the prophets. The waiting for the Messiah marks the very duration of time.[63]

Levinas's way seems to me to be another good way to keep the word "God" in one's vocabulary. But I do wonder whether it would also seem a good way to Rorty. I am sure he would be uncomfortable with Levinas' language of "waiting for the Messiah." But his worry might be alleviated by noting how Levinas characterizes such waiting, not as mere acquiescent passivity, but in terms of the human *capacity* to "master the hostile forces of history" in order to bring about "a reign of justice." As we have seen, Rorty is far from being uncomfortable with that kind of language.

While Rorty continually insists on maintaining a difference between his position and those of religious thinkers like Levinas and Vattimo, the difference between him and such thinkers, as he says in his discussion with Vattimo, is "that between unjustifiable gratitude and unjustifiable hope . . . [,] not a matter of conflicting beliefs about what really exists and what does not."[64] The difference Rorty has in mind here is more subtle, because it involves a different way of construing something that he thinks he and all other intellectuals otherwise share and cannot live without. In the essay "A Pragmatist View of Contemporary Analytic Philosophy," he calls this something "pathos." He continues: "Theists find pathos in the distance between the human and the divine. Realists find it in the abyss separating human thought and language from reality as it really is in itself. Pragmatists find it in the gap between contemporary humanity and a utopian future in which the very idea of responsibility to anything except our fellow-humans has become unintelligible, resulting in the first truly humanistic culture." Rorty goes on to say that if one does not like the word "pathos" to name the sort of general longing he describes here, one might also use the word "romance" or even Nagel's phrase "ambition of transcencence"(!). And finally, because he does not think we are able to appeal to neutral argumentative ground in determining which form of pathos would be better for us to adopt, he echoes Arthur Fine (who in turn echoes Blaise Pascal), concluding that one's choice will be settled "by the reasons of one's heart."[65]

In the final analysis, Rorty's antipathy to the very idea of transcendence does not prevent his politically motivated anticlerical atheism from overlapping in significant ways with the views espoused by such religious thinkers as Vattimo and Levinas. One might conclude, then, that his attitude with respect to religious culture is more ambivalent than completely negative. Yet despite this professed ambivalence, he remained primarily suspicious of religious culture throughout his career. This is because, according to him, the recent and much touted "return to religion" that has falsified Max Weber's "optimistic predictions" of secularization "is driven, at least in part, by a yearning for the sort of conversation-stopping certainty that pragmatists hope human beings will someday cease to want."[66] Here Rorty has "the followers of Falwell and Khomeini" primarily in mind, who loom so large in his imagination that, in spite of his appreciation for thinkers like Vattimo, he habitually uses this rather wide brush to paint over the vast majority of religious observers. Of course, one has only to turn on the television or flip open a newspaper to understand Rorty's concerns about the violently toxic mix of religious fundamentalism and politics that runs rampant today. His response to this state of affairs, more often than not, is to recommend that religion, *in toto*, keep its nose out of politics. Yet, again, given his ambivalent stance toward religion, one wonders why he did not do more to build up conversational solidarity with those forms of religious expression he did in fact appreciate. I will conclude this examination of Rorty and religion with an examination of this question.

RICHARD RORTY

KEEPING RELIGION PRIVATE, OR KEEPING THE CONVERSATION GOING?

"Religion as Conversation-stopper," Rorty's irritated response to Stephen Carter's *The Culture of Disbelief: How American Law and Politics Trivialize Religious Devotion*, is, unfortunately, his best known pronouncement on the legitimacy of religious culture.[67] Yet even in this salvo, he is careful to steer clear of tacitly endorsing the first, epistemological or metaphysical, variant of atheism discussed above. The best parts of Carter's book, Rorty admits, are those parts that point out "the hypocrisy involved in saying that believers have no right to base their political views on their religious faith, whereas we atheists have every right to base ours on Enlightenment philosophy." As he goes on to say: "The claim that in doing so we are appealing to reason, whereas the religious are being irrational, is hokum. Carter is quite right to debunk it."[68] So Rorty's reason for excluding religious voices from the public square has nothing to do with any perceived lack of epistemic warrant, or that religious motivations for public stands are peculiarly illegitimate; no, the main reason Rorty thinks religion must be privatized is because "in political discussion with those outside the relevant religious community, it is a conversation-stopper."[69]

As this last and now very famous quote makes clear, Rorty directs his recommendation for privatizing religion upon the area of "political discussion with those outside the relevant religious community." Here he has in mind those controversial policy discussions that often arise in pluralist democratic societies, such as debates about legalizing abortion or same-sex marriage. In focusing his recommendation for religious privatization upon this special sort of political conversation, he claims he does not intend to trivialize religious devotion (because for him private concerns are far from trivial), nor to deny the inescapable role such devotion plays in motivating a religious believer's public stance on any particular issue; instead, he seems to be claiming that in these political contexts *the expression* of a believer's religious beliefs, in spite of their nontriviality and motivating role, adds little if anything relevant or helpful to political discussions *with those outside the relevant religious community*. Yet this is precisely where such conversations must be joined. In recommending religious privatization in this context, Rorty is expressing a concern with political moves that he thinks only serve to preempt these important conversations before they can even begin.

Given the divisive role that the expression of religious conviction frequently plays in American society, Rorty finds it prudent to recommend that his political community keep *specifically religious* forms of argument out of the public square. But what, according to him, is a "specifically religious" form of argument? He describes it as "a dialogue in which some members cite religious sources for their beliefs," or "an argument whose premises are accepted by some people because they believe that these premises express the will of God."[70] An example of this for Rorty is someone citing Leviticus 18:22 to support a premise (or be a premise) in an argument against legalizing same-sex marriage. Rorty grants that many religious people are against legalizing same-sex marriage because they understand homosexuality to be forbidden by the sacred texts they consider authoritative, texts that on their interpretation tell them that homosexuality is against God's will; and his position also grants that they are within their rights to take this stand for this reason. The problem is that in a pluralist society not everyone in the conversation credits this religious source with the same normative authority, so introducing Leviticus 18:22 as some sort of trump card in a pluralist discussion about legally sanctioning same-sex marriage is, on Rorty's reading, fated to be a move that kills conversation before it starts; it does not give one's differently motivated interlocutor anything to work with. He therefore recommends that all discussants, both religious and secular, drop the reference to the unshared sources that motivate them to hold their respective premises. "Surely the fact that one of us gets his premises in church and the other in the library is, and should be, of no interest to our audience in the public square. The arguments that take place there, political arguments, are best thought of as neither religious nor nonreligious."[71] They are best thought of in this way, Rorty thinks, because it is futile to have to hash out theism vs atheism before being able to continue any meaningful political debate.

Instead of referring to the unshared source of one's argumentative premises, Rorty suggests that the interlocutors continue their discussion on some other basis. In a democracy, he says, the only test for a political proposal should be "its ability to gain assent from people who retain radically diverse ideas about the point and meaning of human life, about the path to private perfection."[72] In saying this, he expresses broad agreement with the opinion of such political philosophers as John Rawls and Jürgen Habermas, who both at one time or another have suggested that democratic political discussion should proceed on the basis of publicly shareable reasons alone.[73] Using this potential consensus as the test of a belief or argumentative premise, Rorty thinks, will helpfully de-emphasize what he takes to be the divisive and conversation-stopping role played by the expression of the religious (or, for that matter, nonreligious) sources motivating it. So what is sauce for the goose is also sauce for the gander; when presenting their arguments, atheists like himself, says Rorty, must also "claim no authority for our premises save the assent we hope they will gain from our audience."[74]

Rorty's position in "Religion as Conversation-stopper" has come under fire from two primary interlocutors: Nicholas Wolterstorff and Jeffrey Stout. In responding to both critiques, Rorty would come to significantly nuance, yet not take back, his position with regard to religious privatization. It therefore pays to look at each critique along with Rorty's responses more closely. For his part, Wolterstorff criticizes the confusing role that the liberal private–public distinction plays in Rorty's discussion. He notes how in "Religion as Conversation-stopper" Rorty agrees with Carter that the expression of religious reasons for holding to a particular political position are indeed likely to end a conversation with "a group of well-educated professionals." Yet for Rorty, unlike Carter, such an outcome is not due to the fact that such people represent a cultural elite who trivialize and belittle religious devotion; rather, he thinks the conversation gets stopped at this point because in expressing such a religious reason the religious person is making an irrelevant comment about his private life, one that is out of place or in "bad taste" in the context of a discussion about public policy. According to Rorty, the silence ensuing a conversation that has been stopped in this way "masks the group's inclination to say, 'So What? We weren't discussing your private life; we were discussing public policy. Don't bother us with matters that are not our concern.'"[75] Wolterstorff, for his part, thinks Rorty's reference to privacy here is "a throw-away reference," one that does not do any real work. He says this because, as we have seen, Rorty quickly proceeds to identify the test of a belief or premise put forward in a political argument with its ability to gain assent from others who hold radically different ideas about the meaning of human life, and in a pluralistic context one will not garner such assent by appealing to reasons that only one's religious cohorts share. For this reason, Wolterstorff concludes that "the problem Rorty sees with offering religious reasons for political positions is not that such reasons are 'private', in any clear sense of that term, but that they are not shared by the citizenry in general."[76]

In distinguishing a private from an unshared reason, Wolterstorff astutely notices that, while it might make sense to describe private beliefs as beliefs that are unshared by everyone, this does not logically entail the opposite—that is, that unshared beliefs, or beliefs not shared by "the citizenry in general," are necessarily "private" in any clear sense of that term. What is more, says Wolterstorff, Rorty's criterion for privacy would also exclude many not-commonly shared secular rationales from entering public discourse (although, as we have seen, this is a point that Rorty admits, although he does not seem to fully register the impoverishing consequences such broad restrictions might have on robust public dialogue).[77] Wolterstorff thus concludes that Rorty's insistence on privatizing religious reasons, if allowed to win the day, would set an intolerable restriction on religious citizens' freedom of expression in a liberal democracy. So, setting Rorty's recommendation of privatization to one side as somewhat ill-considered and confused, Wolterstorff instead points to another claim that Rorty makes in "Religion as Conversation-stopper," one that actually runs counter to this recommendation for privatization. According to Rorty "moral decisions that are to be enforced by a pluralist and democratic state's monopoly of violence are best made by public discussion in which voices claiming to be God's, or reason's, or science's, are put on a par with everybody else's."[78] "Exactly!" exclaims Wolterstorff in response, "Permit the different voices!"[79] Such latitude, thinks Wolterstorff, will provide a truer reflection of the pluralism that actually exists on the ground in liberal democracies, a truer reflection than would a recommendation to exclude proffering reasons that not everyone shares.[80]

Stout's critique of Rorty's position continues in the direction set out by Wolterstorff.[81] Agreeing with Wolterstorff that Rorty's restriction on expressing religious reasons in public is needlessly illiberal, he would remind Rorty of Rorty's own endorsement of the inescapability of final vocabularies in *Contingency, Irony, and Solidarity*, and also of the value Rorty places on the role of "abnormal" conversation in the third and final section of *Philosophy and the Mirrror of Nature*. With these passages in mind, Stout wonders why, when people who hold differing final vocabularies disagree in public, Rorty does not suggest that they pursue "abnormal" conversational strategies:

> The role of edifying philosophy, as Rorty presented it in [*Philosophy and the Mirror of Nature*], is to keep discursive exchange going at those very points where 'normal' discourse—that is, discourse on the basis of commonly accepted standards—cannot straightforwardly adjudicate between competing claims. Conversation is a good name for what is needed at those points where people employing different final vocabularies reach a momentary impasse. But if we do use the term 'conversation' in this way, we shall have to conclude that conversation is the very thing that is not stopped when religious premises are introduced in a political argument.[82]

The introduction of unshared premises will only stop "normal" discourse, says Stout. Because any pluralistic democracy will be rife with people who hold such unshared premises, the political discourse of such a society thus "needs to be a mixture of normal discourse and conversational improvisation."[83]

Stout's second, related line of criticism refers to the way Rorty's thinking about religion is dominated by a monological tendency, one that runs counter to a more dialogical tendency on display in such essays as "Failed Prophecies, Glorious Hopes" and his dialogue with Vattimo, explored above. Stout praises this dialogical strand for its contribution to democratic coalition-building efforts, for showing potential paths that the religious and secular might travel together in the pursuit of social justice. Unfortunately, however, for Stout "most of Rorty's writing on the topic of religion and politics" is monological, and decidedly unpragmatic.[84] In making this latter claim, Stout draws attention to the fact that, when discussing religious matters, Rorty appears to drop his pragmatic, Quinean holism with respect to belief, and instead makes rather sweeping, essentialistic, and unpragmatic-sounding pronouncements. According to this holism, the meaning of any particular belief a person holds is determined by the inferential connections it holds within that person's entire web of belief. For this reason, on

Rorty's own account, "the significance of a given theist's belief in God can be determined only against a background of other commitments held by the same person." It therefore will not do for Rorty to tell us that he persists in thinking "that non-theists make better citizens than theists."[85] It will not do, says Stout, because bare theism, in abstraction from a religious person's other commitments, is, like bare atheism or nontheism, "largely indeterminate in its implications." These labels are too thin, and they do not tell us enough about the individuals so labelled such that we can make sweeping generalizations like those Rorty is wont to make in his more monological moments. We have every reason to complain, says Stout, about hateful, cruel, and sadistic theists, those "who take their God to be a jealous commander of vengeful cruelties"; but we also have every reason to complain about hateful, cruel, and sadistic nontheists, those "who take the historical dialectic to justify mass murder and the crushing of dissent." Stout therefore declares the question "Do theists or nontheists make the better citizens?" a bad one, "the sort of question a pragmatist would be expected to undermine rather than answer."[86]

In spite of these rather trenchant criticisms, in the end Stout, Wolterstorff, and Rorty all agree that in a pluralistic democracy it is important to keep conversation going, and to find dialogical rather than violent ways through our many conversational impasses. This much is clear from Rorty's response to Wolterstorff; agreeing with Stout's criticism that he should not have said that religion is essentially a conversation-stopper, because it is not *essentially* anything, he goes on in this essay to say that "instead of saying that religion was a conversation-stopper, I should have simply said that citizens of a democracy should try to put off invoking conversation-stoppers as long as possible. We should do our best to keep the conversation going without citing unarguable first principles, either philosophical or religious. If we are sometimes driven to such citation, we should see ourselves as having failed, not as having triumphed."[87]

Of course, unlike Rorty, Stout and Wolterstorff advise full disclosure and complete candour from the get go, and not as a final resort. "Cite away!" they say; while the ensuing impasse might signal the arrest of normal conversation, it also invites us to engage in much needed abnormal, improvisational conversation. Heck, maybe each side might even learn something from one another. Given the fact that such an approach is one Rorty recommends in other contexts, one wonders why when it comes to religion in particular he remains so reticent. Rorty hints that it is not the mere *citation* of the religious first principle that bothers him so much, as it is the supposition of that citation's *unarguability*. But as he also says, it is not just theists who are driven, at times, to make such final declarations of their faith, to say "here I stand for I can do no other." So even here he gives his reader reason to doubt that it is unarguability as such that he finds problematic.

The problem with citing unarguable first principles for Rorty, as I see it, has more to do with the way some religious people base this unarguability on an undiscussable appeal to nonhuman *authority*. For this reason, although he eventually accepts Wolterstorff's argument concerning the right of religious believers to cite the religious sources of their premises, he nevertheless wavers: "I am torn . . . between agreement with Wolterstorff's defense of his right to cite Psalm 72 and the feeling that religious believers should not justify their support of or opposition to legislation *simply* by saying 'Scripture says' or 'Rome has spoken; the matter is closed' or 'My church teaches. . . .' It is one thing to explain how a given political stance is bound up with one's religious belief, and another to think that it is enough, when defending a political view, simply to cite authority, scriptural or otherwise."[88] Rorty's problem here, as I have said, is with the way he takes certain religious folk to understand normative authority, rather than with the bare appeal to authority itself. Rorty is objecting to the fact that the religious people he has in mind do not, with him, follow Brandom in describing cultural authority as a thoroughly social-practical affair, to be hashed out in communal dialogue with one's fellow citizens.

According to Rorty, religious believers would not say that God has authority over human society "unless they think they know what God wants human beings to do—unless they can cite sacred scriptures, or the words of a guru, or the teachings of an ecclesiastical tradition, or something of the sort, in support of their own position." Rorty would have such people understand that, whatever authority they think backs up their position, they cannot escape the responsibility that comes with the fact that, at the end of the day, it is still *their own position*.[89] In a pluralist democratic society, illusory pretensions of privileged access to an omniscient supernatural vantage point are decidedly unwelcome, for "from the point of view of both atheists and people whose scripture or guru or tradition is different, what is purportedly said in the name of God is actually said in the name of some interest group—some sect or church, for example." Since no one—theist, atheist, or nontheist—can accede to a vantage point from which to neutrally adjudicate all the views in play, our understanding of what may or may not be authoritative must always be hashed out upon, and can never transcend, the human dialogical plane. "The so-called 'authority' of anything other than the community," Rorty thus proclaims, "can only be more table-thumping."[90]

Yet, as Stout points out, and as Rorty also knows, religious persons can put forward the unshared views they nonetheless hold to be authoritative in ways that are not merely table-thumping. Stout tells us that the pragmatist's "insistence on the priority of the social-practical can be distinguished from the questions of what sorts of persons there are and how divinity is to be conceived." For this reason, he says, "it is possible for thinkers to give the priority of the social-practical a theological twist."[91] They can do so by putting forward an understanding of God as a person who is only known through a covenantal relationship of mutual accountability, and so as someone with whom theists are in a position to talk.[92] In his response to Stout, Rorty admits that his "perfectly secular utopia" would still contain theists of the sort both he and Stout admire. "There would be room for the sort of God worshipped by James, Whitehead, Tillich, and West (and, I suspect, by Rauschenbush, Gutierrez and King), but none of the sort worshipped by St. Paul, Wojtila, Ratzinger, Falwell and Khomeini." Why one would still call such a utopia "perfectly secular" Rorty does not explain (nor does he say why St Paul, the progenitor of both forms of theism he is here comparing, only belongs on the latter list). It could be that he simply doubts the ability of the former, more broadly pragmatist camp of theists to win the day over their more politically powerful counterparts. In response to Stout's suggestion regarding the possibility of a theistic version of pragmatism, one in which God becomes an accountable conversation partner, he offers the following: "The last thing that followers of Falwell and Khomeini are interested in is a tolerant and conversable deity. There are certainly passages here and there in the Christian Scriptures that suggest that accountability between the divine and the human goes both ways, but these passages are taken seriously by only a few liberal theologians."[93]

Given this state of affairs, Rorty finds it politically prudent to make common cause with these liberal theologians only in the near term. "But," he mysteriously adds, "I still think it is important to pursue a long-term, militantly secularist, *philosophical* agenda." So at the end of the day, in spite of his willingness to absorb the criticisms of Wolterstorff and Stout, he remains an anticlerical prophet of a secularist utopia. In spite of the fact that many theists have shown themselves to be as good democratic citizens as their nontheist neighbors, the future inhabitants of his perfect secularist utopia, he says, "will nevertheless be puzzled about how democracy managed to survive in a time when a majority of citizens still professed to believe that the wrong political choices might doom them to the fires of hell and the right ones entitle them to the joys of paradise. They will be as glad not to have been born in those dangerous times as we are not to have lived under the inquisition."[94]

As we have seen in this chapter, and indeed throughout this book, a common, antiauthoritarian streak runs throughout Rorty's criticisms of religion, theology, and metaphysics. The origin of this thread can be traced back to his radical rejection of the correspondence theory of truth, and his concomitant attempt to redefine truth pragmatically in terms of intersubjectivity or conversational solidarity. Our deference to such nonhuman power as Truth, he thinks, is fatal to our humanity, to our freedom and ability to redescribe our circumstances in ways that will help us cope more adroitly with the dynamic world we find ourselves inhabiting. This monological obsession, he thinks, keeps us from being happy. This theme is so central to Rorty's thought that it would seem unthinkable that he would ever come to doubt it. Yet relatively late in his career he engaged in a significant exchange with the philosopher Bjørn Ramberg that did in fact lead him to revisit his dismissive attitude regarding truth (understood in terms of correspondence or objectivity) and alter it quite substantially. In the next and final chapter of this book, we will explore this philosophical exchange and assess its impact on Rorty's long-held and most cherished philosophical positions.

CHAPTER 5

WHAT IS TRUTH *FOR*? THE CONVERSATION CONTINUES

PINNING DOWN RORTY'S PHILOSOPHICAL EVASIONS

Surely one of the most frustrating yet also intriguing aspects of Rorty's philosophy is its apparent evasiveness. Whether under the guise of therapy, irony, or prophecy, he often comes across as a philosopher who refuses to play the game according to the preestablished rules, even though he knows those rules inside and out. Actually, that way of putting his approach is somewhat misleading; it is more accurate to say that Rorty frequently, if not mostly, plays by the rules, engaging with the arguments of various philosophers in ways that they themselves recognize as legitimate, as philosophy; yet in doing so he also attempts to loosen the grip of (some of) those very rules, and perhaps even to convince his peers that they would be better off playing another game (with different rules) altogether. Rorty is enough of a Hegelian to be aware of the fact that discursive norms not only guide our conversations, but are themselves available for debate within them, and as such these norms may be changed or dropped through this communal process of deliberation (although never all at once). His philosophy does not shy away from this dialectic, but vigorously participates in it.

Yet Rorty's dialectical approach can still vex readers, and perhaps nowhere more so than in his various attacks on a representationalist theory of truth. For in arguing against the notion of truth as correspondence to mind-independent reality, he looks like he is doing philosophy, and in a very real sense he is. Yet at the same time that he criticizes this dominant Western philosophical understanding of truth, he denies that he is putting forward an alternative definition, theory, or philosophical account of truth. Many readers can't quite believe this, and those who won't simply write him off as, at worst, a nihilist, or, at best, a quietist, will often read such a theory into his work—and then declare it to be viciously relativist, self-defeating, or incoherent.[1]

But what does Rorty actually say? In "Solidarity or Objectivity?" the first essay in *Objectivity, Relativism, and Truth*, he sets up a somewhat invidious distinction between "two principle ways in which reflective human beings try, by placing their lives in a larger context, to give sense to those lives." He labels one way "objectivity" and the other "solidarity." Those who desire objectivity think that human life only makes sense if it centers on the pursuit of Truth for its own sake, on the attempt to attach oneself to something transcendent, ahistorical, and not merely human. Such people do not trivialize solidarity, says Rorty, but instead consider its very possibility to require the existence of a universal and ahistorical human "essence" or "nature" in which to ground it; they think solidarity must be grounded in objectivity. Then there is the second group, for whom solidarity alone (without anchorage in something objectively transcending human particularity) is enough. Instead of wishing to ground solidarity in objectivity, says Rorty, this second group seeks to turn the tables on the metaphysician and instead reduce objectivity to solidarity.[2]

Rorty gives the label "realist" to those inside the objectivity camp and the label "pragmatist" to those in the solidarity camp. Because realists wish to ground solidarity in objectivity, he says, they must "construe truth as correspondence with reality." This construal of truth invites the construction of a metaphysics "which has room for a special relation between beliefs and objects which will differentiate true from false beliefs," as well as an epistemology "which has room for a kind of justification which is not merely social but natural, springing from human nature itself, and made possible by a link between that part of nature and the rest of nature."[3] In marked contrast to these "realists," the pragmatists, says Rorty, "do not require either a metaphysics or an epistemology." They require neither of these theoretical entities because, with William James, they view truth as "what it is good for *us* to believe." For this reason, they do not need "an account of a relation between beliefs and objects called 'correspondence', nor an account of human cognitive abilities which ensures that our species is capable of entering into that relation."[4]

Rorty argues that we have no choice but to find everything we need with respect to knowledge and truth already embedded in the social practices of our particular tribe, or *ethnos*. For him "there is nothing to be said about either truth or rationality apart from descriptions of the familiar procedures of justification which a given society—*ours*—uses in one or another area of inquiry." So, in reprising James' description of truth as "what is good for *us* to believe," Rorty italicizes the word "us." For him, this inescapable (but not unalterable) ethnocentrism requires him to recast the objectivity prized by the realist in terms of intersubjectivity: "For pragmatists, the desire for objectivity is not the desire to escape the limitations of one's community, but simply the desire for as much intersubjective agreement as possible, the desire to extend the reference of 'us' as far as we can."[5]

Rorty is quick to point out that his pragmatist ethnocentrism is not a form of vicious relativism, so much as it is simply a recognition of our shared human condition. Upon noting that the label "relativist" is the realist's favored slur to throw at the pragmatist, Rorty proceeds to distinguish three rather different views that he sees falling under that heading. "The first is the view that every belief is as good as every other. The second is the view that 'true' is an equivocal term, having as many meanings as modes of justification." The third is the ethnocentric view I have just outlined. Rorty agrees that the first view is self-refuting, and disparages the second view as "eccentric," and only commits the pragmatist to holding the third, ethnocentric view. Yet he does not see why this third view should be considered a species of relativism: "For the pragmatist is not holding a positive theory which says that something is relative to something else. He is, instead, making the purely *negative* point that we should drop the traditional distinction between knowledge and opinion, construed as the distinction between truth as correspondence to reality and truth as a commendatory term for well-justified beliefs."[6] Because according to Rorty all we may ever achieve, like it or not, is the latter (intersubjective agreement, well-justified beliefs), the distinction which makes this inevitable position appear relativistic falls away, thereby losing any contrastive force.

For Rorty, dropping this distinction is a purely negative point, and not a positive proposal for an alternative philosophical theory of truth. In the pragmatist's mouth (*his* pragmatist's), "truth" is not a name for a positive value, something with an "intrinsic nature," but merely a flexible expression of commendation, paid to those beliefs that come to be widely regarded as well-justified. "The reason that the realist calls this negative claim 'relativistic'," says Rorty, "is that he cannot believe that anybody would seriously deny that truth has an intrinsic nature." He continues:

> So when the pragmatist says that there is nothing to be said about truth save that each of us will commend as true those beliefs which he or she finds good to believe, the realist is inclined to interpret this as one more positive theory about the nature of truth: a theory according to which truth is simply the contemporary opinion of a chosen individual or group. Such a theory would of course be self-refuting. But the pragmatist does not have a theory of truth, much less a relativistic one. Not having *any* epistemology, *a fortiori* he does not have a relativistic one.[7]

In passages like this, many readers see Rorty the "artful dodger," the philosopher who always manages to squirm free of those dialectical corners in which his critics attempt to trap him. Of course, from Rorty's point of view, there can be no question about dodging or evasion; for one need not get out of the way of missiles that land far wide of their intended mark. So, in passages like these, Rorty instead understands himself simply to be telling his critics how and why their salvos have missed their intended target.

Yet above and beyond skillfully pointing out the way a good many of his critics tend to misread him, Rorty also demonstrates a willingness to meet philosophical arguments head on, and even to change his position when he feels such arguments *have* struck their mark. At the end of the day, then, he does not desire to be some sort of Teflon philosopher, upon whom nothing sticks, but rather a thinker who appreciates well-placed criticisms that emerge from a deep understanding and sympathetic reading of his work. In this chapter, I will focus on one such exchange, between Rorty and Bjørn Ramberg.[8] I choose this exchange not simply as a telling example of Rorty's ability to respond positively to constructive criticism, but also because, perhaps more than any other exchange Rorty held with a critic on the related questions of truth and objectivity, it moves the conversation forward in a particularly meaningful and useful way. Through sympathetic critique of Rorty's position, Ramberg gets Rorty to nuance his views on truth and objectivity in ways that come across as surprising to even the seasoned Rorty reader.

Before delving directly into this exchange, however, it is once again necessary to provide some stage setting. Ramberg is a skilled reader of Davidson (to say the least) and of Rorty, and in his critique of Rorty he appeals to Davidson's notion of "triangulation" in order to get Rorty to reconsider aspects of his position with respect to the notions of truth and objectivity, including whether or not these can be completely reduced to the terms of intersubjective, ethnocentric solidarity. In the next section, I will lay out the terms of Davidson's understanding of triangulation so that the reader will have a better grasp of the moves and allowances that Rorty makes with respect to Ramberg's sympathetic critique.

NORMATIVE TRIANGULATION: COHERENCE, SOLIDARITY, AND OBJECTIVITY

As we have seen in numerous places throughout this book, Rorty uses the vocabulary of "coherence" to couch his refusal to offer an account of truth as something that possesses an intrinsic nature (defined as correspondence). This vocabulary is perfectly suited to Rorty's holistic, ethnocentric pragmatism, which as we have just seen holds that little more can be said about our use of the word "truth" than that it is a compliment we pay to those views we agree are well-justified, and which in this way cohere with the larger web of beliefs our particular community already holds. This emphasis on coherence over correspondence provides the impetus behind such infamous quips as "truth is what our peers will let us get away with saying"—Rorty's cheerful way of agreeing with Dewey's description of truth as (socially) warranted assertibility. The sky will not fall, says Rorty, if we drop talk of correspondence and instead pick up talk of coherence: "[T]o say that truth and knowledge can only be judged by the standards of the inquirers of our own day is not to say that human knowledge is less noble or important, or more 'cut off from the world', than we had thought. It is merely to say that nothing counts as justification unless by reference to what we already accept, and that there is no way to get outside our beliefs and our language so as to find some test other than coherence."[9]

As I briefly mentioned in the introduction to this volume, Davidson expressly agrees with Rorty's aforementioned statement of the coherence position. For him, as for Rorty, only a belief can justify another belief. After registering this agreement, however, Davidson adds that "where we differ, if we do, is on whether there remains a question how, given that we cannot 'get outside our beliefs and our language so as to find some test other than coherence', we nevertheless have knowledge of, and talk about, an objective public world that is not of our own making."[10] For Davidson, this question remains, while he suspects it does not for Rorty. Rorty seems to want us to talk only about coherence, whereas Davidson is interested in showing how "coherence yields correspondence."[11] Unlike Rorty, apparently, Davidson thinks that accepting the coherence position does not necessarily entail dropping all talk of objective truth.

In the essay "Three Varieties of Knowledge," Davidson attempts to demonstrate not just the possibility, but also the inescapability of retaining the vocabulary of objectivity after one has abandoned, as he has, a correspondence theory of truth (i.e. an epistemological theory that posits a truth-making relationship between objects and our beliefs about them). In this essay, he makes the following rather unRortyan statement: "Someone who has a belief about the world—or anything else—must grasp the concept of objective truth, of what is the case independently of what he or she thinks."[12] In "A Coherence Theory of Truth and Knowledge," he puts the matter as follows: "In order to doubt or wonder about the provenance of his beliefs, an agent must know what belief is. This brings with it the concept of objective truth, for the notion of a belief is the notion of a state that may or may not jibe with reality."[13] For us to even worry over our beliefs, we must know what "beliefs" are; if we use the word correctly at all, says Davidson, we will also grasp the concept of objective truth, because beliefs are the kinds of things that one puts forward as candidates for that feature. At the same time, for Davidson there can be no question of standing outside our web of beliefs in order to demonstrate, from some neutral, transcendent vantage point, the correspondence of a particular belief with a particular item in reality: "[A]ll that counts as evidence or justification for a belief," he insists, "must come from the same totality of belief to which it belongs."[14]

So how does this peculiar combination of coherence and objectivity work? How does one discover, a la Davidson, that an understanding of objectivity comes as part and parcel of what it means to be a believing creature? This is where Davidson's notion of "triangulation" comes in. For him, objective knowledge is analogous to the way we determine the location of an object in space by triangulating from two (or more) points of view on that object: "[E]ach of two people is reacting differentially to sensory stimuli streaming in from a certain direction. If we project the incoming lines outward, their intersection is the common cause."[15] Davidson's position is that, even though we cannot establish individual mind-world correspondence (or consider only one side of the triangle in isolation from the other two), there is nevertheless a way for one to make sense of saying that one knows objective truth, or what is the case independently of what one happens to think. This is so because, in communicating with each other (yet another side of the triangle), two interlocutors may, through triangulation, be confident that they are homing-in on the object in question. Yet it is important to keep in mind that no such homing-in ever occurs without triangulation; that is, Davidson is not saying that, once we have successfully triangulated, we have thereby secured direct access to the object in question such that any further triangulation in this particular case is unnecessary. Just as, for Rorty, all we have is intersubjectivity or "the conversation," for Davidson all we ever have is triangulation: "The triangle which gives content to thought and speech is complete. But it takes two to triangulate. Two, of course, or more."[16]

Davidson's strategy here is to remain (as he thinks we must) "inside" language (although that unhappy term suggests an inside/outside contrast that Davidson rejects). Like Rorty, he considers the philosophical effort to transcend linguistic intersubjectivity futile. Instead, he asks "after the source of the concept of truth." According to him, "Wittgenstein put us on the track of the only possible answer to this question. The source of the concept of objective truth is interpersonal communication." If we follow Wittgenstein's lead, says Davidson, and suppose that language is essential to thought and that there is no such thing as a private language, we must come to the inescapable conclusion that thought depends on communication: "The central argument against private languages is that unless a language is shared there is no way to distinguish between using the language correctly and using it incorrectly; only communication with another can supply an objective check. If only communication can provide a check on the correct use of words, *only communication can supply a standard of objectivity in other domains . . . .*"[17] So while, as I have already stated, there can be no question for Davidson of direct correspondence with objective reality outside of intersubjective communication, he reads Wittgenstein to be saying that the very possibility of communication depends on the fact that in speaking to each other we hold one another accountable for the correct use of language, and such "normative scorekeeping" provides us with a standard of objectivity that we can then apply to other areas of intercourse and inquiry.[18]

The activity of normative scorekeeping is part and parcel of what it means to give meaning to or an interpretation of another speaker's utterances, for we cannot attribute meaning without invoking the norms implicit in our use of language. Stanley Cavell provides an interesting example of this phenomenon: Upon witnessing his infant daughter utter the word "kitty" for the first time while stroking the family pet, he assumes she has successfully learned the correct meaning of that word. Yet later on he witnesses her using the word again while petting a furry pillow. Cavell feels compelled to conclude from these two instances that his daughter, while well on her way, does not yet know what the word "kitty" means; perhaps she is using that word (mistakenly) to refer to any furry object, or perhaps she means the adjective "furry" itself, or even the activity of petting.[19] In the latter case, when she is petting the pillow, Cavell's daughter is not *simply* making a mistake, for she is in the ballpark, and she seems to be intending *something*; yet all the same most parents in this situation would correct their child with a simple "No, that's a pillow" and then point to the cat and say "that's a kitty," while leaving the child to puzzle out all the ensuing inferences implied in this correction.[20] For Stout, such an example illustrates the Davidsonian point that "interpretation is an inherently normative affair. We cannot ascribe meaning to the utterances or inscriptions of our fellow human beings without (implicitly or explicitly) committing ourselves to judgments about how well they are doing at avoiding error."[21] Interpretation thus includes normative scorekeeping, or applying our own norms to the people we are interpreting.

Because of the implication of linguistic norms in our everyday interpretive practices, Davidson insists that such acts of interpretation must include a grasp of the *concept* of objective truth (as opposed to directly grasping objective truth). Linguistic communication, and the interpretation of others' utterances upon which it depends, thus involves possessing "the distinction between what is thought to be the case and what is the case"—a standard that is provided by our shared language. Without this distinction, says Davidson, "there is nothing that can be clearly thought."[22]

In addition to securing a workable understanding of objective knowledge, Davidson also argues that the three points of the triangle involved in the shared act of triangulation represent three *mutually irreducible and mutually supporting* kinds of knowledge: (1) self-knowledge (or direct noninferential knowledge of one's own mental states); (2) other-knowledge (knowledge of others' mental states or propositional attitudes implied in successful communication); and (3) objective knowledge (knowledge of an objective public world that is not of our own making, secured through triangulation). For Davidson, the three types of knowledge are mutually *supporting* because the knowledge named at each corner is not possible without the knowledge that is co-present in the other two corners. This also makes them mutually *irreducible*—reducing the knowledge at any one corner to the type of knowledge found at another corner would be to effectively remove one of the supports of the tripod, undermining the other two types of knowledge in the process. Davidson thus attempts to demonstrate the mutual irreducibility of the three types of knowledge he outlines through a demonstration of their mutual supportability.

We have already come across one example in Davidson's case for the overall mutual supportability of these three kinds of knowledge in his contention that objective knowledge is not possible without the other-knowledge upon which successful acts of triangulation are based: "Until a base line has been established by communication with someone else, there is no point in saying a person's thoughts or words have a propositional content. If this is so, then it is clear that knowledge of another mind is essential to all thought and all knowledge."[23] In the same way, the other-knowledge we possess is not possible without the objective knowledge of a shared world: "Knowledge of another mind is possible, however, only if one has knowledge of the world, for the triangulation which is essential to thought requires that those in communication recognize that they occupy positions in a shared world. So knowledge of other minds and knowledge of the world are mutually dependent; neither is possible without the other."[24] What is true for both objective knowledge and other-knowledge is also true for self-knowledge. Even though such knowledge is direct or noninferred, it still depends for its condition of possibility on the other two forms of knowledge: "Knowledge of the propositional contents of our own minds is not possible without the other forms of knowledge since without communication propositional thought is impossible. . . . Knowledge of our own minds and the minds of others are mutually dependent."[25] As Davidson later elaborates: "Our thoughts are 'inner' and 'subjective' in that we know what they are in a way no one else can. But though *possession* of a thought is necessarily individual, what gives it content is not. The thoughts we form and entertain are located conceptually in the world we inhabit, and know we inhabit with others. Even our thoughts about our own mental states occupy the same conceptual space and are located on the same public map."[26]

Davidson concludes his essay with the following summary of the way these three varieties of knowledge mutually support one another:

> If I did not know what others think I would have no thoughts of my own and so would not know what I think. If I did not know what I think, I would lack the ability to gauge the thought of others. Gauging the thoughts of others requires that I live in the same world with them, sharing many reactions to its major features, including its values. So there is no danger that in viewing the world objectively we will lose touch with ourselves. The three sorts of knowledge form a tripod: if any leg were lost, no part would stand.[27]

As Davidson's argument here suggests, these three types of knowledge co-emerge as human beings are acculturated into their respective linguistic communities. Davidson's case for objective knowledge as an irreducible point on this triangle, then, is not meant to argue for the possibility of an objectivist "view from nowhere," one with the dehumanizing potential to put us out of touch with the irreducibly unique knowledge of our own personal subjectivity; for that personal knowledge, it turns out, is one of the conditions of possibility for any objective knowledge at all, and so no objectivity can exist without it. We can avoid the very real danger of reducing persons to objects, then, once we recognize that we would have no objective knowledge at all if we were not already and irreducibly persons—members of that "community of minds" upon which all of our knowledge is based.[28]

RETRIEVING THE TRIANGLE: RAMBERG ON RORTY

With this understanding of Davidson's notion of normative triangulation in hand, we are now in a position to examine the aforementioned exchange between Ramberg and Rorty. Ramberg begins his essay by first declaring his sympathy for Rorty's Darwinian critique of representationalist epistemology. In particular, he affirms Rorty's attempt to dissipate "any metaphysical puzzle about the relation between thought and reality" by explaining our linguistic abilities in evolutionary terms, as a part of our adapted behavioral equipment. Once we follow Rorty in conceiving of language in these Darwinian terms, says Ramberg, the idea of the world being a certain way *in itself* loses its contrastive force, and language then becomes simply "a (very interesting) feature of the world," as opposed to an ethereal medium that interposes itself between cognizer and world. Ramberg thus agrees that we should drop "the representationalist idea of a world in itself that we cognizers confront." At the same time, however, he goes on to add (in Davidsonian fashion) that "even on Rorty's pragmatic, Darwinian picture of language, a good way to conceive of what we language-users are able, as such, to do for ourselves will invoke the truth-error contrast."[29]

In focusing on the importance of retaining an appeal to the truth-error contrast, Ramberg takes aim at Rorty's attempt to reduce objectivity (or truth) to intersubjectivity (or solidarity) without remainder. So although he is largely sympathetic with Rorty's position, Ramberg thinks that Rorty's antirepresentationalist epistemology misses something important about what we language-users are able to do, something that requires recourse to the very truth-error contrast that Rorty's critique of representationalism would apparently have us forego. As we saw in the previous section, for Davidson invoking the normative "truth-error" distinction involves appealing to a conception of objectivity, or, in Stout's words, a notion of "getting things right," where the word "things" names the furniture of a public world that is not of our own making. On Ramberg's reading, the extreme care Rorty takes to thoroughly repudiate representationalist epistemology leads him to neglect the way in which we must continue to invoke the truth-error contrast, even once we have abandoned any understanding of truth as correspondence.

In order to get Rorty to see the inescapability of continuing to invoke a truth-error contrast (without thereby giving up his holist, coherentist perspective), Ramberg appeals to Rorty's own notion of "redescription." As we saw in Chapter 3, Rorty thinks that once we drop the representationalist idea of the One Right Description, we become free to entertain alternative descriptions (vocabularies), and also to invent new ones, depending on our purposes. After defending Rorty's nonreductive epistemological pluralism against critics who view it as a form of idealism (which holds that the world is however we choose to describe it), Ramberg proceeds to bring out implications of Rorty's vocabulary pluralism that Rorty himself has perhaps not sufficiently registered. Basically, Ramberg tries to pull the Rortyan notion of redescription in a Davidsonian direction, and then see if Rorty will tag along.

Ramberg begins this demonstration by suggesting that Rorty's notion of redescription helpfully highlights our linguistic capacity to engage in "different strategies of description." These strategies, he says, are "ways of bringing salience to different causal patterns in the world, patterns with which we engage." Even if we cannot represent these patterns "in themselves," independent of our descriptive purposes (and our intersubjective communication about these purposes), language still gives us the ability to highlight (or make stand out) different features of that causal nexus with which we are in perpetual engagement. According to Ramberg, the "great ability" that language brings is the ability "to reprogram our causal dispositions through salience-alteration." This special power is one way of marking the uniqueness of the human form of life as we come across it today: "We are the organisms causally engaged with the rest of the world in ways that we have developed this very nifty means—language—of modifying. By changing our causal dispositions, redistributing significance across kinds, we affect how we engage with the world, and thus also the world." Ramberg is here, in part, making the blindingly simple point, a point which representationalist epistemology tends to obscure, that we humans are ourselves part of the world; we are creatures who are just as caught up in its nexus of physical forces as any other, as both agents and patients. At the same time, we are unique creatures who have evolved a special capacity to become profound shapers of and not simply passive responders to that world. Our linguistic capacity to change descriptive strategies to suit different purposes has not just a causal, but also a steering impact on the course of the world's development.[30] Indeed, Ramberg argues, if vocabularies didn't have this impact, "it would be hard to see how language could have evolved as a useful tool. On the pragmatist view I impute to Rorty, changing descriptions matters, just because it makes a causal difference in the world. This it does because it changes *us*, our dispositions."[31] In making this suggestion, Ramberg also fuzzifies Rorty's sharp distinction between reasons (descriptive strategies, justifications, etc.), on the one hand, and causes, on the other, because on this picture our reasons, understood as descriptive strategies, themselves play a causal role in the course of events. So *pace* Rorty, phrases like "true of" and "refers to" which we commonly employ in such descriptive strategies do name word–world relations after all, even if those relations cannot be relied upon to do any epistemic work.

We have yet to pin down, however, how Ramberg's way of glossing the Rortyan notion of redescription involves necessary recourse to the "truth-error" contrast. Simply stated, the truth-error contrast is an essential part of the activity of normative scorekeeping; normative scorekeeping, in turn, is an essential component of intersubjective interpretation and communication; and finally, such communication is an essential part of our ability to deploy different descriptive strategies that suit *our* purposes. As Ramberg reminds us: "*Describing* anything, if Davidson is right, is an ability we have only because it is possible for others to see us as in general conforming to the norms that the predicates of agency embody."[32] Our ability to hold one another to account depends on our ability to know our interlocutors, and to be known ourselves, as agents—persons whose subjectivity is irreducible to objectivist descriptions, descriptions which are not possible without that irreducible subjectivity in the first place.

As I have already stated, Ramberg intends his portrait of Davidson's position, which leads up to an argument for the inescapability of invoking a truth-error contrast, to trouble Rorty's attempt to recast objectivity in terms of intersubjectivity alone. "The possibility of *error*," he says, "generalized in the notion of inappropriateness with respect to purpose, goal, or end, takes the form in (assertively used) language of the possibility of a failure of a claim to be in accord with what it says something about."[33] As Davidson argues, such "failure to be in accord" is a normative status, it signals the result of the fact that in speaking to each other we also inevitably hold each other to account for the things we say, grading each other according to the truth-error standard. The truth-error contrast, then, comes along with the fact that we are linguistic creatures, creatures who can, through redescription, highlight different salience patterns in the causal nexus in which we are always engaged, and who hold each other to account for the various things we say in that process—for we can also get things wrong.

For Ramberg, the fact that we are linguistic creatures, which means (in part) that we are creatures who can get their descriptions right or wrong, is the very thing that opens up the Davidsonian triangle, including all the uniquely human possibilities which it allows. The possibility of error plays a special role here, says Ramberg, for it "marks our ability to get our noises and (the rest of the) world prized locally apart to a sufficient extent to allow for intentionality, for there *being* meaning and mind, that is to say, for there being a point to treating some things as thinkers, with a point of view on the world."[34] For Ramberg, language gives us the ability to stand at a remove from a certain aspect of the world, to be intentional with respect to it, because it opens a gap between our linguistic noises and what those noises are about that is not there for nonlinguistic creatures. This gap creates the space for the power of "variable response" to our environment that Rorty, as we saw in Chapter 3, understands language to give us. But we would not have this power, says Ramberg, if our linguistic capacities did not also bring a truth-error contrast in tow. That is, our descriptions would not be descriptions if they were not available for others to score, for others to make judgments as to the ability of these descriptions to get the local matters to which they pertain right.

In continuity with the above point, Ramberg, in a brilliant flourish, attempts to get Rorty to see that his rejection of representationalism's *global* separation of subject from object does not necessitate a rejection of the *local* separation of subject from object, a separation that our interest in objectivity and the concomitant possibility of error makes possible. For, according to Ramberg, the Davidsonian understanding of objectivity and normativity (scorekeeping according to the truth-error contrast) "inverts the framing assumptions of traditional normative epistemology since Descartes." He continues:

"For the mystery really cannot be, for the Darwinian naturalist, how mind and meaning could possibly connect with, relate to, or correspond with the world. The mystery, a scientific one, is how we have been able to develop this amazing system of behavior that allows us to stand, locally and for particular purposes, at a distance from some aspect of the world, and then exploit that distance to modify our dispositions in systematic ways."[35]

Throughout his criticism of Rorty's efforts to speak of truth and objectivity solely in terms of solidarity or intersubjectivity, Ramberg attempts to articulate a position that Rorty would nevertheless still find sympathetic. Ramberg thus takes no issue with the things Rorty says about our power to redescribe, or our ability to use different descriptive strategies or vocabularies for different purposes. He also has no objection to Rorty's Darwinian analogy of language as a coping tool rather than a representational medium. Unlike Rorty, however, he thinks we need to keep an understanding of objectivity that retains a truth-error contrast in order to explain the very powers that Rorty thinks this tool—language and its power to redescribe (or alter salience)—gives us.

So how does Rorty respond to Ramberg's critique? His response is twofold. To start, he agrees with Ramberg's Davidsonian arguments for the inescapability of normativity. The stress Ramberg places on the themes of agency and normativity in his essay, says Rorty, helps him resituate his qualms with respect to the way Davidson argues for the irreducibility of the intentional (or mental) to the physical: "The key to understanding the relation between minds and bodies is not an understanding of the irreducibility of the intentional to the physical but the understanding of the inescapability of the normative."[36] Rorty admits that his criticisms of Davidson's way of arguing for the special status of human mentality (by means of arguing for the irreducibility of intentional vocabularies to physical ones) had led him to neglect his larger agreement with Davidson's contention that all descriptive strategies depend for their condition of possibility on the prior recognition of human agency implied in the inescapable activity of normative scorekeeping: "[W]e could not have spoken either commonsensical or Aristotelian or corpuscularian unless we were already treating each other as persons who had duties to respond to certain situations with certain words rather than others."[37] In helping him see this, says Rorty, Ramberg helps him appreciate an aspect of Davidson's position that he had not fully registered:

> Davidson, [Ramberg] rightly says, has understood better than I that recognizing some beings as fellow-obeyers of norms, acknowledging them as members of a community, is as much a requirement for using a language as is the ability to deploy a descriptive vocabulary. The recognition establishes, so to speak, a community of tool-users. The various descriptive vocabularies this community wields are the tools in its kit. No toolkit, no community—if we did not describe we would have no criticisms to offer of one another's descriptions. But no community, no toolkit—if we did not criticize each other's descriptions, they would not be descriptions.[38]

As we can see, Rorty's recognition of the mutual irreducibility and supportability of (normative) community and (descriptive) toolkit here chimes quite well with several of the key points Davidson makes in "Three Varieties of Knowledge."

But Rorty is not finished. The second, and perhaps most surprising move he makes in response to Ramberg's essay is to acquiesce to Ramberg's Davidsonian criticisms of his tendency to adopt a dismissive attitude toward the concept of truth: "Ramberg sets me straight here too. He tells me, in effect, that it was a mistake on my part to go from criticism of attempts to define truth as accurate representation of the intrinsic nature of reality to a denial that true statements get things right. What I should have done, he makes me realize, is to grant Davidson's point that most of our beliefs about anything (snow, molecules, the moral law) must be true of that thing—must get that thing right." This *mea culpa* also chimes with Rorty's overall agreement with the Davidsonian notion of triangulation: "That norms are mostly obeyed and objects mostly gotten right are two ways of making a single point: none of the three corners of his process of triangulation can be what they are in independence of the other two."[39] In affirming all the implications of Davidsonian triangulation, Rorty finally admits that he should not have spoken of linguistic or epistemic norms as things that are set solely by one's peers, without remainder. "It was a mistake to locate the norms at one corner of the triangle—where my peers are—rather than seeing them as, so to speak, hovering over the whole process of triangulation. . . . It is not that my peers have more to do with my obligation to say that snow is white than the snow does, or I do."[40]

As Rorty himself realizes, his twofold acceptance of Ramberg's critique makes significant concessions to his realist opponents, concessions that throughout the bulk of his career he doggedly resisted making. In this response, Rorty admits that Ramberg has persuaded him to jettison two long-held doctrines in particular: "that the notion of 'getting things right' must be abandoned, and that 'true of' and 'refers to' are not word-world relations." Rorty's post-Rambergian position, then, is that we must *not* abandon the notion of "getting things right," and also that such phrases as "true of" and "refers to" *do* name word–world relations. At the same time, however, Rorty insists that these concessions, however monumental they may seem, still do not force him to give up very many of his major philosophical positions. In the final section of this chapter, I will assess Rorty's contention that most of these positions remain in place; while Rorty's more fulsome appreciation of Davidsonian triangulation may have made his position on truth less dismissive, that position still remains, he insists, pragmatic.

WHAT IS TRUTH FOR? RETURNING TRUTH TO THE SERVICE OF EDIFYING CONVERSATION

Lest his critics think these concessions imply that he has suddenly "taken it all back," Rorty, at the end of his response to Ramberg, insists that most of his major philosophical positions remain largely unchanged under the light of these concessions. Before he enumerates those, however, he offers a general statement about what he now thinks both his version of pragmatism and the realism of his opponents get right: "*What is true in pragmatism is that what you talk about depends not on what is real but on what it pays you to talk about. What is true in realism is that most of what you talk about you get right.*"[41] So, even after making his concessions, Rorty still insists that our effort to get things right remains in the service of talking about those things we think (or hope) it will pay us to talk about. Rorty thus retains his pragmatist insistence that potential sociocultural benefit (happiness) continues to set the direction and motivate the intellectual activities of description and inquiry, activities that, he now admits, will always and inevitably invoke a truth-error contrast.

With the priority of sociocultural benefit clearly in mind, Rorty lists four of his key, long-held positions that remain in place even after he makes the aforementioned concessions to Ramberg. The first position is that, although it makes sense to say that we can get particulars right or wrong, it still does not make sense to say that Reality as such is something that we can get right or wrong. "There is no such thing as Reality to be gotten right—only snow, fog, Olympian deities, relative aesthetic worth, the elementary particles, human rights, the divine right of kings, the Trinity, and the like." We cannot get something as global and abstract as Reality right because, says Rorty, "there are no norms for talking about it. . . . There are norms for snow-talk and Zeus-talk, but not for Reality-talk. That is because the purposes served by the former, but not those served by the latter, are reasonably clear."[42]

The second position that Rorty thinks remains in place is his contention, *contra* McDowell, that "there is no second norm given us by the facts, in addition to the norms given us by our peers." Yet here, as we saw above, Rorty also gives McDowell the point that these norms are not set *solely* by our peers; rather, it is the entire process of triangulation, involving all three corners, that produces the norms inherent in human discourse, discovery, and description.[43] Discursive norms are social products that arise from the process of triangulation, a process that necessarily invokes or includes a conception of objectivity as one of its vertices.

The third position that remains unscathed, Rorty thinks, is his recommendation to drop all talk of truth in terms of accuracy of representation. "To say that we get snow mostly right is not to say that we represent snow with reasonable accuracy."[44] To say the latter, Rorty argues, still betrays a wish to escape the inescapable, cutting off the corner of Davidson's triangle occupied by one's peers, and "just ask about a relation called 'correspondence' or 'representation' between your beliefs and the world."[45] With Davidson, Rorty maintains that the language of representation goes along with the language of "sentences being made true by facts." Talk of "getting things right," then, does not on Rorty's account participate in any way in the metaphysical or epistemological quest to determine or secure representational accuracy apart from the normative, peer-governed activities through which human beings pursue any form of inquiry at all.[46]

The fourth and final position that remains unchanged, Rorty says, is his "militant anti-authoritarianism." This central aspect of his overall philosophical perspective remains unchanged, he says, because he can still maintain that "there is no such thing as the search for truth, as distinct from the search for happiness. There is no authority called Reality before whom we need bow down." As I mentioned at the beginning of this section, Rorty's position here remains pragmatist insofar as the quest for sociocultural benefit determines our interest in, and so also sets the direction of, objective inquiry (or inquiry with an interest in objectivity, in getting things right), and not the other way around.[47] It would therefore also seem consistent with Rorty's position to say that our discussions about what does or should make us happy will, like any of our other discussions, invoke linguistic norms and word–world relations, and so also involve our ability both to attribute error and get things right; yet happiness *itself*, like reality and truth, does not seem to be something that Rorty thinks we can precisely define, something we can therefore either get right or wrong.

In his response to Ramberg, Rorty says that happiness "in the relevant sense" means "getting more of the things we keep developing new descriptive vocabularies in order to get." While Rorty would agree that this "definition" is imprecise and circular, he would argue that such imprecision and circularity is unavoidable, especially if we would avoid reducing the point of human life to convergence upon a fixed, metaphysical idea of truth. In Rorty's hands, then, "happiness" becomes a general name for our success in getting more of what we want and less of what we don't, leaving the question of what it is that we *should* want immersed in the mud of cultural politics. All the same, happiness, whatever we make that out to be in specifics, is for Rorty the point or goal of inquiry, and it is therefore the value that makes truth preferable to error, the value that tells us why we have an interest in getting things right in the first place:

> Getting snow right—getting still more truth about snow—is not an end in itself but a means to the purposes for which we invented the term 'snow'. Intellectual progress is not progress toward better and better representations of what is out there. . . . It is, in Ramberg's terms, finding more and more useful ways

of 'bringing salience to different causal patterns in the world'. No such pattern . . . is more 'real' than any other such pattern. Utility for human happiness is all that distinguishes them.[48]

While some might still wish to complain of the utter vagueness of the cultural ideal of happiness that Rorty habitually invokes, here and elsewhere, he insists that there is little more to say about it than that it is a result of getting more of what we want, and less of what we do not. Because there is no one cultural goal that trumps all others (like Truth), his understanding of happiness must remain indexed to a pluralistic and shifting conversation concerning the variety of ends that might make any particular human life meaningful.

The social practice of determining, ranking, and critically assessing the variety of cultural desires in play at any given moment is therefore an inescapably messy one, something we "muddle through" rather than directly ascertain.[49] Yet Rorty's use of the word "we" in offering his quasi-definition of happiness is instructive, for it precludes an interpretation that would construe his position as a form of vicious, antidemocratic individualism (as opposed to portraying a healthy respect for individuality). Furthermore, on this definition, one's understanding of happiness, like anything else, remains subject to the normative scorekeeping that automatically takes place when we discuss such matters with one another. We can, because we are social creatures living in the same world, still criticize one another's views of what makes life happy and meaningful.

Rorty's imprecision about happiness can also be seen as consistent with his deflationary, if no longer dismissive, account of truth. That is, while he has come around to thinking that, in our pursuit of happiness, it is important for us to get those particular things we are talking about right, to not be in error with respect to them; the attempt to get *truth* itself right remains a matter he thinks does not repay our concerted intellectual attention. Hanne Andrea Kraugerud and Ramberg effectively sum up Rorty's position on this score, stating that Rorty's critique of correspondence does not intend to dismiss our various uses of the concept of truth, or the virtues we are wont to associate with those uses. Rather, his point, according to them, is that "neither epistemic prudence nor virtuous conduct presupposes an account of truth or will be aided by one. Neither the ways in which we test and modify our accounts of things, nor our insight into what is proper and good and reasonable conduct will be better understood or more fully justified by our coming to understand fully what truth is."[50]

Just as such a full understanding of truth will not help us secure desirable virtues, it will also be of little help in our efforts to combat undesirable vices. For Rorty, in our struggle against vice, "it is of no help to proclaim that truth is on our side, or to attempt clarifying the nature of truth, or to pin our hopes on truth's compelling force."[51] This is because our opponent in this struggle, say a Nazi, will claim the support of a similarly sophisticated (or unsophisticated) account of truth. The epistemological attempt to hone a truth theory will not lead such a person to abandon those values that we, their opponents, find abhorrent. Kraugerud and Ramberg illustrate this point using the example of "cultic practices" associated with New Age superstitions. They point out that such superstitious cultic beliefs and practices "are perfectly compatible with the most ordinary assumptions about truth" and that "cultic creeds are often formulated as a series of unprovable but nonetheless absolute truths." According to Kraugerud and Ramberg, Rorty's philosophical quietism, his doubts about the usefulness of theoretical attempts to clarify the nature of truth, is simply a registration of such a theory's lack of utility in our attempts to encourage virtue and discourage vice. Our criticisms of the cultist should be directed at their beliefs, then, and not their conception of truth: "The metaphysician need not worry that cultists are mistaken about *truth*. Cultists are mistaken about *the world*. Therefore, clarification of the nature of truth will be of no aid against New Age superstitions, just as it is irrelevant to combating denial or trivialization of the Holocaust."[52]

Yet what will help us in these and other efforts to pursue our collective happiness? While he feels compelled to remain imprecise, refusing to define happiness in the same way in which the metaphysician would define truth, Rorty is nevertheless far from remaining a quietest with respect to this question. His answer, to no surprise, is to remind us of the importance of taking care of freedom:

> I have sometimes tried to sum up my views on these matters by saying that Freedom is more important than Truth: that it is better to regard inquiry as enlarging our imagination, and thus our alternatives, than to think of it as getting more and more things right. It does . . . get things like snow and photons and baseball

right. But getting things right is to the point of human life what shooting straight is to the pursuit of happiness. Both are very useful, but they are only means to an ever-changing end. Plato's nerdy conviction that the point of our existence is getting things right *more geometrico* was as blinkered as Achilles' conviction that the point is victory in battle.[53]

Rorty's insistence on construing happiness as an "ever-changing end" is, in part, meant to forestall the efforts of the authoritarian "bad guys" to insist that only one sort of human flower be allowed to bloom: "These guys do not agree . . . that increased freedom and richness of the Conversation is the aim of inquiry, but instead think that there is the further aim of getting Reality right (as opposed to getting, for instance, snow, photons, baseball, Cézanne and the best use of the term 'fact' right)."[54] If nothing else, Rorty's philosophy represents a concerted effort to combat these bad guys.

In order to fight these bad guys, Rorty argues that it is both morally and politically important to insist that our overarching public purpose is to ensure the blossoming of "a hundred private flowers." Brandom summarizes Rorty's moral and political outlook here in the following way: "The point of speaking the common language of the tribe, binding oneself by the shared norms of a public vocabulary, is not limited to the capacity to pursue shared public goals. It consists largely in the private (in the sense of novel and idiosyncratic) uses to which the vocabulary can be put. Not the least of these is the capacity to generate new specialized vocabularies, the way in which private sprouts branch off of the public stem."[55] From this perspective, what most matters to us morally and politically, says Brandom, "is not ultimately to be understood in terms of goals available from the inevitably reductive perspective of the naturalist: paradigmatically the avoidance of mammalian pain." Instead, he says, what matters most is

> the capacity each of us discursive creatures has to say things that no-one else has ever said, things furthermore that would never have been said if we did not say them. It is our capacity to transform the vocabularies in which we live and move and have our being, and so to create new ways of being (for creatures like us). Our moral worth is our dignity as potential contributors to the Conversation.[56]

Rorty's fervent desire to defend and promote this construal of human moral worth leads him to agree with Brandom that simple avoidance of pain should not be considered definitive of, but rather subservient to, human moral worth, and should have only a second-hand, yet still genuine, moral significance.

Speaking from experience, Rorty thinks Brandom's point about the second-hand moral significance of pain prevention or mitigation is worth making, even though it may leave one open to "accusations of pseudo-aristocratic condescension and ivory-tower aestheticism." It is worth making, says Rorty, because the "representationalist totalitarianism" of the bad guys, along with their "attempts to claim 'that some vocabularies possess a special sort of cognitive authority stemming from ontology alone'," is "bolstered by the idea that pain is our best example of contact with reality."[57] As we saw in Chapter 3, Rorty does agree that pain is our best example of our sheer contact with reality.[58] At the same time, he does not think this makes its avoidance our ultimate moral end. He does agree that, because of the sheer salience of pain, its ability to keep us from the full richness of life, "our most pressing moral duty is to relieve the social and economic deprivation which fills so many lives with unnecessary pain." Yet he pushes the matter one step further: If we are asked why this is our most pressing moral duty, he says, "the best answer is that we want everybody to be able to lead a specifically human life: a life in which there is a chance to compose one's own variations on old themes, to put one's own twist on old words, to change a vocabulary by using it."[59] At the end of the day, Rorty's most deep-seated moral concern is for everyone to be granted the chance to live a life that allows them to make a meaningful and unique contribution to our collective, pluriform Conversation.

As his exchange with Ramberg shows, Rorty does not think that his philosophical positions are immune from criticism. While he does in fact intend to circumvent or evade a certain type of philosophical discourse about the nature of truth, his position is still one that both uses and responds to argument. In this sense, he is an obeyer of discursive norms just like everyone else. Rorty's exchange with Ramberg itself presents us with an exemplary instance of normative scorekeeping; Ramberg holds Rorty to account for some of the things he says about truth and objectivity, as well as for some of the ways he reads Davidson. In doing so, he insists that Rorty has missed something important in his critique of truth as correspondence to the intrinsic nature of reality; Rorty, says Ramberg, has gotten something wrong. Rorty's response to Ramberg is also exemplary, insofar as in it he recognizes his responsibility to respond to Ramberg's critique "with certain words rather than others." In Ramberg, Rorty recognizes an authoritative peer to whom he owes an answer regarding his reading of Davidson and his dismissal of the very idea of objective truth. In attempting to provide such an answer, he comes away from the discussion different than he was when he entered it, as one who is less prone to dismiss the concept of objectivity in his own understanding of truth. At the same time, Rorty regards his deeper pragmatic values and commitments to remain relatively unscathed by this encounter. While he has become more open to an understanding of truth *qua* objectivity (nonerror or rectitude), he continues to insist that this sort of truth can never form an ultimate goal or *telos*; objective inquiry remains a means to more pragmatically defined ends. Rorty thereby remains faithful to the "deep sense of vision and conviction" I mentioned in the introduction to this book. In the conclusion that follows, I will attempt to provide a concise articulation of what I take that sense of vision and conviction to be.

CONCLUSION

PRAGMATISM AS THE APOTHEOSIS OF THE FUTURE—RORTY, HOPE, AND THE AMERICAN SUBLIME

In the introduction to this book, I suggested that throughout his career Rorty strove to remain faithful to "a deep sense of vision and conviction." This sense of vision and conviction, I contend, runs through all of the different intellectual *personae* we have just explored. Whether he is practicing philosophical therapy, cultural politics, or intellectual prophecy, Rorty seems to be responding to a deeper exigency, or to be struggling to honor an underlying impetus that persists as a constant theme (even as it matures and evolves over time). One might even go so far as to say that through his work Rorty develops his own sense of "sacred value," in the sense Jeffrey Stout gives that phrase: Rorty uses philosophy to express what he values for its own sake, to articulate what he cares about so deeply that he would count its violation or destruction as horrendous.[1] After the preceding exploration of the various major facets of his work, we are now in a position to give Rorty's sense of sacred value some more precision and definition.

Rorty's autobiographical reflection piece, "Trotsky and the Wild Orchids," stands as a testament to this sense of vision and conviction, for in it he declares his intention to make a serious and meaningful contribution to American intellectual life, and also expresses his dismay with the fact that so many readers take him instead to be a frivolous thinker who would say anything to get a gasp. He strenuously denies being the frivolous, cynical, would-be debunker of cherished truths that many of his critics have taken him to be. While he may indeed end up de-bunking certain cherished "truths," he claims to have serious and important reasons for doing so. In order to stave off the impressions of cynicism and frivolity, then, he proceeds to divulge several key personal details behind his motivation for practicing philosophy. Like his parents before him, and the many pragmatist philosophers he so admires, this motivation involves the (perhaps quintessentially American) attempt to articulate the relationship between the private and public dimensions of human life in a way that does justice to both—an articulation that maintains an appropriate emphasis on the unique, creative potential inherent in each individual person, without thereby undermining one's concomitant responsibility to cooperate in the construction and maintenance of societies of justice, peace, and solidarity.

In "Trotsky and the Wild Orchids" Rorty says that he began pursuing the study of philosophy as a natural continuation of his adolescent quest to find some way of unifying these two different aspects of human life. He then goes on to describe how he would subsequently come to question the desire informing this very attempt to "hold reality and justice in a single vision," thereby giving up his quest for what he calls a "synoptic vision."[2] The modest way in which he describes this intellectual development (as a failure of sorts) masks the fact that his inability to synthesize the private with the public also represents an important discovery about what he thinks makes for a full (or rich) human life, and therefore about what he thinks makes for a society that would optimize the chances for any one of its members to lead such a life.

Rorty critically questions the attempt to unite private and public exigencies in a synoptic vision because he thinks that, if successful, such a synthesis would undermine something important about the private *qua* private (not to mention something important about public solidarity *qua* solidarity). For the wishful attempt to find one's idiosyncratic passions writ large into the structure of the universe not only occludes their potentially game-changing uniqueness and novelty (i.e. the potential public ramifications of unique and singular contributions to the Conversation); this attempt also represents an implicit wish to impose one's particular loves and fascinations on everyone else. Such totalization of the individual or idiosyncratic not only robs this dimension of human life of its individuality or idiosyncrasy, it also robs the totality (or plurality) of our public life of its diversity and richness, construing it instead as monolithic and one-dimensional. Rorty deeply fears the scenario in which the normal discourse of a certain time and place becomes so dominant that it leaves no room for the development of abnormal, idiosyncratic responses and alternatives to it. He would have his readers avoid this scenario at all costs, for to him such a development would represent the "freezing-over of culture," the death of our capacity for innovation and imagination. Our ability to embrace the human capacity for novelty, he suggests in *Philosophy and the Mirror of Nature*, represents our ability to embrace our full humanity (understood as the rich range of human possibility). To refuse this capacity, he says, would be to inaugurate "the dehumanization of human beings."[3]

Although Rorty's antiessentialist philosophical stance leads him to deny that all humans share a universal, atemporal "essence," we can see that this antiessentialism does not prevent him from putting forward a normative understanding of what it means to be human. As we saw at the end of Chapter 5, he articulates this normative understanding through a discussion of human happiness as life's ever-shifting end, something that is achievable only when we recognize and grasp our freedom to constantly reconceive and reinvent our ends (i.e. make unique and idiosyncratic contributions to the Conversation). Put another way, Rorty does not see happiness as a "goal" in any traditionally understood sense (i.e. as something fixed, final, and antecedently—if only ideally—existent), so much as he regards it to be the desirable effect of a life well lived, a life in which we continuously make the most of our freedom, including the freedom to change and reinvent our goals when we feel the need or find the opportunity to do so. For Rorty we do not become happy as the result of reaching some sort of predetermined destination that must be the same for everyone, so much as we become happy when we strive to embrace our full human potential, an effort that includes embracing the freedom we possess to reinvent ourselves, to write our own life's script.

According to Rorty, "the human self is created by the use of a vocabulary rather than being adequately or inadequately expressed in a vocabulary. . . ."[4] As we invent different life scripts to enact, we become different kinds of persons, seizing alternative possibilities to the ones that seem to be fatalistically set out before us. Rorty thus embraces the Romantic idea that human beings who change their vocabularies, their way of describing themselves and the world, are able to become new kinds of human beings. Rorty experiences this capacity for novelty as a kind of grace, something that may save us as a society from travelling down increasingly inhuman roads. For this reason he cherishes the human capacity for novelty and invention as sacred, in that he contemplates the destruction of this capacity as horrendous. Rorty's sense of human fullness thus involves, as perhaps its most important ingredient, an insistence upon the *plasticity* of the human. Rorty's arguments with epistemologically centred philosophy, as well as his defense of liberal political philosophy and his criticisms of religious culture, are all in one way or another directed toward those intellectual forces that would deny the reality of this plasticity, and with it the liberating potential he thinks it represents.

Yet exactly how plastic does Rorty think humans are? Infinitely so? While he does not think we can prescribe a limit to what human beings might be able to become, or to the number of languages they may yet invent to remake or redescribe themselves (because the course of novelty and invention does not follow a determinate or predictable path), at the same time he does ascribe to a robust sense of human finitude and fallibility, one that prevents his thoughts about the human potential for novelty from sliding into a version of wilful subjectivism.[5] He does not think that individuals can remake themselves however they like, whenever they like, through sheer force of will or out of whole cloth. Composing one's own personal script is the project of a lifetime, and requires the material of a cultural inheritance that one does not invent oneself. The parallel process of cultural change on a public scale requires several generations worth of piecemeal, accumulative modifications, not to mention a variety of idiosyncratic contributions from the individuals who compose a given public.[6] A more accurate reading of Rorty's insistence on human plasticity, then, would be to say that he thinks the cultural material available to us at any given moment allows for a richer array of alternative possibilities than we might initially think, and because any cultural pattern short of the absolutely totalitarian allows for such individual variation, any culture is itself wont to change over the course of lengthy spans of time. Human imagination must be encouraged so that we may keep open this possibility for change.

CONCLUSION

In the end, Rorty intends his emphasis on Freedom over Truth to enable us to see the ways in which we need not be mired in current cultural patterns, even if our success in becoming unstuck from them will be a difficult, painstaking purchase. Rorty recognizes this difficulty when he suggests that our freedom to realize such alternatives will include a destructive moment: "Great systematic philosophers, like great scientists," he says, "build for eternity. Great edifying philosophers destroy for the sake of their own generation."[7] That is, great edifying philosophers, the ones Rorty hopes to emulate, wish to keep the space open for a poetic sense of wonder and novelty. To do that, says Rorty, they must follow Dewey's advice and "break through the crust of convention." A sufficient aim for such a philosophy, he says, is "keeping conversation going," an aim that includes seeing human beings as "generators of new descriptions rather than beings one hopes to be able to describe accurately."[8] The edifying form of philosophy he strives to practice thus tries to do no more than send the conversation off in new, promising directions, directions that may themselves settle into new "normal" discourses. But the point of such philosophy is not to achieve the systematic rigour of a research program, but rather to perform the aforementioned social function of breaking with convention, thereby "preventing man from deluding himself with the notion that he knows himself, or anything else, except under optional descriptions."[9]

The delusion that Rorty here alludes to, that of claiming to know ourselves, or anything else, under a *necessary*, nonoptional description, is the delusion of hypostasizing what is after all merely the normal discourse of the day; it is the mistake of thinking that one has discovered the single correct description that finally puts to rest the need to come up with alternative descriptions. For Rorty, life under such a truth-regime would be a reduced, impoverished, and less than fully human life. As we saw in Chapter 5, for him a "specifically human life" would be "a life in which there is a chance to compose one's own variations on old themes, to put one's own twist on old words, to change a vocabulary by using it."[10]

Rorty's Left-leaning, reformist, American patriotism can finally be understood as the orientation that comports best with his sense of sacred value. Invoking Harold Bloom's notion of "the American Sublime," Rorty self-consciously places himself in the tradition of American democratic thought that stretches from Emerson to Dewey. Thinkers in this tradition recognize that, to be fully human, we do need to avail ourselves of all the old themes, words, and vocabularies that come to us as part and parcel of our cultural inheritance. At the same time, these thinkers insist that in our hands this inheritance must not simply be conserved, but rather used as the raw material for our experiments in innovation, our efforts to compose our own variations and twists. In the essay "Circles," Emerson describes this approach to the relationship between the old and the new in a way that Rorty would find congenial: "The new position of the advancing man has all the powers of the old, yet has them all new. It carries in its bosom all the energies of the past, yet is itself an exhalation of the morning."[11] With Emerson, Whitman, and Dewey, Rorty celebrates the American democratic experiment, the American Sublime, as such a new, fresh exhalation. In doing so, he agrees with Whitman that this democratic experiment counts almost entirely on the future for its justification and success.[12] The experiment succeeds insofar as it is able to hold open our chances for making a different and better future for ourselves, at both the individual and societal levels. One catches the sense of sacred value Rorty attaches to the American Sublime when he describes pragmatism, so interpreted, as "the apotheosis of the future."[13]

Emerson similarly apotheosizes the future when in the essay "Circles" he claims that "old age ought not to creep on a human mind." It is thus not difficult to hear Emerson's version of this apotheosis animating Rorty's understanding of the American Sublime: "In nature," says Emerson, "every moment is new; the past is always swallowed and forgotten; the coming only is sacred. Nothing is secure but life, transition, the energizing spirit. No love can be bound by oath or covenant to secure it against a higher love. No truth so sublime but it may be trivial tomorrow in the light of new thoughts. People wish to be settled: only as far as they are unsettled is there any hope for them."[14] Only insofar as we remain unsettled, ever willing to break through the crust of convention, will we be able, in continuity with Emerson's organic metaphor, to "grow" into an open future. Rorty thus agrees with Dewey's fuzzy sentiment that growth, and the maintenance of its continuing possibility, is the only moral end.[15] In order to continue striving for this open-ended end, Rorty concludes that we must preserve within ourselves a precious and vulnerable cultural commodity, hope:

CONCLUSION

"Hope—the ability to believe that the future will be unspecifiably different from, and unspecifiably freer than, the past—is the condition of growth."[16] Encouraging this sense of hope, I suggest, is the thread that connects Rorty's various contributions to philosophy. For such hope is the condition of growth, and growth in the Deweyan sense Rorty intends is only possible if we strive to remain open to an as-yet unwritten future.

NOTES

INTRODUCTION

1. L. S. Klepp, "Every Man a Philosopher King," *New York Times Magazine*, December 2, 1990, 56.
2. For the actual quote, see Richard Rorty, *Philosophy and the Mirror of Nature*, 30th Anniversary edn (Princeton, NJ: Princeton University Press, 2009): 176. "For philosophers like Chisholm and Bergmann, [ontological explanations of the relations between object and subject, nature and its mirror] *must* be attempted if the realism of common sense is to be preserved. The aim of all such explanations is to make truth something more than what Dewey called 'warranted assertability': more than what our peers will, *ceteris paribus*, let us get away with saying. . . . To choose between these approaches is to choose between truth as 'what it is good for us to believe' and truth as 'contact with reality'."
3. Ibid., 178. I will elaborate upon an important critical discussion of Rorty's coherence understanding of truth in Chapter 5.
4. See "Trotsky and the Wild Orchids," in Richard Rorty, *Philosophy and Social Hope* (New York: Penguin, 1999): 4.
5. Neil Gross, *Richard Rorty: The Making of an American Philosopher* (Chicago, IL: University of Chicago Press, 2008). See pp. 5–10 for Gross' discussion of the merits and deficiencies of various approaches to intellectual biography, including the way in which his sociological approach focusing on the formation of intellectual self-concept augments these approaches and ameliorates their deficiencies.
6. I owe the idea of presenting Rorty as a thinker who adopts several different intellectual *personae* to Jeffrey Stout. See Jeffrey Stout, "On Our Interest in Getting Things Right: Pragmatism without Narcissism," in *New Pragmatists*, ed. Cheryl Misak (Oxford: Oxford University Press, 2007).
7. See chapter 6, "Rorty as Elvis: Dewey's Reconstruction of Metaphysics," in John J. Stuhr, *Genealogical Pragmatism: Philosophy, Experience, and Community* (Albany, NY: SUNY Press, 1997): 126, where Stuhr memorably suggests that "Rorty is the Milli Vanilli of liberalism, merely lip-synching the old Elvis refrain: 'Don't Be Cruel'."

NOTES

8. For a discussion of Rorty's description of his philosophy as "therapeutic positivism," see Gross, *Richard Rorty*, 197–8.
9. Richard Rorty, "Response to Bernstein," in *Rorty and Pragmatsim: The Philosopher Responds to his Critics*, ed. Herman J. Saatkamp Jr. (Nashville, TN: Vanderbilt University Press, 1995): 71.
10. Stout, "On Our Interest in Getting Things Right: Pragmatism without Narcissism."
11. Donald Davidson, "A Coherence Theory of Truth and Knowledge," in *The Essential Davidson* (Oxford: Oxford University Press, 2006): 228.
12. See Richard Rorty, *Take Care of Freedom and Truth Will Take Care of Itself: Interviews with Richard Rorty*, ed. Eduardo Mendieta (Stanford, CA: Stanford University Press, 2006): 58.

CHAPTER 1: PHILOSOPHY AS EXISTENTIAL QUEST: RORTY'S LIFE IN THOUGHT

1. See Gross, *Richard Rorty*.
2. See Rüdiger Safranski, *Martin Heidegger: Between Good and Evil* (Cambridge, MA: Harvard University Press, 1999). All quotes from the review are taken from Richard Rorty, "A Master from Germany," *The New York Times Book Review*, May 3, 1998, 12–13. In drawing attention to the issues Rorty raises in this review, I in no way mean to suggest that Rorty's character was similar to Heidegger's, someone Rorty describes as "a resentful, ungenerous, disloyal and deceitful man," over whose thought "the smell of smoke from the crematories" will always linger. In marked distinction to such a characterization, Gross praises Rorty for his "openness and integrity." See Gross, *Richard Rorty*, xix.
3. Rorty, *Philosophy and Social Hope*, 5.
4. Gross, *Richard Rorty*, 16.
5. Ibid., 15.
6. Richard Rorty, *Philosophy and Social Hope*, 5.
7. Ibid., 6.
8. See Gross, *Richard Rorty*, 56.
9. Ror a discussion of this circle, see ibid., 29–36. For a more comprehensive history, see Alan M. Wald, *The New York Intellectuals: The Rise and Decline of the Anti-Stalinist Left from the 1930s to the 1980s* (Chapel Hill, NC: University of North Carolina Press, 1987).
10. Rorty, *Philosophy and Social Hope*, 6.
11. Ibid., 7.
12. Ibid., 7–8.
13. Gross, *Richard Rorty*, 33–4.
14. Ibid., 35.
15. Ibid., 30.
16. Ibid., 31.
17. Ibid., 36. James Rorty's parents were Irish immigrants, and Winifred Raushenbush's father was Walter Rauschenbusch, a key leader in the nineteenth-century Social Gospel movement in the United States.

[18] Ibid.
[19] Ibid., 38.
[20] James Rorty, "Hail-Or Farewell," *The Nation*, September 13, 1919, 365–6. Cited in Gross, *Richard Rorty*, 38.
[21] James Rorty, "The General Says Good-Bye," *The Nation*, July 19, 1919, 83–4. Cited in Gross, *Richard Rorty*, 38.
[22] John Dewey, *Democracy and Education: An Introduction to the Philosophy of Education* (New York: Macmillan, 1916): 305.
[23] See Gross, *Richard Rorty*, 47 ff.
[24] James Rorty, *Where Life is Better: An Unsentimental American Journey* (New York: Reynal & Hitchcock, 1936): 57–8.
[25] Ibid., 380. See also the discussion in Gross, *Richard Rorty*, 47–50.
[26] Ibid., 40. On James Rorty as a "Social Ecologist," see John Michael Boles, "James Rorty's Social Ecology," *Organization & Environment* 11(2) (June 1998): 155–79.
[27] Gross, *Richard Rorty*, 49.
[28] James Rorty, *Where Life is Better: An Unsentimental American Journey*, 128–9. See Gross' discussion in Gross, *Richard Rorty*, 41–50.
[29] James Rorty, *Where Life is Better: An Unsentimental American Journey*, 383.
[30] Gross, *Richard Rorty*, 63.
[31] Ibid., 63–4, note 2.
[32] Ibid., 63.
[33] Ibid., 65–6.
[34] Ibid., 67.
[35] Casey Nelson Blake, "Private Life and Public Commitment: From Walter Rauschenbusch to Richard Rorty," in *A Pragmatist's Progress? Richard Rorty and American Intellectual History*, ed. John Pettegrew (Lanham, MD: Rowman & Littlefield, 2000): 92.
[36] Gross, *Richard Rorty*, 68.
[37] See ibid., 69.
[38] Winifred Raushenbush, "Labor Analysis and Research," *New York Herald Tribune*, October 4, 1931, sec. XI, 15. Cited in Gross, *Richard Rorty*, 73.
[39] Ibid., 75.
[40] Ibid., 80.
[41] See, for example, Rorty's "Universality and Truth" and "Response to Habermas," in *Rorty and His Critics*, ed. Robert Brandom (Malden, MA: Blackwell, 2000b): 17 and 62.
[42] See Winifred Raushenbush, "The Idiot God Fashion," in *Woman's Coming of Age: A Symposium*, ed. Samuel Schmalhausen and V. F. Calverton (New York: Horace Liveright, 1931): 424. "One learns about civilization by studying its gods. Without question the god of our American acquisitive civilization is Things."
[43] Gross, *Richard Rorty*, 75.
[44] Ibid., 78. Gross' citation is from Winifred Raushenbush, *How to Dress in Wartime* (New York: Coward-McCann, 1942): 158.

NOTES

45 Gross, *Richard Rorty*, 82. See Winifred Raushenbush, *Robert E. Park: Biography of a Sociologist* (Durham, NC: Duke University Press, 1979).
46 Blake, "Private Life and Public Commitment: From Walter Rauschenbusch to Richard Rorty," 99.
47 See Gross, *Richard Rorty*, 90.
48 Ibid.
49 Rorty, *Philosophy and Social Hope*, 7.
50 Gross, *Richard Rorty*, 87.
51 See ibid., 88–91.
52 Ibid., 100.
53 Ibid.
54 Ibid., 86.
55 Rorty, *Philosophy and Social Hope*, 8.
56 Ibid., 8–9.
57 Ibid., 9.
58 Gross, *Richard Rorty*, 97; See also 305.
59 Winifred Raushenbush to Richard Rorty, September 30, 1949. Cited in ibid., 102.
60 See James Ryerson, "The Quest for Uncertainty: Richard Rorty's Pilgrammage," in *Take Care of Freedom and Truth Will Take Care of Itself: Interviews with Richard Rorty*, ed. Eduardo Mendieta (Stanford, CA: Stanford University Press, 2006): 4.
61 Gross, *Richard Rorty*, 105. Ryerson gives a somewhat different account of Rorty's decision to stay on at Chicago. Whereas Gross suggests Rorty made this decision after eventually concluding that he was unlikely to gain admittance to other prestigious graduate programs, Ryerson suggests that Rorty's decision was more intentional ("tantamount to a career choice"), and that Rorty reported to him that his father was "surprised and dismayed" by the decision. See Ryerson, "The Quest for Uncertainty: Richard Rorty's Pilgrammage," 5.
62 Gross, *Richard Rorty*, 106. The philosophical subfield called analytic philosophy finds its origin in the late nineteenth and early twentieth centuries, especially in the logical studies of such philosophers as Gottlob Frege and Bertrand Russel, whose work sought to provide a firm basis for human knowledge on the principles of logic. This logical emphasis encouraged an investigation into the supposed building blocks of language, with the dissecting method of philosophical "analysis" being perceived as the way to dig down through language to this more basic, logical level. A fundamental principle at work here is that of logical atomism, the idea that philosophical problems can be solved by showing the simple constituents of more complex notions. Such digging finally reaches some basic "unanalyzable" or "given" level, however conceived. Analytic approaches also tend to favor an empiricist paradigm, one that inherits the modern epistemological problem of discerning how the inner mental events to which our linguistic competence points might correspond to or mirror independent, external reality, thus serving as an incorrigible basis for knowledge. In America, this approach to the study of philosophy was deeply influenced by the

philosophers of the so-called Vienna Circle (such as Rudolf Carnap and Herbert Feigl), who emigrated to America in the late 1930s. Their program of logical positivism, with its "principle of verification," insisted that, with the exclusion of so-called analytic propositions (propositions that are true by definition, such as "all bachelors are unmarried"), only those statements that are empirically verifiable through human observation (paradigmatically, those able to be tested via the scientific method of investigation) are meaningful. This radical approach implied, not the falsity, but rather the meaninglessness of huge ranges of human language, including metaphysical, ethical, artistic, and religious statements. While much analytic philosophy would distance itself from positivism's radical empiricism, the emphasis on conceptual clarity, logical rigour, and science as the paradigm of human knowledge still retain a lasting impress in the movement. As Gross notes, Rorty's basic philosophical pluralism, combined with a pragmatic impulse to address common concerns, would constantly color his engagement with the work of analytic philosophers.

[63] Ibid., 111.
[64] Ibid., 112.
[65] Ibid., 113. Rorty discusses Hegel's influence on the development of his thought in Rorty, *Philosophy and Social Hope*, 11.
[66] Gross, *Richard Rorty*, 115.
[67] See the interview by Andrzej Szahaj, "Biography and Philosophy," in *Take Care of Freedom and Truth Will Take Care of Itself: Interviews with Richard Rorty*, ed. Eduardo Mendieta (Stanford, CA: Stanford University Press, 2006): 150.
[68] Rorty, *Philosophy and Social Hope*, 9.
[69] Cited in Gross, *Richard Rorty*, 123.
[70] Ibid., 125.
[71] Ibid., 129. In reciting the historical development of philosophy at Yale and Harvard during the period that extends from James to W. V. O. Quine (both of whom taught at Harvard), Gross relies on Bruce Kuklick, *A History of Philosophy in America, 1720–2000* (Oxford: Clarendon Press, 2001).
[72] Gross, *Richard Rorty*, 131.
[73] Bruce Kuklick, "Philosophy at Yale in the Century after Darwin," *History of Philosophy Quarterly* 21 (2004): 320 and 323. Cited in Gross, *Richard Rorty*, 132.
[74] Ibid., 134.
[75] Ibid.
[76] Ibid., 142.
[77] Ibid., 144.
[78] Charles Hartshorne, "Whitehead's Metaphysics," in *Whitehead and the Modern World: Science, Metaphysics, and Civilization: Three Essays on the Thought of Alfred North Whitehead* (Boston: Beacon Press, 1950): 25. Cited in Gross, *Richard Rorty*, 123.
[79] Ryerson, "The Quest for Uncertainty: Richard Rorty's Pilgrammage," 5. Gross, *Richard Rorty*, 146.

80 For a detailed discussion of Rorty's research program a this time, see ibid., 149–59.
81 Ibid., 152.
82 See the discussion in ibid., 154–6.
83 Richard Rorty, "Pragmatism, Categories, and Language," *Philosophical Review* 70 (1961): 197–8. Cited in Gross, *Richard Rorty*, 159.
84 Ibid., 158.
85 Ryerson, "The Quest for Uncertainty: Richard Rorty's Pilgrammage," 6.
86 Gross, *Richard Rorty*, 160.
87 Ibid., 161.
88 Ibid., 308–14.
89 Ibid., 189.
90 Richard Rorty to Michael and Dorothea Frede. Cited in ibid., 197; see also 317.
91 Ibid., 162. James Rorty's comments on his son's paper are from a letter cited on the same page.
92 Ibid., 226. Another telling episode involves Rorty's actions as President of the Eastern Division of the American Philosophical Association (APA), an organization dominated by analytic philosophers. Rorty declined to use his authority as President to quash a challenge leveled by nonanalytic philosophers to the legitimacy of the APA's 1979 executive elections, which resulted in the overturning of the election results and the election of nonanalytic philosophers to the APA's executive. Rorty's Presidential Address to the same congress is also memorable for mounting a criticism of the dominance of analytic philosophy that was in broad agreement with many of the complaints of the dissenters. See ibid., 216–27.
93 See ibid., 232–4. The quotation is from a letter from Richard Rorty to Gerald Freund, March 22, 1982, cited on 233.
94 Rorty, *Philosophy and Social Hope*, 12.

CHAPTER 2: THE PHILOSOPHICAL THERAPIST: RORTY'S CRITIQUE OF "PHILOSOPHY-AS-EPISTEMOLOGY"

1 Ludwig Wittgenstein, *Philosophical Investigations*, ed. G. E. M. Anscombe, 3rd edn (New York: Macmillan, 1958): 51e, §133. Rorty invokes this passage at the very conclusion of his essay, "The World Well Lost," in Richard Rorty,*Consequences of Pragmatism* (Minneapolis, MN: University of Minnesota Press, 1986): 3–18.
2 See Wittgenstein, *Philosophical Investigations*, 103e, §309.
3 Ibid., 51e, §133.
4 See Richard Rorty, "Intellectual Autobiography," in *The Philosophy of Richard Rorty*, ed. Randall E. Auxier and Lewis Edwin Hahn, vol. XXXII, The Library of Living Philosophers (Chicago, IL: Open Court, 2010): 13.
5 I should here point out that Michael Williams, in his "Introduction to the Thirtieth Anniversary Edition" of *Philosophy and the Mirror of Nature*, warns against reading too much into Rorty's sympathy with the therapeutic approach of thinkers like Wittgenstein or J. L. Austin:

NOTES

"Rorty is suspicious of the idea that philosophical problems are 'nonsensical' or result from abuses (or misunderstandings) of ordinary language. Anything has a sense if you give it one; and who knows where ordinary ways of talking end and philosophical theory takes over?" See Richard Rorty, *Philosophy and the Mirror of Nature*, xiv. While it is important to keep this caveat in mind, Rorty's therapeutic persona remains a key ingredient of his intellectual make-up, even if this particular characterization fails to provide an exhaustive description of his contribution to philosophy.

6 "Pathological" is perhaps too strong a word here, and I use it rather loosely, in extension of the philosophy as therapy metaphor. I should also take this opportunity to point out that, far from understanding himself to be undercutting the very *raison d'être* of analytic philosophy (that is to say, "stopping" it *tout court*), Rorty instead simply considers himself to be following through the dialectical consequences of its "post-positivist" strain, which he sees set in motion by philosophers like Sellars, and Quine. See Rorty's "Introduction" to Wilfrid Sellars, *Empiricism and the Philosophy of Mind* (Cambridge, MA: Harvard University Press, 1997): 5–6.

7 Rorty makes this point in an early (although only recently published) essay, entitled "The Philosopher as Expert." See Rorty, *Philosophy and the Mirror of Nature*, 395–421, esp. 413.

8 See ibid., 392–3.

9 See Rorty, "The World Well Lost."

10 Rorty, *Philosophy and the Mirror of Nature*, 8, 257, 269, 272, 315, and 380.

11 See "A Pragmatist View of Contemporary Analytic Philosophy," in Richard Rorty, *Philosophy as Cultural Politics: Philosophical Papers Volume 4* (Cambridge, MA: Cambridge University Press, 2007): 134–5.

12 Rorty's position here resembles that of the French philosopher Michel Foucault, who argues that once we understand the historically contingent character of any state of affairs, and therefore no longer accept its necessity, we may take up a freer relationship with it, and even alter it. See "What is Enlightenment?" in Michel Foucault, *The Foucault Reader*, ed. Paul Rabinow (Toronto: Random House, 1984): 46, where Foucault distinguishes his genealogical approach from Kant's "transcendental" one (which sought to discover the necessary preconditions of human knowledge): "[My] critique will be genealogical in the sense that it will not deduce from the form of what we are what it is impossible for us to do and to know; but it will separate out, from the contingency that has made us what we are, the possibility of no longer being, doing, or thinking, what we are, do, or think. It is not seeking to make possible a metaphysics that has finally become a science; it is seeking to give new impetus, as far and wide as possible, to the undefined work of freedom."

13 Rorty, *Philosophy and the Mirror of Nature*, 7.

14 Although I here use Wittgenstein's "picture" analogy, the reader should keep in mind Rorty's agreement with Donald Davidson's

rejection of a dualism of scheme and content (or interpretive paradigm and uninterpreted reality, picture frame and what it pictures, etc.). The important point of agreement between Rorty and Wittgenstein here is on the idea of something holding us captive, not necessarily on the idea of something being pictured. See Donald Davidson, "On the Very Idea of a Conceptual Scheme," in *The Essential Davidson* (Oxford: Oxford University Press, 2006): 196–208; Rorty, "The World Well Lost."

15 Wittgenstein, *Philosophical Investigations*, 48e, § 115.
16 I borrow the felicitous descriptive phrase "diagnostic narrative" from Williams' "Introduction to the Thirtieth Anniversary Edition" in Rorty, *Philosophy and the Mirror of Nature*, xvii.
17 Ibid., 11.
18 Ibid. On the historicist notion of "styles of reasoning," see Ian Hacking, *Historical Ontology* (Cambridge, MA: Harvard University Press, 2004): 159 ff.
19 See Thomas S. Kuhn, *The Structure of Scientific Revolutions* (Chicago, IL: University of Chicago Press, 1996). See also Rorty, *Philosophy and the Mirror of Nature*, 333.
20 See ibid., 131–6.
21 Ibid., 6–7.
22 See ibid., 176. Here Rorty suggests that he might have simply called this position "pragmatism," were that term not "a bit overladen." See the discussion in James Tartaglia, *Rorty and the Mirror of Nature* (London: Routledge, 2007): 128. As Tartaglia correctly notes, Rorty's linking of epistemological behaviorism to pragmatism here shows the ongoing and continuous influence of pragmatist philosophy in his work. The fact that he would only later fully embrace the term should not then be interpreted to mean that he only turned to pragmatism after writing *Philosophy and the Mirror of Nature*.
23 Rorty, *Philosophy and the Mirror of Nature*, 176. See also Rorty's "Introduction" to Sellars, *Empiricism and the Philosophy of Mind*, 6–7.
24 See Rorty, *Philosophy and the Mirror of Nature*, 133–6.
25 All citations in this paragraph are from ibid., 45.
26 In referring to "the Greeks" I think it is safe to say that Rorty means primarily the Aristotelian tradition (including of course the extension of the Aristotelian into the Middle Ages and into the sixteenth century). While it is true to say that the Aristotelian tradition assigned sensation to body in contradistinction to soul, this is not true of the neo-Platonism of a thinker like Augustine. According to this neo-Platonism, the soul takes up the data of the external senses, as collated in the inner wits by the imagination, and forms a phantasm (this is the soul's power of sensation). The neo-Platonic notion of phantasm thus makes the presentation of sensation a power of the soul, a characterization that is closer to the Cartesian understanding of representation than Aristotelian hylopmorphism. Rorty recognizes that there may be "more continuities in the history of these topics than the

story I am telling" in ibid., 50–1, n. 21. I thank my colleague Robert Sweetman for pointing out this nuance.

27 Ibid., 46–50. In his intriguing reading of Descartes' *Meditations*, Rorty follows the historical observations of Wallace Matson and Anthony Kenny, who both argue for the novelty of the modern use of such notions as "idea" and "sensation."

28 All citations in this paragraph are from ibid., 51–4.

29 A. G. A Balz, "Concerning the Thomistic and Cartesian Dualisms: A Rejoinder to Professor Mourant," *Journal of Philosophy* 54 (1957): 387; cited in Rorty, *Philosophy and the Mirror of Nature*, 57–8. Rorty suggests that one reason Descartes must cast about for a new way of formulating the mind-body distinction is because Aristotle's hylomorphic epistemology is "impossibly difficult to reconcile with the explanatory power of Galilean mechanics" (p. 57).

30 Rorty, *Philosophy and the Mirror of Nature*, 56. Here Rorty also cites the following quote from Descartes' *Third Meditation*: "Now as to what concerns ideas, if we consider them only in themselves and do not relate them to anything else beyond themselves, they cannot properly speaking be false; for whether I imagine a goat or a chimera, it is not the less true that I imagine the one rather than the other."

31 Ibid., 58.

32 Ibid., 61.

33 Ibid., 48. The two Locke citations contained in this passage are from the *Essay Concerning Human Understanding* (I, i, 8) and the "Letter to the Bishop of Worcester," respectively.

34 Ian Hacking, *Why Does Language Matter to Philosophy?* (Cambridge: Cambridge University Press, 1975): 12.

35 Rorty, *Philosophy and the Mirror of Nature*, 143–4.

36 All citations in this paragraph are from ibid., 144.

37 Ibid., 146.

38 Ibid., 140.

39 See ibid., 141.

40 Ibid., 146.

41 Immanuel Kant, *Critique of Pure Reason*, trans. Paul Guyer and Allen W. Wood (Cambridge: Cambridge University Press, 1999): 193–4 (A 51, B 75). The fuller quote reads: "Without sensibility no object would be given to us, and without understanding none would be thought. Thoughts without content are empty, intuitions without concepts are blind. . . . The understanding is not capable of intuiting anything, and the senses are not capable of thinking anything. Only from their unification can cognition arise."

42 See Rorty, *Philosophy and the Mirror of Nature*, 154–5. Here Rorty argues that Kant also shares the assumption, common to both rationalists and empiricists in the Modern era, that sensibility presents us with a manifold of intuitions or presentations to sense. Yet if, as Kant argues, we cannot be aware of or know anything about unsynthesized intuitions, how can we know that a manifold which cannot be presented as

NOTES

a manifold (because synthesis unifies it) *is* a manifold? Rorty concludes that Kantian terms like "intuition" and "concept" can only be defined contextually and not wholesale; they are theoretical posits designed to address lingering seventeenth-century epistemological issues, and make little sense when considered outside of that context.

43. Ibid., 148.
44. Ibid., 151.
45. Ibid., 161.
46. All quotations in this paragraph are from ibid., 159.
47. Ibid., 163.
48. Ibid., 176. My emphasis.
49. See Gilbert Ryle, *The Concept of Mind*, 60th Anniversary edn (New York: Routledge, 2009): 30–3. A simple example of a dispositional concept that Ryle uses is the "brittleness" of glass. Brittleness names a disposition or propensity of the glass to behave or act in a certain way under certain conditions, even if those conditions do not now in fact obtain. (A glass may be brittle even if it is not presently being shivered.) Ryle considers such mental concepts as "knowing" and "believing" to be dispositional in a similar, if more complex, sense. Our belief that the earth is round (to use another one of his examples) reveals itself in and through a complex variety of behavioral dispositions, without these being necessarily accompanied by any private, inner state, or an interior mental "harping" on the belief in question.
50. All citations in this paragraph are from Rorty, *Philosophy and the Mirror of Nature*, 109–10.
51. Ibid., 110–11, 182–3. Rorty's way of keeping these two different senses of knowledge apart has the apparently counterintuitive consequence that a prelinguistic infant can know it is in pain while at the same time not know what a pain is. Yet, as Stanley Cavell points out, such an infant can also pet kitties without yet knowing what kitties are. See Stanley Cavell, *The Claim of Reason: Wittgenstein, Skepticism, Morality, and Tragedy* (Oxford and New York: Oxford University Press, 1999): 172. Rorty treats the difficult matter of prelinguistic awareness in Rorty, *Philosophy and the Mirror of Nature*, 182–92.
52. Ibid., 183.
53. Tartaglia, *Rorty and the Mirror of Nature*, 114. Tartaglia's fourth chapter, "Linguistic Holism" (from which this quote is taken), provides an excellent explanatory summary of the way Rorty uses the work of Sellars and Quine.
54. Rorty, *Philosophy and the Mirror of Nature*, 170.
55. Ibid. Tartaglia describes the common message that Rorty draws from both Sellars and Quine as "the lynch-pin" of *Philosophy and the Mirror of Nature*'s "destructive case," adding that "Rorty has boiled down and reshaped it so much since then that it has effectively become his own." See Tartaglia, *Rorty and the Mirror of Nature*, 113.
56. See Rorty's introduction to Sellars, *Empiricism and the Philosophy of Mind*, 3. Rorty affirms that the "fundamental thought" running

NOTES

throughout Sellars' essay is Kant's suggestion that "intuitions without concepts are blind." For a discussion of this ambiguity in Rorty's presentation of Sellars, see Tartaglia, *Rorty and the Mirror of Nature*, 116–17.
57 Sellars, *Empiricism and the Philosophy of Mind*, 62. Emphasis in original.
58 Ibid., 63.
59 Rorty's "Introduction," in ibid., 3–4.
60 Ibid., 76.
61 Rorty's "Introduction," in ibid., 4.
62 Ibid., 14.
63 Rorty's "Introduction," in ibid., 4–5. See ibid., 107, where Sellars offers the following gloss: ". . . concepts pertaining to such inner episodes as thoughts are primarily and essentially intersubjective, as intersubjective as the concept of a positron, and . . . the reporting role of these concepts—the fact that each of us has a privileged access to his thoughts—constitutes a dimension of the use of these concepts which is built on and presupposes this intersubjective status."
64 Rorty's "Introduction," in ibid., 6.
65 W. V. O. Quine, "Two Dogmas of Empiricism," in *From a Logical Point of View* (Cambridge, MA: Harvard University Press, 1953): 41.
66 Sellars, *Empiricism and the Philosophy of Mind*, 79. Emphases in original.
67 See Quine, "Two Dogmas of Empiricism," 42–3: ". . . the total field is so underdetermined by its boundary conditions, experience, that there is much latitude of choice as to what statements to reëvaluate in the light of any single contrary experience."
68 Rorty, *Philosophy and the Mirror of Nature*, 211–12.
69 See ibid., 389–94.
70 Rorty, *Philosophy as Cultural Politics: Philosophical Papers Volume 4*, 3.
71 Ibid., 5. See also x.

CHAPTER 3: THE LIBERAL IRONIST: RORTY'S CULTURAL POLITICS

1 See "Trotsky and the Wild Orchids," in Rorty, *Philosophy and Social Hope*, 3–5. Here Rorty lists and describes the criticisms he has received from both ends of the political spectrum, suggesting that "[i]f there is anything to the idea that the best intellectual position is one which is attacked with equal vigour from the political right and the political left, then I am in good shape."
2 For an example of such Left-leaning criticism, see Richard J. Bernstein, "One Step Forward, Two Steps Backward: Richard Rorty on Liberal Democracy and Philosophy," *Political Theory* 15(4) (November 1987): 538–63.
3 See Rorty, *Philosophy and Social Hope*, 3, where he cites Neal Kozody's charge that "it is not enough for [Rorty] that American students

NOTES

should be merely mindless; he would have them positively mobilized for mindlessness."

4 See Richard Rorty, "Thugs and Theorists: A Reply to Bernstein," *Political Theory* 15(4) (November 1987): 564–80. I will explore this response in more detail below.
5 Rorty, *Philosophy and Social Hope*, 5.
6 Ibid., 20.
7 John Dewey, *Democracy and Education: An Introduction to the Philosophy of Education* (New York: Macmillan, 1916): 340–7.
8 Ibid., 347.
9 Richard Rorty, *Essays on Heidegger and Others: Philosophical Papers, Volume 2* (Cambridge: Cambridge University Press, 1991): 121; Rorty, *Philosophy and Social Hope*, 20.
10 Richard Rorty, *Objectivity, Relativism, and Truth: Philosophical Papers Volume 1* (Cambridge: Cambridge University Press, 1991): 14.
11 Richard Rorty, *Contingency, Irony, and Solidarity* (Cambridge: Cambridge University Press, 1989): xv. Rorty invokes the labels "historicism" and "nominalism" to describe his general rejection of what he views as lingering Platonic tendencies in the Western philosophical tradition. His historicism temporalizes those items Plato considered eternal (and so should not be confused with Sir Karl Popper's critique of Marxist historicism, which holds that history reveals the operation of determinate laws that preordain the outcome of historical processes); his nominalism rejects a philosophical realism that (1) only accepts unchanging universals as truly real (as opposed to being simply abstract linguistic predicates, or "names" for these abstract predicates), and (2) holds the world of ordinary appearance, of time and change, to be deficient and illusory.
12 Ibid., xiii.
13 John Dewey, *Reconstruction in Philosophy* (Boston: Beacon Press, 1957): 156.
14 Rorty, *Philosophy as Cultural Politics: Philosophical Papers Volume 4*, 6–7.
15 Dewey, *Reconstruction in Philosophy*, 158.
16 Ibid., 159.
17 Rorty, *Contingency, Irony, and Solidarity*, 8.
18 Ibid., xvi.
19 See ibid., 6. Here Rorty clarifies that he is not suggesting we replace objective criteria of choice with subjective criteria, or reason with will. The freedom to develop alternatives he would have his reader recognize, then, is not the freedom of wilful, arbitrary, individual choice, but more like the room or space a culture experiences, over time, to lose the habit of playing certain language games and to acquire the habit of playing new ones. His notion of freedom is thus reminiscent of Dewey's emphasis on the possibility of retail, piecemeal change, change that, cumulatively and over time, may indeed become revolutionary.

NOTES

[20] Ibid., 10. For Rorty's primary engagement with Davdison's philosophy, see Rorty, *Objectivity, Relativism, and Truth: Philosophical Papers Volume 1*, pt. II.

[21] Ibid.

[22] Ibid., 10–11. See also Rorty's "Response to Farrell," in *Rorty and Pragmatism: The Philosopher Responds to his Critics*, ed. Herman J. Saatkamp (Nashville, TN: Vanderbilt University Press, 1995): 191: "I have been trying to mark out a position that does not take sides between subject and object, mind and world, but that instead tries to erase the contrast between them. I have, so to speak, been trying to lose *both* us and the world. . . . I want to stop using the us-world contrast, and thus to get rid of the realism-antirealism issue." Rorty here agrees with Davidson that, because our "touch" with the world can never really be in doubt, the question of its very possibility should not trouble us very long. See Davidson, "A Coherence Theory of Truth and Knowledge, 236–8.

[23] Ibid., 228. As we have already seen, Rorty puts this point by contrasting coercion and conversation. The world causes us to have beliefs, but it does not coercively decide for us which ones we must adopt in response to its causal pressures. That matter is only decided in the logical space of reasons, in the arena of ongoing human conversation. The difference between Davidson's and Rorty's views of objectivity is the focus of Chapter 5.

[24] Rorty, *Contingency, Irony, and Solidarity*, 5. As Rorty himself notes on several occasions, his use and interpretation of Davidson is controversial, and has been contested by several scholars, including Davidson himself.

[25] See "Texts and Lumps" in Rorty, *Objectivity, Relativism, and Truth: Philosophical Papers Volume 1*, 81.

[26] All citations in this paragraph are from ibid. Rorty here reveals the rather "Promethean" side of his pragmatism, one much in evidence in the work of his fellow pragmatist, Roberto Unger. See Roberto Mangabeira Unger, *The Self Awakened: Pragmatism Unbound* (Cambridge, MA: Harvard University Press, 2007). To what extent Rorty recognizes any limitation to "language as a way of grabbing hold of causal forces and making them do what we want," or any way that a certain inevitable passive receptivity limits the range of human spontaneity, is not easy to determine. We will have cause to further examine this Promethean or antiauthoritarian side of Rorty's thinking in the remaining two chapters.

[27] This interpretation is mainly due to the critical reception of Rorty's essay "The World Well Lost" in Richard Rorty, *Consequences of Pragmatism: Essays 1972–1980* (Minneapolis, MN: University of Minnesota Press, 1986). See Susan Haack, "Vulgar Pragmatism: An Unedifying Prospect," in Saatkamp, *Rorty and Pragmatism*; and Frank B. Farrell, "Rorty and Antirealism," in ibid.

NOTES

28 See Davidson, "On the Very Idea of a Conceptual Scheme," 196–208; Donald Davidson, "A Nice Derangement of Epitaphs," in *The Essential Davidson* (Oxford: Oxford University Press, 2006): 251–65.
29 Davidson, "A Nice Derangement of Epitaphs," 265.
30 Davidson, "On the Very Idea of a Conceptual Scheme," 208.
31 In "The Very Idea of Human Answerability to the World" Rorty describes Davidson's position as follows: "Brandom, Sellars, and Davidson can all agree that the space of reasons as we find it is also, by and large, the shape of the world. Because most of our beliefs must be true, we can make no sense of the idea that a great gulf might separate the way the world is and the way we describe it." Richard Rorty, *Truth and Progress: Philosophical Papers Volume 3* (Cambridge: Cambridge University Press, 1998): 147–8. I thank Barry Allen for sage advice regarding the preceding reading of Davidson. As mentioned, I explore Davidson's position in more detail in Chapter 5.
32 Rorty, *Contingency, Irony, and Solidarity*, 17.
33 Ibid., 13.
34 Ibid., 25.
35 Ibid., 25–6.
36 Ibid., 29.
37 Ibid., 37–9.
38 Ibid., 39–40.
39 Ibid., 40.
40 Ibid., 53.
41 Ibid., 59–60. See also Wilfrid Sellars, *Science and Metaphysics* (London: Routledge & Kegan Paul, 1968): chapters 6 and 7. For more on Rorty's understanding of the contingency as opposed to the necessity of our sense of "we," see "Solidarity or Objectivity?" "The Priority of Democracy to Philosophy," and "On Ethnocentrism: A Reply to Clifford Geertz," in Rorty, *Objectivity, Relativism, and Truth: Philosophical Papers Volume 1*.
42 Rorty, *Contingency, Irony, and Solidarity*, 61.
43 See Charles Taylor, *A Secular Age* (Cambridge, MA: Harvard University Press, 2007): chapter 16.
44 Rorty, *Contingency, Irony, and Solidarity*, 73.
45 Ibid., 75.
46 Ibid.
47 Ibid., 77.
48 Ibid., 87–8.
49 My gloss here somewhat obscures the fact that Rorty's way of describing the ironist's predicament remains rather silent regarding the ironist's ongoing reliance on the resources provided by a public, inherited final vocabulary for her efforts to fashion a private, idiosyncratic one.
50 Ibid., 37.
51 See ibid., 61–8. As Rorty notes, Habermas often expresses a worry about the antisocial consequences of both romantic expressive

NOTES

individualism and modern "subject-centred reason." See Jürgen Habermas, *The Philosophical Discourse of Modernity: Twelve Lectures* (Cambridge, MA: MIT Press, 1990).

52 Rorty, *Contingency, Irony, and Solidarity*, 89.
53 See ibid., 120 and 194. In contrasting irony to metaphysics, Rorty opts for the former because he does not think it possible to develop a final vocabulary that will not break up into a public and a private portion. Yet he insists that these theoretically nonsythesizable imperatives can and should be combined in an individual life. Even so, he rejects the idea that public moral concerns must automatically trump private aesthetic ones: ". . . our responsibilities to others constitute *only* the public side of our lives, a side which competes with our private affections and our private attempts at self-creation, and which has no *automatic* priority over such private motives. Whether it has priority in any given case is a matter for deliberation, a process which will usually not be aided by appeal to 'classical first principles'. Moral obligation is . . . to be thrown in with a lot of other considerations, rather than automatically trump them" (p. 194).
54 Ibid., 35.
55 Ibid., 91.
56 Ibid., 65.
57 Ibid., xv.
58 Rorty, *Consequences of Pragmatism*, 168.
59 Rorty, *Contingency, Irony, and Solidarity*, 94.
60 Ibid., 141.
61 Ibid., 144.
62 Ibid., 160.
63 Ibid., 161.
64 Ibid., 163.
65 Ibid., 164. Of course, if Humbert had cared to notice Lolita as someone who has her own story, someone capable of suffering, he would not have been so ready to enfold her into his own story, and then he may well have kept his hands off her.
66 Ibid., 173.
67 Ibid., 183.
68 Ibid., 181–2.
69 Ibid., 182.
70 Rorty, *Contingency, Irony, and Solidarity*.
71 Ibid., 184–5.
72 Ibid., 196.
73 See "Protests and Power," *The New Republic*, November 3, 2011.
74 See Richard Rorty, "Two Cheers for Elitism," *The New Yorker*, January 30, 1995, 88.
75 See Richard Rorty, *Achieving Our Country: Leftist Thought in Twentieth Century America* (Cambridge, MA: Harvard University Press, 1998): 102–5.
76 Rorty, "Thugs and Theorists: A Reply to Bernstein," 569–70.

NOTES

77 Ibid., 569.
78 Rorty, *Philosophy and Social Hope*, 18.
79 See Rorty, "Thugs and Theorists: A Reply to Bernstein," 570. Rorty would surely have shared Stout's critique of such Left-wing theorists as Žižek and Alain Badiou, who appear to prefer the revolutionary political muscle of a Lenin or a Stalin to the "weak" force of grassroots democratic reform. See Jeffrey Stout, *Blessed Are the Organized: Grassroots Democracy in America* (Princeton, NJ: Princeton University Press, 2010): 249–50.
80 Address, June 29, 1966, to United States Junior Chamber of Commerce, Detroit, Michigan.

CHAPTER 4: THE ANTICLERICAL PROPHET: RORTY AND RELIGION

1 Richard Rorty, *Contingency, Irony, and Solidarity* (Cambridge: Cambridge University Press, 1989): 45.
2 Ibid.
3 See Rorty's "The Very Idea of Human Answerability to the World: John McDowell's Version of Empiricism," in Rorty, *Truth and Progress: Philosophical Papers Volume 3*. Here Rorty claims the work of Robert Brandom in support of his view that the epistemic norms of correctness and incorrectness are the products of conferred social status, a status that results from our ongoing answerability to one another as opposed to our answerability to the nonhuman world.
4 See Rorty's conclusion to "Trotsky and the Wild Orchids," briefly discussed in the previous chapter, in Rorty, *Philosophy and Social Hope*.
5 John Dewey, *A Common Faith* (New Haven, CT: Yale University Press, 1934): 46.
6 Richard Rorty, "Anticlericalism and Atheism," in *The Future of Religion*, ed. Santiago Zabala (New York: Columbia University Press, 2005): 33.
7 Rorty, *Philosophy and Social Hope*, 20.
8 Rorty, "Anticlericalism and Atheism," 32–3. For a thorough treatment of the difference Rorty's distinction between these two types of atheism makes for future work in the philosophy of religion and theology, see G. Elijah Dann, *After Rorty: The Possibilities for Ethics and Religious Belief* (London: Continuum, 2006). Dann argues that by obviating the possibility of the first type of atheism, Rorty's critique of philosophy-as-epistemology creates room for like-mindedly antirepresentationalist and "edifying" approaches to the study and practice of religion.
9 Rorty, "Anticlericalism and Atheism," 33.
10 Ibid.
11 See Richard Rorty, *Objectivity, Relativism, and Truth: Philosophical Papers Volume 1*, 66–7. For an opposite and highly capable interpretation of the net social impact of historical Christianity, see David

NOTES

Bentley Hart, *Atheist Delusions: The Christian Revolution and Its Fashionable Enemies* (New Haven, CT: Yale University Press, 2009).

[12] This is the title of an excellent book on Rorty. See D. Vaden House, *Without God or His Doubles: Realism, Relativism, and Rorty* (Leiden: Brill, 1994).

[13] Rorty, *Objectivity, Relativism, and Truth: Philosophical Papers Volume 1*, 7.

[14] See Hanne Andrea Kraugerud and Bjørn Ramberg, "The New Loud: Richard Rorty, Quietist?" *Common Knowledge* 16(1) (December 25, 2010): 54.

[15] Rorty, *Objectivity, Relativism, and Truth: Philosophical Papers Volume 1*, 5.

[16] Thomas Nagel, *The View from Nowhere* (Oxford: Oxford University Press, 1989): 9.

[17] Rorty, *Objectivity, Relativism, and Truth: Philosophical Papers Volume 1*, 12.

[18] Rorty, *Philosophy and the Mirror of Nature*, 139 ff. On the emergence of skepticism as a pressing intellectual concern in the seventeenth century, see Louis Dupré, *Passage to Modernity: An Essay in the Hermeneutics of Nature and Culture* (New Haven, CT: Yale University Press, 1995): 86.

[19] Jeffrey Stout, "On Our Interest in Getting Things Right: Pragmatism Without Narcissism," in *New Pragmatists*, ed. Cheryl Misak (Oxford: Oxford University Press, 2007): 9–10.

[20] Ibid., 10.

[21] See the "Introduction" and "Is Truth a Goal of Inquiry?" in Rorty, *Truth and Progress: Philosophical Papers Volume 3*.

[22] Stout, "On Our Interest in Getting Things Right: Pragmatism Without Narcissism," 8.

[23] Richard Rorty, "Response to Bernstein," 71. Cited in Stout, "On Our Interest in Getting Things Right: Pragmatism Without Narcissism," 9.

[24] Stout, "On Our Interest in Getting Things Right: Pragmatism Without Narcissism."

[25] Cornel West et al., "Pragmatism and Democracy: Assessing Jeffrey Stout's Democracy and Tradition," ed. Jason Springs, *Journal of the American Academy of Religion* 78(2) (June 2010): 423. I should point out that, in spite of these misgivings concerning Stout's attempt to salvage a pragmatist understanding of objectivity, Rorty had already significantly nuanced his views on objectivity by the time of this exchange. See his "Response to Ramberg" in Brandom, *Rorty and His Critics*, 370–7. I address this issue in the following chapter.

[26] Rorty, *Philosophy and the Mirror of Nature*, 376–7.

[27] See Karl Marx, "Theses on Feuerbach," in *The Marx-Engels Reader*, ed. Robert C. Tucker, 2nd edn (W. W. Norton, 1978): 145. Here Rorty also echoes Dewey's concerns regarding conservative fears of growth and change, and the concomitant longing for fixed, antecedent order (cited above in Chapter 3, note 16).

NOTES

28 Rorty, *Philosophy and the Mirror of Nature*, 377.
29 Ibid., 388–9.
30 Rorty, *Contingency, Irony, and Solidarity*, 5.
31 Rorty, *Philosophy and the Mirror of Nature*, 182–8.
32 See "Deconstruction and Pragmatism: Is Derrida a Private Ironist or a Public Liberal?" and "Metaphysics in the Dark: A Response to Richard Rorty and Ernesto LaClau," in Simon Critchley, *Ethics, Politics, Subjectivity: Essays on Derrida, Levinas and Contemporary French Thought* (London: Verso, 1999). I thank James Olthuis for bringing these essays to my attention.
33 Rorty, *Objectivity, Relativism, and Truth: Philosophical Papers Volume 1*, 199.
34 Ibid., 201.
35 Ibid., 201–2. My emphasis. I wish Rorty had used the word "object" here instead of "animal," insofar as his usage tacitly affirms our habitual mistreatment of animals.
36 Rorty, *Contingency, Irony, and Solidarity*, xv.
37 Emmanuel Levinas, *Totality and Infinity: An Essay on Exteriority* (Pittsburgh: Duquesne University Press, 1969): 50–1.
38 Ibid., 50.
39 See Critchley, *Ethics, Politics, Subjectivity*, 98. My emphasis.
40 Ibid., 97.
41 Ibid., 98.
42 Richard Rorty, "Response to Simon Critchley," in *Deconstruction and Pragmatism*, ed. Chantal Mouffe (London: Routledge, 1996): 42.
43 Richard Rorty, "Comments on Taylor's 'Paralectics'," in *On the Other: Dialogue And/or Dialectics*, ed. Robert P. Scharlemann (Lanham, MD: University Press of America, 1991): 75–8.
44 Rorty, "Response to Simon Critchley," 42.
45 See Jeffrey Metzger, "Richard Rorty's Disenchanted Liberalism," *Contemporary Pragmatism* 7(1) (June 2010): 109–0: "Apparently there is nothing for us to do, theoretically or practically, except to 'thank our lucky stars' for the current of history in which we presently happen to be drifting along."
46 Rorty, "Comments on Taylor's 'Paralectics'," 75.
47 Ibid., 76.
48 As I explore to some extent in the following section, I think Rorty's caricature of Levinas's interpretation of transcendence here misses the mark significantly. Levinas's transcendence is more fragile and "immanent" than Rorty's portrayal admits. See Levinas, *Totality and Infinity: An Essay on Exteriority*, 52; Emmanuel Levinas, "Difficult Freedom," in *The Levinas Reader*, ed. Seán Hand (Oxford: Blackwell, 1989): 251.
49 J. Wesley Robbins, "'You Will Be Like God': Richard Rorty and Mark C. Taylor on the Theological Significance of Human Language Use," *The Journal of Religion* 72(3) (July 1992): 389.
50 Ibid., 392.

NOTES

51 Dewey, *A Common Faith*, 52–3. Cited in Rorty, *Objectivity, Relativism, and Truth: Philosophical Papers Volume 1*, 69–70.

52 Rorty, *Objectivity, Relativism, and Truth: Philosophical Papers Volume 1*, 70.

53 For an astute analysis of Rorty's ambivalent attitude toward religion, see Nicholas H. Smith, "Rorty on Religion and Hope," *Inquiry* 48(1) (2005): 76–98.

54 See Rorty, *Philosophy and Social Hope*, 202–4.

55 Peter Dews, "'The Infinite Is Losing Its Charm': Richard Rorty's Philosophy of Religion and the Conflict Between Therapeutic and Pragmatic Critique," in *The Philosophy of Richard Rorty*, vol. xxxii, The Library of Living Philosophers (Chicago and La Salle: Open Court, 2010): 647.

56 See Rorty, "Anticlericalism and Atheism," 34–6. Rorty's desire to take religion and transcendence out of the epistemic arena also forms a nonpolitical rationale for his conclusion that religious devotion properly belongs in the private sphere. I explore his privatization thesis in the next section of this chapter.

57 Dews, "The Infinite Is Losing Its Charm," 646.

58 Rorty, "Anticlericalism and Atheism," 40. Dews reading of this passage is less conciliatory than mine: "[Rorty's position] is said with his characteristic blend of ingenuousness and irony, that 'any millennium now' destroys—as much as it expresses—hope. But if, as Rorty ardently believed, 'hope for social justice is . . . the only basis for a worthwhile human life', then the consequences of such destruction must be grave indeed." Dews, "The Infinite Is Losing Its Charm," 652. The latter quote is from the essay "Failed Prophecies, Glorious Hopes," in Rorty, *Philosophy and Social Hope*, 204.

59 See also Rorty, *Philosophy and Social Hope*, 203. Here Rorty suggests that parents and teachers should encourage young people to read the New Testament as well as the Communist Manifesto, adding: "The young will be morally better for having done so."

60 Dewey, *A Common Faith*, 52–3. My emphasis.

61 Dews, "The Infinite Is Losing Its Charm," 651.

62 Richard Kearney, *The God Who May Be: A Hermeneutics of Religion* (Indianapolis, IN: Indiana University Press, 2001); Richard Kearney, *Anatheism: Returning to God After God* (New York: Columbia University Press, 2011).

63 Levinas, "Difficult Freedom," 252.

64 Rorty, "Anticlericalism and Atheism," 40.

65 Rorty, *Philosophy as Cultural Politics: Philosophical Papers Volume 4*, 135. See also "Religious Faith, Intellectual Responsibility, and Romance" in Rorty, *Philosophy and Social Hope*, 161.

66 Richard Rorty, "Reply to Jeffrey Stout," in *The Philosophy of Richard Rorty*, vol. xxxii, The Library of Living Philosophers (Chicago and La Salle: Open Court, 2010): 548.

NOTES

67 Rorty, *Philosophy and Social Hope*, 168–74; Stephen L. Carter, *The Culture of Disbelief: How American Law and Politics Trivialize Religious Devotion* (New York: Basic Books, 1993).
68 Rorty, *Philosophy and Social Hope*, 172.
69 Ibid., 171.
70 Ibid., 172.
71 Ibid. For an elaboration of Rorty's views on the problematic nature of dogmatically religious conversation-defeaters in political discussion, especially those of the "because God says so" variety, see Dann, *After Rorty*, 64–6.
72 Rorty, *Philosophy and Social Hope*, 173.
73 See Jürgen Habermas, *The Theory of Communicative Action, Volume 2: Lifeworld and System: A Critique of Functionalist Reason*, trans. Thomas McCarthy (Boston: Beacon Press, 1985): 89; John Rawls, "The Idea of Public Reason Revisited," in *The Law of Peoples* (Boston: Harvard University Press, 2001). As Stout notes, Rorty's recommendation on this score is more pragmatic than that of Rawls or Habermas, focusing on premises shared *in fact* as opposed to proposing an epistemological standard for public reasons that can be universally shared *in principle*. See Jeffrey Stout, *Democracy and Tradition* (Princeton, NJ: Princeton University Press, 2004): 85.
74 Rorty, *Philosophy and Social Hope*, 173.
75 Ibid., 171. Rorty's "bad taste" comment is found at Rorty, *Philosophy and Social Hope*, 169.
76 Nicholas Wolterstorff, "An Engagement with Rorty," *Journal of Religious Ethics* 31(1) (March 2003): 132.
77 Ibid., 136–7.
78 Rorty, *Philosophy and Social Hope*, 172.
79 Wolterstorff, "An Engagement with Rorty," 135.
80 In the final two sections of his paper, Wolterstorff also offers a description of Rorty's "pragmatist Darwinism" that highlights its particularist character, one that includes a rather religious-sounding celebration of Deweyan democracy under the heading of the "American Sublime." Wolterstorff thus suggests that Rorty's desire for religion to behave itself through privatization might really be a "menacing" attempt to claim cultural authority for his particular conception of the good. See ibid., 136–9.
81 The following are the primary sources of Stout's critique: Stout, *Democracy and Tradition*, 85–91; West et al., "Pragmatism and Democracy: Assessing Jeffrey Stout's Democracy and Tradition," 434–7; Jeffrey Stout, "Rorty on Religion and Politics," in *The Philosophy of Richard Rorty*, vol. xxxii, The Library of Living Philosophers (Chicago and La Salle: Open Court, 2010): 523–45.
82 Stout, *Democracy and Tradition*, 90.
83 Ibid.
84 Stout, "Rorty on Religion and Politics," 529.

NOTES

85. West et al., "Pragmatism and Democracy: Assessing Jeffrey Stout's Democracy and Tradition," 419.
86. Stout, "Rorty on Religion and Politics," 537–8.
87. Richard Rorty, "Religion in the Public Square: A Reconsideration," *Journal of Religious Ethics* 31(1) (March 2003): 148–9. The other major amendment Rorty makes to his privatization recommendation in this essay is to restrict his anticlericalism to ecclesiastical organizations "beyond the parish level": "Only the latter are the target of secularists like myself. Our anti-clericalism is aimed at the Catholic bishops, the Mormon General Authorities, the televangelists, and all the other religious professionals who devote themselves not to pastoral care but to promulgating orthodoxy and acquiring economic and political clout. We think that it is mostly religion above the parish level that does the damage. For ecclesiastical organizations typically maintain their existence by deliberately creating ill-will toward people who belong to other such organizations, and toward people whose behavior they presume to call immoral. They thereby create unnecessary human misery." Rorty, "Religion in the Public Square: A Reconsideration," 142. Stout criticizes this position for displaying the same unpragmatic essentialism with regard to ecclesiastical organizations beyond the parish level as Rorty often displays toward theism in general. See Stout, "Rorty on Religion and Politics," 536.
88. Rorty, "Religion in the Public Square: A Reconsideration," 147.
89. For a discussion of the Deweyan provenance of this point, see "Pragmatism as Romantic Polytheism," in Rorty, *Philosophy as Cultural Politics: Philosophical Papers Volume 4*, 38–9.
90. "Cultural Politics and the Question of the Existence of God," in ibid., 8–9. Dann agrees that table-thumping appeals to a final nonhuman authority only mask human interpretive choices that are deeply colored by contingent historical sentiment. It therefore follows that a Christian, for example, can claim to hold a biblically oriented view without denying the fallibility and reformability of their particular, historically inflected interpretation of what they nevertheless take to be authoritative sacred scripture. See Dann, *After Rorty*, 104 ff.
91. West et al., "Pragmatism and Democracy: Assessing Jeffrey Stout's Democracy and Tradition," 440.
92. Stout, "Rorty on Religion and Politics," 548–9.
93. Rorty, "Reply to Jeffrey Stout," 548–9.
94. Ibid., 549.

CHAPTER 5: WHAT IS TRUTH *FOR*?
THE CONVERSATION CONTINUES

1. This, at least, is Rorty's take on the situation. See "Solidarity or Objectivity?" in Richard Rorty, *Objectivity, Relativism, and Truth: Philosophical Papers Volume 1*, 30.
2. Ibid., 22.
3. Ibid.

NOTES

4 Ibid. Rorty's emphasis on "us" in the previous quote.
5 Ibid., 23.
6 Ibid., 23–4.
7 Ibid., 24.
8 See Bjørn Ramberg, "Post-Ontological Philosophy of Mind: Rorty versus Davidson," in *Rorty and His Critics*, ed. Robert B. Brandom (Malden, MA: Blackwell, 2000): 351–70; Richard Rorty, "Response to Bjørn Ramberg," in *Rorty and His Critics*, ed. Robert B. Brandom (Malden, MA: Blackwell, 2000): 370–7.
9 Rorty, *Philosophy and the Mirror of Nature*, 178.
10 Donald Davidson, "A Coherence Theory of Truth and Knowledge," 228.
11 Ibid., 225.
12 Donald Davidson, "Three Varieties of Knowledge," in *A. J. Ayer: Memorial Essays*, ed. A. Phillips Griffiths, vol. 30, Royal Institute of Philosophy Supplements (Cambridge: Cambridge University Press, 1992): 156–7.
13 Davidson, "A Coherence Theory of Truth and Knowledge," 237.
14 Ibid., 238.
15 Davidson, "Three Varieties of Knowledge," 159–60.
16 Ibid., 160.
17 Ibid., 157. Wittgenstein first raises the hypothetical notion of a strictly private language, and then proceeds to argue for its impossibility, because he thinks that something like this impossible notion is implicit in mainstream Western epistemology since Descartes. See Wittgenstein, *Philosophical Investigations*, §§244–71.
18 The phrase "normative scorekeeping" is Stout's label for a position Brandom develops at length. See Robert B. Brandom, *Making It Explicit: Reasoning, Representing, and Discursive Commitment* (Cambridge, MA: Harvard University Press, 1998): 180–98. See also Jeffrey Stout, "Radical Interpretation and Pragmatism: Davidson, Rorty, and Brandom on Truth," in *Radical Interpretation in Religion*, ed. Nancy K. Frankenberry (Cambridge: Cambridge University Press, 2002).
19 See chapter 7, "Excursus on Wittgenstein's Vision of Language," in Stanley Cavell, *The Claim of Reason: Wittgenstein, Skepticism, Morality, and Tragedy* (Oxford and New York: Oxford University Press, 1999): 172–3 ff. This example forms part of Cavell's larger argument for the conclusion that linguistic competence entails a mastery of the norms that implicitly govern the use of concepts.
20 Cavell's gloss on this situation is much more eloquent than mine: "Kittens—what we call 'kittens'—do not exist in her world yet, she has not acquired the forms of life which contain them. They do not exist in something like the way cities and mayors will not exist in her world until long after pumpkins and kittens do; or like the way God or love or responsibility or beauty do not exist in our world; we have not mastered, or we have forgotten, or we have distorted, or learned through fragmented models, the forms of life which could make utterances like 'God exists' or 'God is dead' or 'I love you' or 'I cannot do

otherwise' or 'Beauty is but the beginning of terror' bear all the weight they could carry, express all they could take from us. We do not know the meaning of the words." Ibid., 172–3.
21. Stout, "Radical Interpretation and Pragmatism: Davidson, Rorty, and Brandom on Truth," 26. For a more detailed account of this position, Stout here refers the reader to Brandom, *Making It Explicit*, 623–50.
22. Davidson, "Three Varieties of Knowledge," 157. As Ramberg helpfully explains, while Davidson's semantic theory of truth does invoke a relation between language and the world, it does not rely on this relation to do any epistemic work (because only a belief can justify another belief). A relation of correspondence is thus simply "a postulate of the theory" that is "derived from its theorums" and not "the source of the empirical content of a theory of truth." While "epistemologically useless," Ramberg argues that correspondence for Davidson nevertheless remains "semantically necessary." See Bjørn T. Ramberg, *Donald Davidson's Philosophy of Language: An Introduction* (New York: Blackwell, 1989): 44 ff; cf. 75–6, 124.
23. Davidson, "Three Varieties of Knowledge," 160.
24. Ibid.
25. Ibid.
26. Ibid., 165. This is essentially the same point Sellars makes in "Empiricism and the Philosophy of Mind," explored in Chapter 2, and roughly what Wittgenstein is driving at in his private language argument.
27. Ibid., 166.
28. Ibid., 164. As we have already seen, Rorty too worries about the dehumanizing consequences of a reductionistic objectivism in Rorty, *Philosophy and the Mirror of Nature*, 376–7. Ramberg also emphasizes this point in his exchange with Rorty, much of which is devoted to defending Davidson's particular way of arguing for the irreducibility of mental vocabularies to the vocabularies of the physical sciences. See Ramberg, "Post-Ontological Philosophy of Mind: Rorty versus Davidson."
29. Ramberg, "Post-Ontological Philosophy of Mind: Rorty versus Davidson," 362.
30. Although Ramberg does not use the language of "steering," I choose this word in order to evoke the uniqueness of the causal role humans are able to play in the world, a power to alter the environment that is qualitatively different in kind than the power of, say, the beaver to alter her environment through dam building.
31. Ramberg, "Post-Ontological Philosophy of Mind: Rorty versus Davidson," 363.
32. Ibid., 362.
33. Ibid., 363.
34. Ibid.
35. Ibid.
36. Rorty, "Response to Bjørn Ramberg," 371.
37. Ibid., 372.

[38] Ibid., 373.
[39] Ibid., 374.
[40] Ibid., 376.
[41] Ibid., 374. Rorty's emphasis.
[42] Ibid., 375. Ramberg might say that there is no sense in which we can (locally) separate ourselves from a global nexus (Reality) in which we must remain perpetually immersed and engaged, and so we cannot become intentional with respect to it, and therefore cannot say anything meaningful about it, or anything that could be submitted to our intersubjective activity of normative scorekeeping. Our linguistic capacities only open up local intentional spaces, not global ones. But Rorty is right: *pace* Descartes' attempts to doubt everything, inhabiting a global intentional space is both unthinkable and impossible.
[43] Ibid., 376.
[44] Ibid.
[45] Ibid., 374.
[46] Ibid., 376.
[47] Ibid.
[48] Ibid.
[49] See "Pragmatism without Method" in Rorty, *Objectivity, Relativism, and Truth: Philosophical Papers Volume 1*, 67.
[50] Kraugerud and Ramberg, "The New Loud: Richard Rorty, Quietist?" 59.
[51] Ibid.
[52] Ibid., 63.
[53] Richard Rorty, "Response to Robert Brandom," in *Rorty and His Critics*, ed. Robert B. Brandom (Malden, MA: Blackwell, 2000): 188.
[54] Ibid., 187.
[55] Robert B. Brandom, "Vocabularies of Pragmatism: Synthesizing Naturalism and Historicism," in *Rorty and His Critics*, ed. Robert B. Brandom (Malden, MA: Blackwell, 2000a): 178.
[56] Ibid.
[57] Rorty, "Response to Robert Brandom," 189. The interior quote is from Brandom, "Vocabularies of Pragmatism: Synthesizing Naturalism and Historicism," 180.
[58] See Rorty, *Contingency, Irony, and Solidarity*, 39–40.
[59] Rorty, "Response to Robert Brandom," 189.

CONCLUSION: PRAGMATISM AS THE APOTHEOSIS OF THE FUTURE—RORTY, HOPE, AND THE AMERICAN SUBLIME

[1] For Stout's discussion of sacred value, see Jeffrey Stout, *Blessed Are the Organized: Grassroots Democracy in America*, 211. On 221, Stout argues further that the possession and cultivation of a sense of sacred value is not restricted to religious observers.
[2] See Rorty, *Philosophy and Social Hope*, 19–20.

NOTES

3. Rorty, *Philosophy and the Mirror of Nature*, 377.
4. Rorty, *Contingency, Irony, and Solidarity*, 7.
5. See ibid., 6. This sense of finitude and fallibility sits in tension with what in Chapter 3 I describe as his more "promethean" side, evident in the following passage from the "Afterword" to *Philosophy and Social Hope*: "The environment in which we human beings live poses problems to us but, unlike a capitalized Reason or a capitalized Nature, we owe it neither respect nor obedience. Our task is to master it, or to adapt ourselves to it, rather than to represent it or correspond to it." See Rorty, *Philosophy and Social Hope*, 269.
6. See Kraugerud and Ramberg, "The New Loud: Richard Rorty, Quietist?" 56. "We can better understand Rorty's engagement with truth if we view it not as an incessantly repeated invitation to drop the topic but as an attempt to co-opt the discussion. He wants not to end the conversation but to change it. Truth is a topic that serves Rorty well, allowing him to perform just the sort of conversational reversal that is his characteristic strategy for bringing change to philosophy. Rorty responds to so many philosophers in such detail over so many years, on a topic that he claims to find futile, because only by sustained engagement can he dig mental tracks along which we will not find our commonsensical values and commitments leading us to the question 'What is truth?' While explicitly saying that we can abandon metaphysics as a matter of choice, an act of will, Rorty by his own practice indicates that he well knows that it is not so. We attend to theories of truth because representationalist metaphysics has or is an entrenched vocabulary, and vocabularies are not simply tools at our disposal; they are aspects of our practice, changeable only by changing our practice."
7. Rorty, *Philosophy and the Mirror of Nature*, 369.
8. Ibid., 378.
9. Ibid., 379.
10. Richard Rorty, "Response to Robert Brandom," 189.
11. Ralph Waldo Emerson, *Selected Writings of Ralph Waldo Emerson* (New York: Random House, 1992): 261.
12. Rorty, *Philosophy and Social Hope*, 27.
13. Ibid.
14. Emerson, *Selected Writings of Ralph Waldo Emerson*, 261.
15. Rorty, *Philosophy and Social Hope*, 28.
16. Ibid., 120.

BIBLIOGRAPHY

Because there are already several excellent comprehensive bibliographies of Rorty's work on the market, the following bibliography lists only works cited and consulted in the writing of the present book. The Library of Living Philosophers volume dedicated to Rorty's work, entitled *The Philosophy of Richard Rorty* and edited by Lewis Edwin Hahn and Randall E. Auxier (Lasalle and Chicago: Open Court, 2010), contains a complete bibliography of Rorty's published works. This volume also contains previously unpublished material by Rorty, and many excellent critical secondary essays. As far as secondary bibliographies go, the reader may wish to consult Richard Rumana's *Richard Rorty: An Annotated Bibliography of Secondary Literature* (Amsterdam: Editions Rodopi, 2002), as well as the bibliography found in *Richard Rorty*, edited by Charles Guignon and David R. Hiley (Cambridge: Cambridge University Press, 2003). *The Rorty Reader*, edited by Christopher J. Voparil and Richard Bernstein (Malden, MA: Blackwell, 2010), also includes an excellent guide to key secondary texts, in addition to an effective selection of important primary texts.

There are also several volumes of essay collections devoted to Rorty's work. In addition to the Library of Living Philosophers volume mentioned above, the most notable of these are *Rorty and His Critics*, edited by Robert Brandom (Malden, MA: Blackwell, 2000), the four-volume *Richard Rorty*, edited by Alan Malachowski (London: Sage, 2002), *Rorty and Pragmatism: The Philosopher Responds to his Critics*, edited by Herman J. Saatkamp (Nashville, TN: Vanderbilt University Press, 1995), and *Reading Rorty: Critical Responses to* Philosophy and the Mirror of Nature *and Beyond*, edited by Alan Malachowski (Cambridge, MA: Blackwell, 1990).

Balz, A. G. A., "Concerning the Thomistic and Cartesian Dualisms: A Rejoinder to Professor Mourant," *Journal of Philosophy* 54(12) (1957): 383–90.

Bernstein, Richard J., "One Step Forward, Two Steps Backward: Richard Rorty on Liberal Democracy and Philosophy," *Political Theory* 15(4) (November 1987): 538–63.

Blake, Casey Nelson, "Private Life and Public Commitment: From Walter Rauschenbusch to Richard Rorty," in *A Pragmatist's Progress? Richard*

Rorty and American Intellectual History, ed. John Pettegrew (Lanham, MD: Rowman & Littlefield, 2000): 85–101.
Boles, John Michael, "James Rorty's Social Ecology," *Organization & Environment* 11(2) (June 1998): 155–79.
Brandom, Robert B., ed., *Making It Explicit: Reasoning, Representing, and Discursive Commitment* (Cambridge, MA: Harvard University Press, 1998).
—*Rorty and His Critics* (Malden, MA: Blackwell, 2000).
—"Vocabularies of Pragmatism: Synthesizing Naturalism and Historicism," in *Rorty and His Critics*, ed. Robert B. Brandom (Malden, MA: Blackwell, 2000): 156–83.
Carter, Stephen L., *The Culture of Disbelief: How American Law and Politics Trivialize Religious Devotion* (New York: Basic Books, 1993).
Cavell, Stanley, *The Claim of Reason: Wittgenstein, Skepticism, Morality, and Tragedy* (Oxford and New York: Oxford University Press, 1999).
Critchley, Simon, *Ethics, Politics, Subjectivity: Essays on Derrida, Levinas and Contemporary French Thought* (London: Verso, 1999).
Dann, G. Elijah, *After Rorty: The Possibilities for Ethics and Religious Belief* (London: Continuum, 2006).
Davidson, Donald, "A Coherence Theory of Truth and Knowledge," in *The Essential Davidson* (Oxford: Oxford University Press, 2006): 225–41.
—"A Nice Derangement of Epitaphs," in *The Essential Davidson* (Oxford: Oxford University Press, 2006): 251–65.
—"On the Very Idea of a Conceptual Scheme," in *The Essential Davidson* (Oxford: Oxford University Press, 2006): 196–208.
—"Three Varieties of Knowledge," in *A. J. Ayer: Memorial Essays*, ed. A. Phillips Griffiths, 30: 153–66. Royal Institute of Philosophy Supplements (Cambridge: Cambridge University Press, 1992).
Dewey, John, *A Common Faith* (New Haven, CT: Yale University Press, 1934).
—*Democracy and Education: An Introduction to the Philosophy of Education* (New York: Macmillan, 1916).
—*Reconstruction in Philosophy* (Boston: Beacon Press, 1957).
Dews, Peter, "'The Infinite Is Losing Its Charm': Richard Rorty's Philosophy of Religion and the Conflict Between Therapeutic and Pragmatic Critique," in *The Philosophy of Richard Rorty*, xxxii: 635–55. The Library of Living Philosophers (Chicago and La Salle: Open Court, 2010).
Dupré, Louis, *Passage to Modernity: An Essay in the Hermeneutics of Nature and Culture* (New Haven, CT: Yale University Press, 1995).
Emerson, Ralph Waldo, *Selected Writings of Ralph Waldo Emerson* (New York: Random House, 1992).
Foucault, Michel, *The Foucault Reader*, ed. Paul Rabinow (Toronto: Random House, 1984).
Gross, Neil, *Richard Rorty: The Making of an American Philosopher* (Chicago, IL: University of Chicago Press, 2008).
Habermas, Jürgen, *The Philosophical Discourse of Modernity: Twelve Lectures* (Cambridge, MA: MIT Press, 1990).

—*The Theory of Communicative Action, Volume 2: Lifeworld and System: A Critique of Functionalist Reason*, trans. Thomas McCarthy (Boston: Beacon Press, 1985).
Hacking, Ian, *Historical Ontology* (Cambridge, MA: Harvard University Press, 2004).
—*Why Does Language Matter to Philosophy?* (Cambridge: Cambridge University Press, 1975).
Hart, David Bentley, *Atheist Delusions: The Christian Revolution and Its Fashionable Enemies* (New Haven, CT: Yale University Press, 2009).
Hartshorne, Charles, "Whitehead's Metaphysics," in *Whitehead and the Modern World: Science, Metaphysics, and Civilization: Three Essays on the Thought of Alfred North Whitehead* (Boston: Beacon Press, 1950).
House, D. Vaden, *Without God or His Doubles: Realism, Relativism, and Rorty* (Leiden: Brill, 1994).
Kant, Immanuel, *Critique of Pure Reason*, trans. Paul Guyer and Allen W. Wood (Cambridge University Press, 1999).
Kearney, Richard, *Anatheism: Returning to God After God* (New York: Columbia University Press, 2011).
—*The God Who May Be: A Hermeneutics of Religion* (Indianapolis, IN: Indiana University Press, 2001).
Klepp, L. S. "Every Man a Philosopher King," *New York Times Magazine* (December 2, 1990): 56.
Kraugerud, Hanne Andrea and Bjørn Ramberg, "The New Loud: Richard Rorty, Quietist?" *Common Knowledge* 16(1) (December 2010): 48–65.
Kuhn, Thomas S., *The Structure of Scientific Revolutions* (Chicago, IL: University of Chicago Press, 1996).
Kuklick, Bruce, *A History of Philosophy in America, 1720–2000* (Oxford: Clarendon Press, 2001).
—"Philosophy at Yale in the Century After Darwin," *History of Philosophy Quarterly* 21 (2004): 313–36.
Levinas, Emmanuel, "Difficult Freedom," in *The Levinas Reader*, ed. Seán Hand (Oxford: Blackwell, 1989): 249–66.
—*Totality and Infinity: An Essay on Exteriority* (Pittsburgh: Duquesne University Press, 1969).
Marx, Karl, "Theses on Feuerbach," in *The Marx-Engels Reader*, 2nd edn, ed. Robert C. Tucker (New York: W. W. Norton, 1978): 143–5.
Metzger, Jeffrey, "Richard Rorty's Disenchanted Liberalism," *Contemporary Pragmatism* 7(1) (June 2010): 107–28.
Nagel, Thomas, *The View from Nowhere* (Oxford: Oxford University Press, 1989).
"Protests and Power," *The New Republic*, November 3, 2011.
Quine, W. V. O., "Two Dogmas of Empiricism," in *From a Logical Point of View: Nine Logico-Philosophical Essays* (Cambridge, MA: Harvard University Press, 1980): 20–46.
Ramberg, Bjørn T., *Donald Davidson's Philosophy of Language: An Introduction* (New York: Blackwell, 1989).

—"Post-Ontological Philosophy of Mind: Rorty versus Davidson," in *Rorty and His Critics*, ed. Robert B. Brandom (Malden, MA: Blackwell, 2000): 351–70.
Raushenbush, Winifred, *How to Dress in Wartime* (New York: Coward-McCann, 1942).
—"The Idiot God Fashion," in *Woman's Coming of Age: A Symposium*, ed. Samuel Schmalhausen and V. F. Calverton (New York: Horace Liveright, 1931): 424–46.
—"Labor Analysis and Research," *New York Herald Tribune,* October 4, 1931, sec. XI.
—*Robert E. Park: Biography of a Sociologist* (Durham, NC: Duke University Press, 1979).
Rawls, John, "The Idea of Public Reason Revisited," in *The Law of Peoples: With "The Idea of Public Reason Revisited"* (Boston: Harvard University Press, 2001): 129–80.
Robbins, J. Wesley, "'You Will Be Like God': Richard Rorty and Mark C. Taylor on the Theological Significance of Human Language Use," *The Journal of Religion* 72(3) (July 1992): 389–402.
Rorty, James, "The General Says Good-Bye," *The Nation,* July 19, 1919.
—"Hail-Or Farewell," *The Nation,* September 13, 1919.
—*Where Life Is Better: An Unsentimental American Journey* (New York: Reynal & Hitchcock, 1936).
Rorty, Richard, *Achieving Our Country: Leftist Thought in Twentieth Century America* (Cambridge, MA: Harvard University Press, 1998).
—"Anticlericalism and Atheism," in *The Future of Religion*, ed. Santiago Zabala (New York: Columbia University Press, 2005): 29–41.
—"Comments on Taylor's 'Paralectics'," in *On the Other: Dialogue And/or Dialectics*, ed. Robert P. Scharlemann (Lanham, MD: University Press of America, 1991).
—*Consequences of Pragmatism: Essays 1972–1980* (Minneapolis, MN: University of Minnesota Press, 1986).
—*Contingency, Irony, and Solidarity* (Cambridge: Cambridge University Press, 1989).
—*Essays on Heidegger and Others: Philosophical Papers, Volume 2* (Cambridge: Cambridge University Press, 1991).
—"Intellectual Autobiography," in *The Philosophy of Richard Rorty*, ed. Randall E. Auxier and Lewis Edwin Hahn, vol. xxxii, The Library of Living Philosophers (Chicago, IL: Open Court, 2010): 3–24.
—"A Master From Germany," *The New York Times Book Review,* May 3, 1998.
—*Objectivity, Relativism, and Truth: Philosophical Papers Volume 1* (Cambridge: Cambridge University Press, 1991).
—*Philosophy and Social Hope* (New York: Penguin, 1999).
—*Philosophy and the Mirror of Nature*, 30th Anniversary edn (Princeton, NJ: Princeton University Press, 2009).
—*Philosophy as Cultural Politics: Philosophical Papers Volume 4* (Cambridge, MA: Cambridge University Press, 2007).

- "Pragmatism, Categories, and Language," *Philosophical Review* 70 (1961): 197–223.
- "Religion in the Public Square: A Reconsideration," *Journal of Religious Ethics* 31(1) (March 2003): 141–9.
- "Reply to Jeffrey Stout," in *The Philosophy of Richard Rorty*, xxxii: 546–9. The Library of Living Philosophers (Chicago and La Salle: Open Court, 2010).
- "Response to Richard Bernstein," in *Rorty and Pragmatsim: The Philosopher Responds to His Critics*, ed. Herman J. Saatkamp Jr. (Nashville, TN: Vanderbilt University Press, 1995): 68–71.
- "Response to Bjørn Ramberg," in *Rorty and His Critics*, ed. Robert B. Brandom (Malden, MA: Blackwell, 2000): 370–7.
- "Response to Robert Brandom," in *Rorty and His Critics*, ed. Robert B. Brandom (Malden, MA: Blackwell, 2000): 183–90.
- "Response to Simon Critchley," in *Deconstruction and Pragmatism*, ed. Chantal Mouffe (London: Routledge, 1996): 41–6.
- "Thugs and Theorists: A Reply to Bernstein," *Political Theory* 15(4) (November 1987): 564–80.
- *Truth and Progress: Philosophical Papers Volume 3* (Cambridge: Cambridge University Press, 1998).
- "Two Cheers for Elitism," *The New Yorker*, January 30, 1995.
- "The World Well Lost," in *Consequences of Pragmatism* (Minneapolis, MN: University of Minnesota Press, 1986): 3–18.

Ryerson, James, "The Quest for Uncertainty: Richard Rorty's Pilgrammage," in *Take Care of Freedom and Truth Will Take Care of Itself: Interviews with Richard Rorty*, ed. Eduardo Mendieta (Stanford, CA: Stanford University Press, 2006): 1–17.

Ryle, Gilbert, *The Concept of Mind,* 60th Anniversary edn (New York: Routledge, 2009).

Saatkamp, Herman J., ed., *Rorty and Pragmatism: The Philosopher Responds to His Critics* (Nashville, TN: Vanderbilt University Press, 1995).

Safranski, Rüdiger, *Martin Heidegger: Between Good and Evil* (Cambridge, MA: Harvard University Press, 1999).

Sellars, Wilfrid, *Empiricism and the Philosophy of Mind* (Cambridge, MA: Harvard University Press, 1997).
- *Science and Metaphysics* (London: Routledge & Kegan Paul, 1968).

Smith, Nicholas H., "Rorty on Religion and Hope," *Inquiry* 48(1) (2005): 76–98.

Stout, Jeffrey, *Blessed Are the Organized: Grassroots Democracy in America* (Princeton, NJ: Princeton University Press, 2010).
- *Democracy and Tradition* (Princeton, NJ: Princeton University Press, 2004).
- "On Our Interest in Getting Things Right: Pragmatism Without Narcissism," in *New Pragmatists*, ed. Cheryl Misak (Oxford: Oxford University Press, 2007): 7–31.

—"Radical Interpretation and Pragmatism: Davidson, Rorty, and Brandom on Truth," in *Radical Interpretation in Religion*, ed. Nancy K. Frankenberry (Cambridge: Cambridge University Press, 2002): 25–52.

—"Rorty on Religion and Politics," in *The Philosophy of Richard Rorty*, xxxii: 523–45. The Library of Living Philosophers (Chicago and La Salle: Open Court, 2010).

Stuhr, John J., *Genealogical Pragmatism: Philosophy, Experience, and Community* (Albany, NY: SUNY Press, 1997).

Szahaj, Andrzej, "Biography and Philosophy," in *Take Care of Freedom and Truth Will Take Care of Itself: Interviews with Richard Rorty*, ed. Eduardo Mendieta (Stanford, CA: Stanford University Press, 2006): 148–60.

Tartaglia, James, *Rorty and the Mirror of Nature* (London: Routledge, 2007).

Taylor, Charles, *A Secular Age* (Cambridge, MA: Harvard University Press, 2007).

Unger, Roberto Mangabeira, *The Self Awakened: Pragmatism Unbound* (Cambridge, MA: Harvard University Press, 2007).

Wald, Alan M., *The New York Intellectuals: The Rise and Decline of the Anti-Stalinist Left from the 1930s to the 1980s* (Chapel Hill, NC: University of North Carolina Press, 1987).

West, Cornel, Richard Rorty, Stanley Hauerwas, and Jeffrey Stout, "Pragmatism and Democracy: Assessing Jeffrey Stout's Democracy and Tradition," ed. Jason Springs. *Journal of the American Academy of Religion* 78(2) (June 2010): 413–48.

Wittgenstein, Ludwig, *Philosophical Investigations*, ed. G. E. M. Anscombe, 3rd edn (New York: Macmillan, 1958).

Wolterstorff, Nicholas, "An Engagement with Rorty," *Journal of Religious Ethics* 31(1) (March 2003): 129–39.

INDEX

abnormal discourse (or science) 52–4, 125–6, 144–5, 175
   see also Kuhn, Thomas
acculturation 132
Achieving Our Country 111
Adler, Mortimer 32–3
Adorno, Theodor 13
agency 163
alienation 100–1
American sublime 177–9, 199n. 80
analytic philosophy 7, 8, 15, 34, 35, 36, 38–44, 66, 72–3, 75, 183n. 62, 185n. 92, 186n. 6
analytic-synthetic distinction 72, 74–6
   see also Quine
anthropocentrism 122–3
antiauthoritarianism 148, 167, 192n. 26
anticlericalism 9, 117, 200n. 87
   see also atheism
antirepresentationalism 84, 93, 120
argument 29, 66, 81, 102, 171
   inadequacy for sensitizing one to suffering of others 107
   religious forms of 141
Aristotle 56–7, 61, 62, 76, 187n. 26, 188n. 29
atheism 9, 114–18, 129, 133, 140, 145–7

atomism 71
Augustine, St 187n. 26
authenticity 21, 79, 99, 102, 106
   see also individuality, individualism
authoritarianism 22–3, 122–4, 132, 170
authority 10, 81–2, 141, 171, 199n. 80
   religious understanding of 146–7
   as socially determined 146–7
autonomy 79, 102, 106
   see also freedom
Ayer, A. J. 56

Balz, A. G. A. 58
being 37, 87, 170
belief 66, 72, 77
   Davidson on justification of 91
   holism and 75–6, 144–5
   as including a conception of objectivity 154–5
   as justified by objects in the world 150, 166
   as Rylean disposition 69
   see also knowledge; proposition
Berkeley, Bishop George 73
Bernstein, Richard 112
Blake, Casey Nelson 27
Bloom, Allan 35
Bloom, Harold 7, 177

body 57–9, 187n. 26
  see also mind-body problem; physical
Brandom, Robert 10, 122, 146, 170–1, 195n. 3

capitalism 21, 22, 23, 24, 108, 110–11
Carnap, Rudolph 8, 34, 35, 40, 183n. 62
Carter, Stephen 140, 142
category 64, 74
  see also Kant, Immanuel
cause 61–3, 65, 70–1, 91–3, 96–7, 124, 126, 155, 160–1, 168
  Rorty's distinction of reason or justification from 62–3, 65–8, 71, 91, 161, 192n. 23
Cavell, Stanley 156, 189n. 51, 201n. 20
censorship 111
certainty 48, 49, 60, 67, 77, 121, 139
chance 85–6, 90, 94
  see also contingency
change 49–50, 53, 87, 112, 125, 133, 176, 191n. 19, 204n. 6
  see also novelty (natality, new); reformist politics vs revolutionary politics
Christianity 9, 128–9
civil rights 112
cognition 63, 68
  exceeded or preceded by ethical relation to another person 130
coherence 153–9
  see also objectivity (normative triangulation and)
commitment 101
  contingency of 98–9
communication 155–7
  see also conversation; intersubjectivity; language
communism 108

community, balancing individualism and 22, 113
  contingency of 90, 95, 97–8
  knowledge and linguistic competence dependent upon 73, 159, 164
  moral recognition dependent on membership of 128–9
concept 64–5, 68, 72, 73, 74, 188n. 41
  dispositional 189n. 49
  see also Kant, Immanuel
confrontation 66–7, 72, 75
  see also correspondence; reference
conscience 98
  see also morality
consciousness 58–61, 73
  and ethics 130
  see also mind
consequences 87–8
Consequences of Pragmatism 48
conservatism 87, 124
  Rorty and 80
constructivism 93
contingency 49–51, 53–4, 83–5, 90–8, 99, 103, 128, 129, 132, 186n. 12, 200n. 90
Contingency, Irony, and Solidarity 7, 83–5, 90–110, 143
conversation 123, 126, 148, 155, 168–72, 177
  with a capital 'C' 174–5
  vs coercion or confrontation 8, 66–7, 72, 192n. 23
  as context for justification 77
  as edifying and abnormal 125, 145
  stopped by religion 9, 140–1
  see also communication; intersubjectivity; language
correspondence 9, 10, 108, 121–2, 148, 150–1, 163
  vs coherence 155

Davidson and 91, 166
see also metaphysics; objectivity; reality; reference; truth; world
creativity 37, 38, 113
Critchley, Simon 126, 129–31
criticism, Rorty's ability to both evade and respond to 149–59
cruelty 83, 102–3, 105–7, 129–30, 180n. 7
cultural politics 8, 77–8, 117–18, 167

Dann, G. Elijah 195n. 8, 199n. 71, 200n. 90
Darwinism 120, 159, 163, 199n. 80
Davidson, Donald 10, 11, 153, 186n. 14, 192n. 22, 193n. 31, 202n. 22
  influence on Rorty 90–3, 120, 164–5
  and 'normative triangulation' 153–9, 161, 165
democracy 9, 22, 23, 29, 80–1, 83, 112, 140, 143–6, 148
Derrida, Jacques 1, 41, 83, 112, 127
Descartes, René 51, 54, 56–60, 61, 64, 68–9, 76, 120, 162, 188nn. 29, 30, 203n. 42
description 91–2, 113, 124, 126, 164
  freedom from inherited 95–6, 177
  'thick' 105
Dewey, John 8, 9, 22, 32–3, 44, 49, 81–3, 86–8, 113, 116, 131, 134–5, 137, 153, 177, 178, 180n. 2, 191n. 19, 196n. 27
Dews, Peter 135–7, 198n. 58
dignity 122–3, 128–9, 170
discovery (finding), vs creating or making 97, 100, 104
divinity 115–18, 137–9
  see also God
Dostoevsky, Fyodor 33

doubt 66, 101
dualism 49, 54, 58, 68
  of scheme and content 93, 187n. 14
  see also mind-body problem

Elliot, T. S. 33
emancipation 135–6
  see also freedom; liberation
Emerson, Ralph Waldo 22, 178
empiricism 62, 64, 72, 117
  analytic philosophy and 183n. 62
Enlightenment 97, 140
epistemological behaviorism 55, 67–76
  as another name for pragmatism 187n. 22
epistemology 2, 7, 42, 44, 49, 54, 60, 66, 77, 120–1, 159
  pragmatist lack of 150–2
  see also justification; knowledge
equality 102, 108
essentialism 144–5
eternality, eternalization 52–4, 59–60
ethnocentrism 151, 153
  see also intersubjectivity; solidarity
explanation 63, 65, 67, 91–2
  see also cause

fact 75, 91–2
faith 117, 145
  see also religion
fallibility, fallibilism 49–50, 67, 176
false 94, 150
Falwell, Jerry 139
feeling 58
Feigl, Herbert 183n. 62
feminism 26
Feuerbach, Ludwig 25

final vocabulary 99–101, 143–4, 194n. 53
Fine, Arthur 139
finitude 81, 176, 204n. 5
flourishing 135
Foucault, Michel 1, 186n. 12
foundation, foundationalism 49–50, 54, 55, 58, 65, 70, 76, 84, 96, 114–15, 117, 127
  see also permanent framework
freedom 9, 10, 11, 22, 31, 36, 37, 76, 80, 83, 90, 91, 97, 102, 110–11, 113, 116, 122
  expressive 29, 30, 143, 170, 191n. 19
  to pursue novel possibility 124, 175
  as a result of the recognition of contingency 95–6, 98, 186n. 12
  as substitute for truth 84–9, 108–9, 113, 169–70, 177
  see also emancipation; liberation
Frege, Gottlob 183n. 62
Freud, Sigmund 95–6
future 89, 98, 108, 113, 115, 118, 135–7
  pragmatism as the apotheosis of 177–9
  see also consequences; growth; hope; transcendence (temporal interpretation of); utopia, utopianism

Galileo 94, 188n. 29
Geertz, Clifford 42
genealogy 50, 54, 56, 186n. 12
given 65, 68, 70–2, 74, 94
God 38, 114, 116–18, 123, 141, 145, 146, 147
  Rorty on keeping the word in one's final vocabulary 133–9

Gross, Neil 6, 20, 38–43, 181n. 1, 183n. 61, 184n. 62
  on Rorty's "intellectual self-concept" 12–17
growth 87
  as moral end 178–9

Habermas, Jürgen 41, 142, 193–4n. 51, 199n. 73
Hacking, Ian 61
happiness 148, 165, 167–70, 175
Hart, David Bentley 195–6n. 11
Hartshorne, Charles 34, 35, 37
Hegel, G. W. F. 56, 86, 94, 95, 129, 184n. 65
Heidegger, Martin 13, 41, 49, 181n. 2
historicism 53, 80, 84, 86, 89, 191n. 11
history of philosophy, Rorty's interest in 35, 36, 41, 42
holiness 115, 118, 136
holism 71–2, 75, 144–5
  see also Quine
homosexuality 141
Hook, Sidney 34, 38
hope 25–6, 77, 89, 106, 108, 113, 118, 134–8, 178–9, 198n. 58
  see also future; transcendence (temporal interpretation of); utopia, utopianism
human nature (or human essence) 85–6, 102, 104, 129
  as universal ground of ethics and solidarity 107, 131, 150
human rights 129
Hume, David 63, 73, 117
humiliation 102, 104
  see also cruelty; pain
Humphrey, Hubert 112–13
Hutchins, Robert Maynard 31

idea 61–3, 71–2, 188nn. 27, 30
ideal 137
  God as union of actual and 134–5

INDEX

idealism 160
ideologiekritik 111
ideology 25
imagination 58–9, 77, 83, 111, 175–6
immediacy 65
 see also given
impression 61, 63, 73
incorrigibility 49, 67
incuriosity, unethical result of 106
individuality, individualism 21, 22, 23, 24, 29, 30, 81–3, 103, 113, 168, 194n. 51
indubitability 59–60, 67, 71
 see also certainty
inference 66
 see also judgment; predication
Institute of Advanced Study (Princeton) 41–2
intellectualism 28–9
intentionality 156, 162, 203n. 42
 irreducibility to the physical 163
 see also meaning
interpretation 156–7
intersubjectivity 41, 119, 148, 153, 190n. 63
 as opposed to objectivity 2, 151
 see also solidarity
intuition 63–5, 68, 72, 74, 188nn. 41, 42
 see also Kant, Immanuel
invariance 65
 see also permanent framework
irony 83, 98–103, 194n. 53

James, William 8, 87, 150–1
Jeffers, Robinson 20
Jesus Christ 31
Johnston, Lyndon 112
Johnston, Mark 122
Judaism 128–9
judgment 62–4, 73, 156

justice 6, 17–19, 21, 22, 81, 102, 130, 136, 138, 144, 174
justification 8, 65–6, 71–2, 76, 77, 202n. 22
 confusion of causes with 61–3, 91
 and ethnocentrism 151, 153
 knowledge as product of 68, 73–4
 of political arrangements 97
 of self 99
 truth as 150–1
 see also epistemology; knowledge; warranted assertability

Kant, Immanuel 51, 54, 56, 63–5, 68, 72, 74, 117, 188nn. 41, 42, 190n. 56
Kearney, Richard 137
Kenny, Anthony 188n. 27
Khomeini, Ayatollah 139
Kierkegaard, Søren 56
knowledge 2, 3, 48, 50, 59, 81, 85, 93, 121, 189n. 51
 as accuracy of representation or correspondence 51, 66
 Aristotle's hylomorphic conception of 56
 as diagnostically reinterpreted by Rorty's "epistemological behaviorism" 67–75
 as justified true belief or warranted assertability 8, 65, 66, 153
 and Locke's "idea" 61–3
 mutual irreducibility and supportability of Davidson's three types (self, other, and objective) 157–8
 vs opinion 151
 subordinate to claims to justice 130
 see also epistemology; representation

INDEX

Kraugerud, Hanne Andrea 168–9, 204n. 6
Kuhn, Thomas 42, 52–4
Kuklick, Bruce 37

language 91–2, 96, 102, 131, 155–7
  analytical philosophy and 183n. 62
  contingency of 94–5
  as coping tool 92, 94, 159, 160–1, 163, 165
  innovation in as defining Rorty's "residual theology" 133–4
  as medium of representation 92–4, 159, 163
  Quine's rejection of analytic-synthetic distinction in 75–6
  recognizing communal discursive norms as condition for the possibility of 73–4, 164
language game 71–2, 92, 94
Levinas, Emmanuel 127, 129–32, 138, 197n. 48
liberalism 9, 19, 80, 83, 98, 100–1, 143
  as aversion to cruelty 103, 127, 129–30, 132, 180n. 7
  ethical influence of Judeo-Christian tradition on 128–30, 132
  vs radicalism 110
  and secularization 115
  see also private-public distinction
liberation 19, 27, 31, 47, 50, 85, 176
  see also freedom
Linguistic Turn, The 41
literature, moral role in sensitizing to pain and suffering 105–10
Locke, John 56, 60–3, 65, 68, 72, 73, 92, 120
logical positivism 8, 34, 35, 39, 184n. 62
love 136

McDowell, John 166
McKeon, Richard 33, 35
material, materialism 58–9, 69
Matson, Wallace 188n. 27
meaning 75, 156, 162–3
  see also interpretation; intentionality
memory 137
mental introspection 70–1
metaphor 94, 96
metaphysics 9, 10, 11, 35–7, 50, 54, 84, 88, 97, 113, 121, 123, 150, 159, 186n. 12, 204n. 6
  as contrasted to irony 102–3, 104, 105, 114–15, 194n. 53
  as demobilizing 135
  see also correspondence; objectivity; representation; transcendence; truth
mind 48–52, 54, 56–61, 63, 64, 67, 68, 74, 76, 82, 84, 162–3, 192n. 22
mind-body problem 49, 50, 58, 68, 188n. 29
mirroring 49, 51, 52, 55, 56, 76, 84, 124
  see also representation, representationalism
morality 104–5, 106–7, 129, 137, 143
  contingency of 98
  as loyalty 127, 131
mystery 136, 163

Nabokov, Vladimir 105–7, 110
Nagel, Thomas 120
narcissism 122–3
narrative 89, 94, 98
natural science 54, 59–60, 105, 124
  belief in God and 117
  as the paradigm of human knowledge 184n. 62
naturalism 131–2, 134, 163, 170
naturalistic fallacy 63

nature 18, 24, 137
necessity 49–50, 90
New York Intellectuals 17, 19–20
Nietzsche, Friedrich 56, 102, 103
   on self-creation 95–6, 100
nominalism 84, 89, 191n. 11
normal discourse 52–4, 125–6, 144–5, 177
   see also Kuhn, Thomas
normativity, norms 73–4
   and Davidsonian triangulation 153–9, 164–5
   discursive 149, 162, 166–7, 171
   Rorty's acceptance of Davidson's emphasis on 163–4
   as set by peers vs the objective world 164, 166, 195n. 3
   see also agency; responsibility
novelty (natality, new) 37, 48, 53, 87, 88, 96, 100–1, 123–7, 132, 174–7
   and Rorty's "residual theology" 133–4
   see also freedom; possibility

object 57–8, 61, 63, 66, 71, 72, 74, 90–1, 94, 162, 192n. 22
objectivity 8–11, 93, 121–2, 150, 191n. 19
   as basis for solidarity 150
   normative triangulation and 153–9, 166
   recast as increasing intersubjectivity 2, 151, 159, 161, 163
   Rorty's parents' political suspicions of 24–5
   see also correspondence; truth
Objectivity, Relativism, and Truth 119, 149–52
obligation 129, 194n. 53
   see also morality; responsibility
"occupy wall street" protests 110–13

ontology 84, 171
order 87
ordinary language 50
Orwell, George 105–6, 107–10

pain 170, 189n. 51
   as brute contact with reality 96–7, 171
   caused by ironic redescription 102
   as mental representation 58–9, 69–72
   moral significance of 101, 170–1
paradigm 48, 52, 54
   see also Kuhn, Thomas
Park, Robert E. 27, 28, 30
Pascal, Blaise 139
pathos 138–9
patriotism 15, 29–30, 32, 177
perception 59–60, 64, 70
permanent framework (also "permanent neutral framework") 49, 53, 67, 76, 84
   see also certainty; foundation, foundationalism
pessimism 108
   see also hope
philosophy 105, 131, 149
   quarrel between poetry and 95, 97
   systematic vs edifying 125, 144, 177
Philosophy and the Mirror of Nature 7, 8, 14, 43, 45–78, 79, 90, 91, 144, 175, 180n. 2, 202n. 28
physical 57, 59
Pierce, Charles Sanders 37, 39
Plato 57, 59, 84, 95, 170
   appearance-reality distinction in 119
plurality, pluralism 113, 143, 145, 146, 160, 168

poet, poetry 79, 131
  tension with philosophy 95, 97, 100, 126, 177
politics 8, 9, 32, 131
  Rorty and 80–113
  Rorty's anticlericalism as 117
  Rorty's view of the relationship of philosophy and 16, 80–1
Popper, Sir Karl 191n. 11
possibility 53–4, 87, 88, 96, 134, 137, 175–6
  see also potentiality
potentiality 36–7
  see also possibility
power 96–7, 112, 116, 136
pragmatism 8, 10, 33, 37, 92–3, 145, 167
  compared to realism 165
  and pathos 139
  Rorty's embrace of 15, 39, 43
  Rorty's "epistemological behaviorism" as a version of 67
  and self-reliance 122–3
  truth in 11, 150–1
predication 64–5
  see also judgment
privacy, private 17, 27, 44, 79, 85, 141
  effect upon others of concern for 83, 105–6
  as idiosyncracy and novelty 101, 170
  irony as 101–2
  language and 155
  mental representations as 69–70
  religion and 140–8
private-public distinction 80, 82, 99–101
  religion and 140–8
  Rorty's concern to keep distinct yet hold together 44, 81, 103, 174, 194n. 53
  see also liberalism
progress 53, 82, 86

prophecy 138
  as characterizing one Rortyan persona 10, 118, 121–3
  see also hope; future
proposition 66
public 27, 34, 44, 79, 83, 85, 101–2
  knowledge justification as 71, 73, 88
  religion and 140–8
  see also democracy; private-public distinction; responsibility; solidarity
Putnam, Hilary 120

quietism 8, 9, 80, 169
Quine, W. V. O. 7, 39, 40, 41, 55–6, 68, 71–2, 74–6, 186n. 6

Ramberg, Bjørn 7, 10, 11, 148, 152–3, 159–65, 166–8, 171–2, 202nn. 22, 28, 203n. 42, 204n. 6
Rauschenbusch, Walter 26, 31
Raushenbush, Winifred 19–20, 26–30, 42
raw feels 69, 71
Rawls, John 142, 199n. 73
realism 91, 139, 180n. 2, 191n. 11, 192n. 22
  as foil to pragmatism 93, 150
  Rorty's concessions to 91, 165
reality 18, 48, 67, 75, 81, 87, 90, 91, 93, 94, 105, 113, 121, 126, 139, 166–7, 170, 174
  contact with vs coping with 124, 125
  as distinct from appearance 84, 107
  see also object; world
Reason (rationality) 58, 97, 140
  as equivalent to procedures of justification 74, 151
reasons 62–5, 67–8, 71, 73, 91
  of the heart 139

recognition 128
  of common susceptibility to suffering 103–5, 110
  of persons as normative agents in linguistic community 164
redescription 69, 96, 102, 107, 114–15, 160–3
reductionism 55, 69, 71, 94, 158, 170, 202n. 28
reference 50
  see also correspondence
reformist politics vs revolutionary politics 110–12
  vs theoretical purism 112
relativism 3, 80, 93, 97, 98, 151–2
religion 9, 10, 33, 54, 113, 114–48
  as dependence 134, 136–7
  as detrimental to the health of democratic society 113, 116–17
  fundamentalism in 113, 139
  in public 139–48, 198n. 56
  and violence 139
  wars of 54
"Religion as Conversation-Stopper" 9, 140–2
representation, representationalism 49, 51, 54–5, 56, 63–4, 68, 71, 72, 76, 90, 94, 95, 120–1, 125, 159, 166, 171, 187n. 26, 204n. 6
  involving global as opposed to local separation of subject and object 162–3
  see also correspondence; epistemology
responsibility 9–10, 33–4, 42, 44, 76, 79, 83, 88, 100–2, 116, 122, 123–8, 130, 138, 139, 146, 174, 194n. 53
Robbins, J. Wesley 133–4
Romanticism 24, 95, 100, 175–6, 193n. 51
Rorty, James 19–20, 21–6, 42

Russel, Bertrand 183n. 62
Ryerson, James 183n. 61
Ryle, Gilbert 68–9, 189n. 49

sacred value 173, 176–7, 203n. 1
salvation 133–4
same-sex marriage 141
Sartre, Jean-Paul 124
scientism 125–6
secular, secularization 115, 139, 147, 148
self 90–1, 96
  contingency of 95
  as divinized 115
self-creation 95, 101, 103, 175
  and human plasticity 176
self-knowledge 158
self-reliance 9, 114, 117, 122–3, 133–4
  see also autonomy
Sellars, Wilfrid 7, 39–41, 55–6, 63, 68–9, 71–4, 76, 94, 186n. 6, 190nn. 56, 63
  and "logical space of reasons" 126, 193n. 31
  and "we-intentions" 98
sensation 57–8, 73, 188n. 27
sense 57–9, 63, 64, 74–5, 119
  as pre-reflective basis for ethics 130–1
sentence 91, 93
Shklar, Judith 103, 129
skepticism 67, 120–1
Skinner, Quentin 42
socialism 20
socialization 86, 101
solidarity 2, 9, 22, 80–1, 85, 102, 103–10, 112, 113, 116, 127, 148, 150, 153–9, 174
  see also intersubjectivity
Stout, Jeffrey 10, 121–3, 142, 143–5, 147, 148, 156, 159, 173, 180n. 6, 195n. 79, 196n. 25, 199n. 73, 203n. 1

Strauss, Leo 35
Stuhr, John J. 180n. 7
subject 57–8, 60, 90, 91, 93, 162, 192n. 22
  see also self
subjectivism 176, 194n. 51
subjectivity 108, 191n. 19
substance 59
supernaturalism 114, 116, 135
  see also religion; theology; transcendence
synoptic vision 81
  see also private-public distinction
synthesis 63–5, 68, 74
  see also concept; intuition; Kant, Immanuel
synthetic a priori 64
  see also judgment; Kant, Immanuel

Tartaglia, James 189nn. 53, 55
Taylor, Charles 99
Taylor, Mark C. 131, 133
theism 117, 123, 138, 145–8
  see also divinity; God; theology
theology 86, 88, 105, 113, 114, 147, 148
  Rorty's "residual" 133–4
theory 89, 90, 105, 107
  commensurating private and public 103
  and politics 111–12
  see also metaphysics; philosophy
therapy (philosophy as) 7, 8, 45–78, 185n. 5, 186n. 6
  compared to prophecy 118–23
thinking 61, 69, 86
  three points of Davidson's triangle as condition of possibility for 157
Thomas, Norman 18–19

time (or temporality) 85–6, 90, 94
  messianic 138
tolerance 54, 81, 116
totalitarianism 108
tradition 81–2, 137, 146
  and moral inclusion 128
transcendence 95, 100, 136
  as ethical alterity 127–33, 197n. 48
  as heteronomy 124
  Rorty's critique of the Western ambition of 9–10, 84–6, 114–15, 118–23, 124, 125–6
  temporal interpretation of 118, 135–6, 139
Trotsky, Leon 17
truth 2, 7, 9, 11, 115, 121, 124, 204n. 6
  as correspondence 10, 91–2, 122
  as goal of inquiry 113, 168, 170, 172
  and happiness 167
  importance of normative contrast with error 159–60, 162, 164, 165
  pragmatist account of 148, 150–3, 180n. 2
  purpose of 149–72
  Rorty's refusal to offer a philosophical account of 149–51, 169
  substitution of freedom for 84, 86–9, 108–9
  as warranted assertability 3, 180n. 2
  see also correspondence; objectivity

Unger, Roberto 192n. 26
United States 6
universality 95, 101, 102, 103
utopia, utopianism 10, 28–9, 89, 97, 122, 139, 147

Vattimo, Gianni 10, 136–7
Veblen, Thorstein 21
verificationism 184n. 62
Vietnam War 112
violence 139, 145

warranted assertability 8
  see also justification; truth
Weber, Max 139
Weiss, Paul 37
White, Morton 39, 41
Whitehead, Alfred North 34, 36, 37
Whitman, Walt 22, 178
Williams, Michael 185n. 5
wisdom 60, 77
Wittgenstein, Ludwig 8, 41, 51, 74, 186n. 14
  impossibility of private language 155–6, 201n. 17
  Philosophical Investigations 39, 45–6
Wolterstorff, Nicholas 10, 142–3, 145, 146, 148, 199n. 80
world 48, 49, 57, 82, 85, 90, 91–3, 96, 120, 122, 126, 154, 160, 162, 166, 169, 192n. 22, 193n. 313
  as divinized 115–16
  relationship of words or language to 165, 167, 202n. 22
  as shared 157
  see also being; objectivity; reality

Yeats, W. B. 18

Žižek, Slavoj 111, 195n. 79

www.ingramcontent.com/pod-product-compliance
Ingram Content Group UK Ltd.
Pitfield, Milton Keynes, MK11 3LW, UK
UKHW021901220326
469204UK00008B/103